The Big Book of

baby knitting

by MARY HEALEY

Additional material by
Eugenie Hammond and Grace Paull
Line drawings by Caroline Clegg

Photographs by W. J. Moore

BOOK CLUB ASSOCIATES, LONDON

This edition published 1974 by
Book Club Associates
By arrangement with Wolfe Publishing Limited

Children's accessories by Mothercare

Shoes by Dolcis, Curtess and Lilley & Skinner

To my mother Mary,
and with thanks to my sister Eva
and my friend Eugenie
for all their help

Printed by Oxley Printing Group Limited, London and Edinburgh

Contents

(continued)

Contents (continued)

An International Guide

In this book the use of speciality yarns (these are yarns which usually produce a textured fabric and are subject to change in accordance with fashion trends) has been avoided and only the more standard yarns, that is to say, Double Knitting, Chunky, three- and four-ply and Quickerknit (lightly twisted baby yarn) which are easily recognised have been used.

Even between these, there is no regular standard of thickness, and yarns of different manufacturers do vary a little, thus producing the slight variation in the amount of yarn to each ball.

Whilst in Britain the description of Double Knitting or Ply is a clear indication of the thickness, this does not apply abroad and knitters should seek the advice of retailers and manufacturers regarding foreign equivalents to British yarns.

Knitting needles also are not standard throughout the world. In Britain, the higher the number the finer the needle, whereas, in America, the opposite is the case; there the highest number refers to the largest needle.

International Sizes in crochet hooks have already been introduced and it is to be hoped that yarns and knitting needles will eventually become universal.

It is because of these difficulties that such importance is attached to tension. Providing you can obtain the correct tension with alternative yarn and size of needle and produce a satisfactory fabric which is neither too loose nor too tight, you should have successful results.

CONVERSION OF OUNCES TO 25-GRAMME BALLS

1 ounce ball = 28.35 grammes
(Difference is 3.35 grammes)

A general rule is to add one 25-gramme ball to every eight ounces.

1 to 7 ounces require 1 extra 25-gramme ball

8 to 16 ounces require 2 extra 25-gramme balls

CONVERSION CHART OF INCHES TO CENTIMETRES

Inches	Approximate Centimetres
1	$2\frac{1}{2}$
2	5
3	$7\frac{1}{2}$
4	10
5	$12\frac{1}{2}$
6	15
7	$17\frac{1}{2}$
8	20
9	$22\frac{1}{2}$
10	$25\frac{1}{2}$
12	$30\frac{1}{2}$
14	$35\frac{1}{2}$
16	$40\frac{1}{2}$
18	$45\frac{1}{2}$
20	51
22	56
24	61
26	66

COMPARISON CHART OF NEEDLE SIZES

British	American	French
14	00	2.00
13	0	2.25
12	1	2.50
11	2	3.00
10	3	3.25
—	4	3.50
9	5	4.00
8	6	4.50
7	7	4.75
6	8	5.00
5	9	5.50
4	10	6.00
3	$10\frac{1}{2}$	7.00
2	11	8.00
1	13	9.25

Introduction

I hope, in this book, you will find all you need to knit for baby from birth to three years, going on four.

With the basic garments I have included a few 'fun' clothes which gave me a great deal of pleasure to design and make. The children who modelled them were delighted to wear them, too, as you can see.

All the designs, even the lacy patterns, are as simple as possible. So don't worry if you are not a very experienced knitter; you will be surprised how easy the stitches are.

I have avoided any complicated shapings by changing to simple stocking stitch before the shaping occurs.

Successful hand-knits depend more on the care taken in making up the garment than on your being an even knitter.

It is a mistake to rush the finishing, as many people do, just to see the end result. Far better to make a fresh start next day and take your time, as I do.

On the following pages you will find a few useful hints for a professional finish.

You will appreciate that this book has taken some time to prepare and, as manufacturers are constantly changing the colours in their range to keep up to date with fashion trends, the shades used may not always be obtainable.

However, with the wide variety of colours always available in hand knitting yarns, you are sure to find many eye-catching shades to suit your individual taste.

I sincerely hope this book will prove invaluable to you during baby's first years and may I wish you every success with your knitting.

Mary Healey

For a Professional Finish

KNITTING NEEDLES ☐ Craftsmen always take great care of their tools; knitting needles are yours. Left lying around, needles are easily bent. It is possible to buy needle boxes or zipped cases to keep them in good shape.

CASTING ON ☐ There are two ways of casting on stitches; one is known as the 'thumb method' using only one needle (in case you are not familiar with this, I have given diagrams on page 11). This method gives a good firm edge to welts on sweaters and cardigans. For finer work however, especially baby clothes, you will find that lacy patterns very often fall naturally into a scalloped edge. You will need the little extra 'give' along the cast-on edge to allow for this, therefore the usual two-needle method should be used. Where a pattern states cast on loosely, use the two-needle method.

CASTING OFF ☐ Never cast off too tightly; be especially careful on neck bands and shaping sleeve tops. If your casting off is too tight you will lose the natural stretch of the knitted fabric and have difficulty in fitting sleeve heads into armholes. It is a good idea to use a size larger needle for the final cast-off group.

TENSION ☐ Checking your tension is most important. Rather than trying to knit either more tightly or loosely it is better to change to a size smaller or larger needle. Knit up a sizeable square; if you get fewer stitches to the measurement quoted try needles a size smaller, if more stitches, then a size larger.

JOINING ON YARN ☐ Never join on another ball of yarn in the middle of a row. Join at the side seam edge where the join can be taken into the seam. There are, of course, exceptions to this rule. Pram covers, cot covers, etc., usually have a border. In this case, join the new yarn at inner edge of the border where it can, more easily, be darned through on the wrong side and avoid spoiling the even line along the outer edge.

YOU HAVE DROPPED STITCHES ☐ Use a finer needle for picking them up, or use a crochet hook if just one stitch has run down a few rows. Never put your knitting aside in the middle of a row; this causes the stitches to stretch and will mar the surface of the work. It also makes stitches more likely to drop.

MARKING THREADS ☐ All the patterns in this book are given in the number of rows to be worked rather than a measurement in inches. It is a good idea to insert a coloured thread and take this up the work at convenient intervals, say every 10 rows.

MAKING UP ☐ Pin out and press each piece. Always use a bodkin for sewing knitted pieces together. Make a flat seam. Using a firm, but not too tight, back stitch, sew one stitch in from the edge. With the bodkin and fingers of the other hand you can feel your way along the knitting, taking the bodkin between each alternate row and back again through the row you have missed. Work carefully and you will have a perfectly straight seam, with none of those wavy lines caused by going through the stitches at each side of the regular line. When sewing in a 'set in' sleeve follow the line along the straight rows of armhole rather than the shaped edge of sleeve top.

ALTERATIONS ☐ It is quite a simple job on plain knitteds (fancy patterns prove a little more difficult) to add an inch or two on a hand-knitted garment. Undo the seams, cut a stitch at one side above the welt and pull the thread tightly across the knitting. Break off thread and put the stitches of the main part onto the needle. You can now knit the extra length required and re-knit the welt. If you do not have any extra yarn, a band of contrast colour is quite effective. Garments can be shortened in the same way.

CARING FOR KNITTEDS □ Most yarns now carry washing instructions, but two points are worth remembering. *Never* let the garments get so soiled that they need rubbing. And *never* dry a white woollen outside in sunlight; this will mar the colour and give it a yellow tinge.

ECONOMISING □ Hand-knits for children are usually out-grown while the yarn remains in very good condition . . . another reason why careful sewing together is important. With a little time and patience, the garments can always be unravelled and made into something else. Carefully unpick the seams then wind the yarn into skeins. A hardback book or the back of a chair are quite useful for this. Tie threads round the skeins at intervals to avoid tangles and press with a warm iron through a damp cloth. This removes all the wrinkles and the yarn can then be used again.

INSERTING COLOURS ON RIBBED BORDERS □ When changing to another colour in rib, always knit the first row on the right side of work and rib back. This will give a very neat finish and avoid the loops of main colour showing through to the right side when the rib is stretched.

ABOUT YARNS □ Different brands of yarn do vary from each other, even when of the same ply, some being more tightly spun than others. This results in a thinner or thicker thread which varies slightly the number of yards to the weight of ball.

Manufacturers are now changing the weight of yarn from ounce to gramme balls in readiness for the Metrication.

Until the system is well in operation you may find, in some shops, yarns made up in both ounce and gramme balls. Retailers will have conversion charts, but for your guidance one 50 gramme ball is approximately $1\frac{3}{4}$ ounces of yarn.

TWISTED CORD □ Take a length of yarn and fold in half. Secure the cut ends to a hook or get a friend to hold it firmly. Slip a pencil through the looped end and, holding yarn taut, twist the pencil. Let yarn go slack to test the tightness of the 'twist' and, when firm enough, fold the length in half again and smooth the hands over the length – the yarn will twist together and hold. For your guidance, $2\frac{1}{2}$ yards of yarn will make approximately 18 inches of cord.

TASSEL FRINGE □ Cut yarn into lengths. Fold in half and, using a crochet hook, draw the looped end through the work. Put the cut ends through the loop and pull tight to form tassel.

POM-PON □ Cut two circles of cardboard each approximately $2\frac{1}{2}$ inches in diameter. Cut a circle in centre of each piece about $\frac{1}{2}$ inch in diameter. Place both circles of card together then take yarn through centre circle, over the outer edges and through centre again until circle is completely filled (see Fig. 1). Cut through yarn between the outer edges of the two discs (see Fig. 2). Slip a strand of yarn between the two and tie securely (see Fig. 3). Remove cardboard and trim pom-pon to shape.

Fig. 1   Fig. 2   Fig. 3

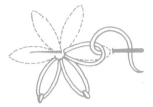

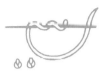

Lazy Daisy   Chain Stitch   French Knot

Herringbone Stitch Casing

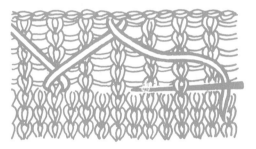

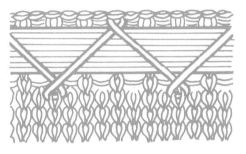

CASTING ON – THUMB METHOD ☐
Measure a length of yarn from ball ($1\frac{1}{2}$ yards for 100 stitches). Make a slip knot and, with the needle in the right hand put this knot on the needle (Fig. 1). Hold the short length of yarn in the left hand and yarn from the ball in the right hand (Fig. 2). Make a loop round the left thumb and insert the needle (Fig. 3). Take the yarn in the right hand round the needle, through the loop and onto the needle (Fig. 4). Continue in this way for the required number of stitches,

Fig. 1   Fig. 2   Fig. 3   Fig. 4

Vest and Pilch

Materials

One ounce of Patons Beehive Baby Wool 3-ply for 1st size; two ounces for 2nd and 3rd sizes. For any one size; a pair of No. 11 knitting needles.

Tension

Work at a tension of 8 stitches and 10 rows to 1 inch, with ribs stretched, to obtain the following measurements:

Measurements

	INCHES		
	1st size	2nd size	3rd size
All round at under-arms-stretched	17	19	21
Side seam	$6\frac{3}{4}$	$7\frac{1}{4}$	$7\frac{1}{2}$
Length	$9\frac{1}{4}$	10	11
Sleeve seam	1	$1\frac{1}{4}$	$1\frac{1}{2}$

Abbreviations

K., knit; p., purl; st., stitch; tog., together; w.fwd., wool forward to make a st.

● *The instructions are given for 1st size. Where they vary, work figures in first brackets for 2nd size; work figures in second bracket for 3rd size.*

SPECIAL NOTE: For 2nd and 3rd sizes – 3 ounces will make two vests.

White Ribbed Vest
in 3-ply

To Make (worked in one piece)

With No. 11 needles cast on 68 (76) (84) sts.

1st row: K.1, * p.2, k.2; repeat from * ending last repeat with k.1.

2nd row: P.1, * k.2, p.2; repeat from * ending last repeat with p.1.

Repeat these 2 rows 33 (35) (37) times more.

Mark each end of work with a coloured thread to denote end of side seam, then work a further 12 (16) (20) rows.

Next (slot) row: Rib 15 (19) (23), * w.fwd., take 2 sts.tog., rib 2; repeat from * 8 times more, take 2 sts.tog., w.fwd., rib 15 (19) (23).

Rib 3 rows.

Now divide sts. for neck.

Next row: Rib 15 (19) (23), w.fwd., take 2 tog., rib 1, cast off next 32 sts. very loosely – 1 st. left on right-hand needle, take 2 tog., w.fwd., rib to end and work on these 18 (22) (26) sts. for 1st side.

1st side: Rib 3 rows, then make a hole at neck edge, as before, on next and the 2 (3) (4) following 4th rows.
Rib 3 rows. Break off wool.

2nd side: Rejoin wool to inner edge of sts. at other side and rib 12 (16) (20) rows making holes at neck edge on every 4th row to match 1st side.
Rib 4 rows, making hole at neck edge at end of last row.

Next row: Cast on 32 sts. loosely, then rib across the sts. of 1st side making a hole at neck edge.
On these 68 (76) (84) sts. rib 3 rows.
Work holes across centre neck edge on next row then rib 13 (17) (21) rows.
Mark each end of work with a coloured thread, then rib 68 (72) (76) rows.
Cast off.

The Sleeves (both alike)

With right side of work facing, rejoin wool to marking thread and pick up and k.48 (56) (64) sts. evenly along side edge to other marking thread.
Work 11 (13) (15) rows in rib as given at beginning.
Cast off.

To Make Up The Vest

Join sleeve and side seams. Make a length of twisted cord and thread through holes all round neck edge.

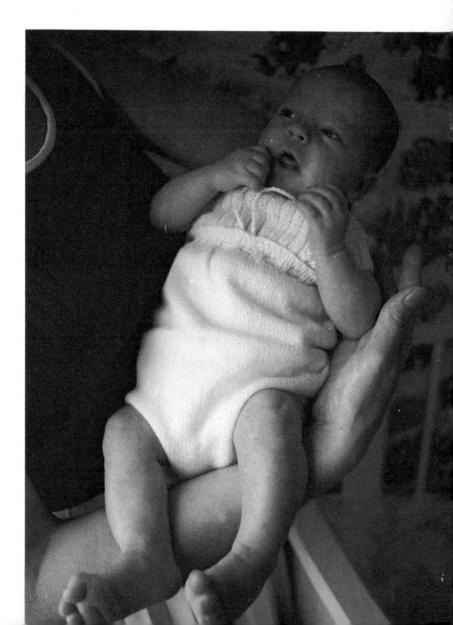

White Pilch — 3-ply

Materials

One ounce of Patons Beehive Baby Wool 3-ply for each size; a pair of No. 11 knitting needles; waist length of elastic.

Tension

Work at a tension of 8 stitches and 10 rows to 1 inch, over the stocking stitch, to obtain the following measurements:

Measurements

	INCHES	
	1st size	2nd size
All round at widest part	19	20
Side seam	7	7½

Abbreviations

K., knit; p., purl; st., stitch; tog., together; dec., decrease (by working 2 sts.tog.); inc., increase (by working twice into same st.); w.fwd., wool forward to make a st.; st.st., stocking st. (k. on right side and p. on wrong side); single rib is k.1 and p.1 alternately.

● *The instructions are given for 1st size. Where they vary, work figures in brackets for 2nd size.*

To Make

Begin at waist edge by casting on 76 (80) sts. and work 5 rows in single rib.

Next (slot) row: K.1, p.1, k.1, * w.fwd., k.2 tog., p.1, k.1; repeat from * to last st., p.1.

Rib a further 4 rows.

Beginning with a k. row, st.st. 56 (60) rows.

To shape for leg openings: Dec. 1 st. at each end of the next 24 (26) rows – 28 sts.

Work 30 rows straight.

Inc. 1 st. at each end of next 24 (26) rows – 76 (80) sts.

Work 56 (60) rows straight.

Work 4 rows in single rib; work slot row, then rib a further 5 rows.

Cast off loosely in rib.

The Leg Bands (both alike)

With right side of work facing, rejoin wool at side edge and pick up and k.78 (82) sts. along entire leg edge.

Work 4 rows in single rib.

Cast off.

To Make Up The Pilch

Press on wrong side, avoiding the ribbing, using a warm iron over a damp cloth. Join side seams. Insert elastic.

Yellow Button Front Vest
in 4-ply

Materials

Two ounces of Patons Beehive Baby Wool 4-ply for each size; a pair of No. 10 knitting needles; 1 button.

Tension

Work at a tension of 7 stitches and 9 rows to 1 inch, over the stocking stitch, to obtain the following measurements:

Measurements

INCHES

	1st size	2nd size	3rd size
All round at underarms	17	18¾	20½
Side seam	6¾	7¾	8½
Length	10¼	11½	12½
Sleeve seam	3	3	3

Abbreviations

K., knit; p., purl; st., stitch; tog., together; w.fwd., wool forward to make a st.; dec., decrease (by working 2 sts. tog.); inc., increase (by working twice into same st.); st.st., stocking st., (k. on right side and p. on wrong side); single rib is k.1 and p.1 alternately; garter st. is every row k.

● *The instructions are given for 1st size. Where they vary, work figures in first brackets for 2nd size; figures in second brackets for 3rd size.*

The Back

With No. 10 needles cast on 60 (66) (72) sts. and work 8 rows in single rib.

Beginning with a k. row, st.st. 54 (62) (70) rows.

To shape the armholes: Cast off 3 (4) (5) sts. at beginning of the next 2 rows, then dec. 1 st. at each end of next row and following 2 right-side rows – 48 (52) (56) sts.

Work 8 (10) (12) rows, ending with a k. row.

Now divide sts. for back neck.

Next row: P. 18 (19) (20) and leave these sts. on a spare needle for left back shoulder, cast off next 12 (14) (16) sts., p. to end and work on these 18 (19) (20) sts. for right back shoulder.

The right back shoulder: To shape back neck: Dec. 1 st. at neck edge on the next row and following 6 alternate rows – 11 (12) (13) sts.

Work 1 row to finish at armhole edge.

To slope the shoulder: Cast off 6 sts. at beginning of next row; work 1 row, then cast off remaining 5 (6) (7) sts.

The left back shoulder: With right side of work facing, rejoin wool to the sts. left on spare needle and k. to end of row.

Now work as given for right shoulder to end.

The Front

With No. 10 needles cast on 60 (66) (72) sts. and work 8 rows in single rib.

The popular Envelope Vest

Materials

Two 25-gramme balls of Patons Beehive Baby Wool 3-ply for each size; a pair of No. 11 knitting needles.

Tension

Work at a tension of 8 stitches and 10 rows to 1 inch, over the stocking stitch, to obtain the following measurements:

Measurements

INCHES

	1st size	2nd size	3rd size
All round at under-arms	17	19	21
Side seam	$6\frac{1}{2}$	$7\frac{1}{4}$	8
Length	$9\frac{3}{4}$	$10\frac{3}{4}$	$11\frac{3}{4}$
Sleeve seam	$1\frac{1}{4}$	$1\frac{1}{2}$	$1\frac{3}{4}$

Abbreviations

K., knit; p., purl; st., stitch; tog., together; dec., decrease (by working 2 sts. tog.); inc., increase (by working twice into same st.); st.st., stocking st. (k. on right side and p. on wrong side); single rib is k.1 and p.1 alternately.

● *The instructions are given for 1st size. Where they vary, work figures in first brackets for 2nd size; figures in second brackets for 3rd size.*

The Back

With No. 11 needles cast on 68 (76) (84) sts. and work 4 rows in single rib.

Beginning with a k. row, st.st. 62 (70) (78) rows **.

Mark each end of last row with a coloured thread to denote end of side seam, then work a further 20 (22) (24) rows.

Now divide sts. for back neck.

Next row: K.22 (24) (26), cast off next 24 (28) (32) sts., k. to end and work on these 22 (24) (26) sts. for 1st side.

1st side: Dec. 1 st. at neck edge on each of next 20 (22) (24) rows.

Take remaining 2 sts. tog. and fasten off.

2nd side: With wrong side of work facing, rejoin wool to the 22 (24) (26) sts. and dec. 1 st. at neck edge on each of next 20 (22) (24) rows.

Take remaining 2 sts. tog. and fasten off.

The Neck Edging: With right side of work facing, rejoin wool to point and pick up and k. 20 (22) (24) sts. along shaped edge, 22 (26) (30) sts. along centre back and 20 (22) (24) sts. along other shaped edge.

Work 4 rows in single rib increasing 1 st. at each end of every row.

Cast off these 70 (78) (86) sts. in rib.

The Front

Work as given for back to **.

Mark each end of work with a coloured thread to denote end of side seam, then work a further 14 (16) (18) rows. Mark each end of work to denote point of overlap.

Now divide sts. for front neck.

Next row: K.24 (26) (28), cast off next 20 (24) (28), k. to end and work on these 24 (26) (28) sts. for 1st side.

1st side: Dec. 1 st. at neck edge on each of next 22 (24) (26) rows.

Take remaining 2 sts. tog. and fasten off.

2nd side: With wrong side of work facing, rejoin wool to the 24 (26) (28) sts. and dec. 1 st. at neck edge on each of next 22 (24) (26) rows.

Take remaining 2 sts. tog. and fasten off.

The Neck Edging: With right side of work facing, rejoin wool to point and pick up and k.22 (24) (26) sts. along shaped edge, 18 (22) (26) from centre front and 22 (24) (26) sts. along other shaped edge.

Work 4 rows in single rib increasing 1 st. at each end of every row.

Cast off these 70 (78) (86) sts. in rib.

The Sleeves (both alike)

First overlap shoulders by placing point of back to the marking thread on front and pin in position. With right side of work facing, rejoin wool to marking thread which denotes end of side seam and pick up and k.58 (66) (74) sts. along edge to marking thread at other side, working through both thicknesses across shoulder.

Work 12 (14) (16) rows in single rib.

Cast off.

To Make Up The Vest

Press on wrong side, avoiding the ribbing, using a warm iron over a damp cloth. Join side and sleeve seams.

Shawl
in 3-ply

Contributed by Grace Paull

Materials

Eleven ounces of Hayfield Beaulon 3-ply; a pair of No. 9 knitting needles.

Tension and Size

Worked at a tension of 20 stitches and 27 rows to 3 inches, over the lacy pattern, the shawl will measure approximately 41 inches square.

To Make

With No. 9 needles cast on 274 sts.
1st row: K.2, * p.2, k.2; repeat from * to end.
2nd row: As 1st row.
3rd row: P.2, * k.2, p.2; repeat from * to end.
4th row: As 3rd row.
These 4 rows form the d.m.st. pattern; repeat them 12 times more, then work the 1st row again.
Next row: D.m.st.40, up 1, d.m.st. to end— 275 sts.
Now work in lace pattern with d.m.st. borders as follows:
1st row: D.m.st.40, k.3, * p.1, k.3; repeat from * to last 40 sts., d.m.st.40.

Abbreviations

K., knit; p., purl; st., stitch; tog., together; sl., slip; p.s.s.o., pass slipped st.over; y.r.n., yarn round needle to make a st.; y.o.n., yarn over needle to make a st.; d.m.st., double moss st.; up 1 (pick up the thread which lies between the needles and k. into back of it, thus making a st.).

2nd row: D.m.st.40, p. 3, * k.1, p.3; repeat from * to last 40 sts., d.m.st.40.
3rd row: D.m.st.40, * y.o.n., sl.1, k.2 tog., p.s.s.o., y.r.n., p.1; repeat from * to last 39 sts., d.m.st.39.
4th row: As 2nd row.
Repeat these 4 rows 64 times more when work should measure 35 inches.
Next row: D.m.st. to last 42 sts., p.2 tog., d.m.st.40.
Work 53 rows in d.m.st.
Cast off in d.m.st.

To Complete The Shawl

Pin out to 41 inch square and press carefully with a cool iron over a dry cloth.

21

Shawl
in quickerknit nylon
(see illustration p. 28)
Contributed by Grace Paull

Materials

Sixteen 20-gramme balls of Patons Brilliante Quickerknit Baby; a pair of No. 8 knitting needles.

Tension and Size

Worked at a tension of 21 stitches and 32 rows to 4 inches, over the centre pattern, the shawl will measure approximately 41 inches square.

Abbreviations

K., knit; p., purl; st., stitch; tog., together; inc., increase (by working twice into same st.); sl., slip; p.s.s.o., pass slipped st. over; k. or p.2 tog.b., k. or p.2 sts. tog. through back of loops; y.fwd., yarn forward to make a st.; y.r.n., yarn round needle to make a st.; garter st. is k. on every row.

To Make

With No. 8 needles cast on 229 sts. and k.4 rows.

Now work in pattern with garter st. borders as follows:

1st row: K.4 * y.fwd., k.2 tog.b., k.1, k.2 tog., y.fwd., k.1; repeat from * to last 3 sts., k.3 more.

2nd row: K.3, p.2, * y.r.n., p.3 tog., y.r.n., p.3; repeat from * to last 8 sts., y.r.n., p.3 tog., y.r.n., p.2, k.3.

3rd row: All k.

4th row: K.3, * p.1, p.2 tog.b., y.r.n., p.1, y.r.n., p.2 tog; repeat from * to last 4 sts., p.1, k.3.

5th row: K.3, k.2 tog., * y.fwd., k.3, y.fwd., sl.1, k.2 tog., p.s.s.o.; repeat from * to last 8 sts., y.fwd., k.3, y.fwd., k.2 tog.b., k.3.

6th row: K.3, p. to last 3 sts., k.3.

Repeat these 6 rows 5 times more.

Next row: Pattern 28 turn and leave remaining 201 sts. on a spare needle.

Beginning with the 2nd pattern row and omitting the k.3 at beginning of wrong-side rows and end of right-side rows continue in pattern until 43 patterns more have been worked (49 complete patterns from cast-on edge).

Break off yarn and leave sts. on a stitch-holder.

With right side of work facing, rejoin yarn to the 201 sts. on spare needle, k.171, k.2 tog. turn and leave remaining 28 sts. on a spare needle.

On 172 sts. p.1 row, then work centre pattern as follows:

1st row: K.1, * k.2 tog., y.fwd., k.1, y.fwd., sl.1, k.1, p.s.s.o., k.5; repeat from * to last st., k.1 more.

2nd row: P.8, * sl.1, p.wise, p.9; repeat from * to last 4 sts., sl.1, p.wise, p.3.

3rd and 4th rows: As 1st and 2nd rows.

5th row: All k.

6th row: All p.

7th row: K.1, * k.5, k.2 tog., y.fwd., k.1, y.fwd., sl.1, k.1, p.s.s.o.; repeat from * to last st., k.1.

8th row: P.3, * sl.1, p.wise, p.9; repeat from * to last 9 sts., sl.1, p.wise, p.8.

9th and 10th rows: As 7th and 8th rows.

11th row: All k.

12th row: All p.

Repeat these 12 rows 20 times more, increasing 1 st. at beginning of last row — 173 sts.

Break off yarn and leave sts. on a spare needle.

With right side of work facing, rejoin yarn to the 28 sts. on spare needle.

Beginning with the 1st pattern row omitting the k.3 border at inside edge, work a further 13 complete border patterns.

Break off yarn.

Sl. all sts. onto one needle and with right side of working facing, rejoin yarn and work 5 complete border patterns then work the first 5 rows again.

K.4 rows.

Cast off.

To Complete The Shawl

Join side borders to centre. Pin out and press carefully with a cool iron over a dry cloth.

Cot Blanket
in Courtelle
(see illustration p. 32)

Materials

Eight 20-gramme balls of Sirdar Wonderland Courtelle Quick Knit; a pair of No. 8 knitting needles.

Tension and Size

Worked at a tension of 6 stitches and 9 rows to 1 inch, over the pattern, the cover will measure 24×34 inches.

Abbreviations

K., knit; st., stitch; tog., together; y.fwd., yarn forward to make a st.

To Make

Cast on 143 sts. and k.10 rows.
Now work in pattern as follows:
1st row: K.5, * k.2 tog., y.fwd.; repeat from * to last 6 sts., k.6.
2nd row: As 1st row.
3rd row: All k.
4th row: All k.

Repeat these 4 rows 73 times more when work should measure 33 inches.
K.8 rows.
Cast off.
To neaten side edges: Rejoin yarn to side edge and pick up and k.1 st. from each loop along edge.
Cast off.
DO NOT PRESS.

Opposite – Trellis pram cover in yellow (pattern p. 26); reversible pram cover in blue (pattern p. 27); bells (pattern p. 242); carry-all shoulder bag (pattern p. 243); pushchair bag (pattern p. 245); rabbit (pattern p. 246); ball (pattern p. 248); hot water bottle cover (pattern p. 249); pyjama case (pattern p. 251).

Trellis Pattern Pram Cover

(see illustration p. 25)

Materials

Eight 50-gramme balls of Wendy Diabolo Double Double Knit; a pair of No. 5 knitting needles; a cable needle.

Tension and Size

Worked at a tension of 2 repeats of the trellis stitch pattern to $3\frac{1}{4}$ inches in width and $4\frac{1}{2}$ inches in depth, the cover will measure, after pressing, $22\frac{1}{2}$ inches wide and $25\frac{1}{2}$ inches long.

Abbreviations

K., knit; p., purl; st., stitch; cr.2 rt., cross 2 right (k. into front of 2nd st. on left-hand needle then k. into front of 1st st. and slip both sts. off needle together); cr.2 lt., cross 2 left (slip next st. onto cable needle and leave at front of work, k.1, then k. st. from cable needle); sl., slip.

SPECIAL NOTE: Slip all sts. p.wise and take yarn loosely across the work or the knitting will pucker. The cr.2 lt. is worked over a slipped st. and you will find, if you work carefully, it is possible to leave the st. free at front of work and avoid the use of the cable needle.

To Make

With No. 5 needles cast on 104 sts. and k.12 rows.

Foundation row: K.7, p.4, * sl.2 p.wise, p.6; repeat from * to last 13 sts., sl.2, p.4, k.7.

Now work the 16-row pattern as follows:

1st row: K.10, * cr.2 rt., cr.2 lt., k.4; repeat from * to last 14 sts., cr.2 rt., cr.2 lt., k.10.

2nd row: K.7, p.3, * sl.1, p.2, sl.1, p.4; repeat from * to last 14 sts., sl.1, p.2, sl.1, p.3, k.7.

3rd row: K.9, * cr.2 rt., k.2, cr.2 lt., k.2; repeat from * to last 7 sts., k.7 more.

4th row: K.7, p.2, * sl.1, p.4, sl.1, p.2; repeat from * to last 7 sts., k.7.

5th row: K.8, * cr.2 rt., k.4, cr.2 lt.; repeat from * to last 8 sts., k.8.

6th row: K.7, p.1, sl.1, * p.6, sl.2; repeat from * to last 15 sts., p.6, sl.1, p.1, k.7.

7th row: K.15, * cr.2 rt., k.6; repeat from * to last 9 sts., k.9 more.

8th row: As 6th row.

9th row: K.8, * cr.2 lt., k.4, cr.2 rt.; repeat from * to last 8 sts., k.8.

10th row: As 4th row.

11th row: K.9, * cr.2 lt., k.2, cr.2 rt., k.2; repeat from * to last 7 sts., k.7 more.

12th row: As 2nd row.

13th row: K.10, * cr.2 lt., cr.2 rt., k.4; repeat from * to last 14 sts., cr.2 lt., cr.2 rt., k.10.

14th row: K.7, p.4, * sl.2, p.6; repeat from * to last 13 sts., sl.2, p.4, k.7.

15th row: K.11, * cr.2 rt., k.6; repeat from * to last 13 sts., cr.2 rt., k.11.

16th row: K.7, p.4, * sl.2, p.6; repeat from * to last 13 sts., sl.2, p.4, k.7.

Repeat these 16 rows 8 times more, then work first 13 rows again.

K.11 rows.

Cast off.

Pin out and press using a warm iron over a damp cloth.

Reversible Pattern Pram Cover

(see illustration p. 25)

Materials

Five 50-gramme balls of Patons Capstan; a pair of No. 6 knitting needles.

Abbreviations

K., knit; p., purl; st., stitch; tog., together; w.fwd., wool forward to make a st.; sl., slip; p.s.s.o., pass slipped st. over; w.t.b., wool to back.

Tension and Size

Worked at a tension of 1 repeat of the pattern to $2\frac{3}{4}$ inches in width and $1\frac{3}{4}$ inches in depth, the cover will measure, after pressing, 20 inches wide and 29 inches long.

To Make

With No. 6 needles cast on 89 sts. and k.12 rows.

Now work in pattern as follows:

1st row: K.9, * w.fwd., k.2, p.7, k.2, w.fwd., k.1; repeat from * to last 8 sts., k.8 more.

2nd row: K.8, p.4, * k.2, sl.1, k.2 tog., p.s.s.o., k.2, p.7; repeat from * to last 19 sts., k.2, sl.1, k.2 tog., p.s.s.o., k.2, p.4, k.8.

3rd row: K.10, * w.fwd., k.2, p.5, k.2, w.fwd., k.3; repeat from * to last 7 sts., k.7 more.

4th row: K.8, p.5, * k.1, sl.1, k.2 tog., p.s.s.o., k.1, p.9; repeat from * to last 18 sts., k.1, sl.1, k.2 tog., p.s.s.o., k.1, p.5, k.8.

5th row: K.11, * w.fwd., k.2, p.3, k.2, w.fwd., k.5; repeat from * to last 6 sts., k.6 more.

6th row: K.8, p.6, * w.t.b., sl.1, k.2 tog., p.s.s.o., p.11; repeat from * to last 17 sts., w.t.b., sl.1, k.2 tog., p.s.s.o., p.6, k.8.

7th row: K.8, p.4, * k.2, w.fwd., k.1, w.fwd., k.2, p.7; repeat from * to last 17 sts., k.2, w.fwd., k.1, w.fwd., k.2, p.4, k.8.

8th row: K.8, k.2 tog., * k.2, p.7, k.2, sl.1, k.2 tog., p.s.s.o.; repeat from * to last 21 sts., k.2, p.7, k.2, k.2 tog., k.8.

9th row: K.8, p.3, * k.2, w.fwd., k.3, w.fwd., k.2, p.5; repeat from * to last 18 sts., k.2, w.fwd., k.3, w.fwd., k.2, p.3, k.8.

10th row: K.8, k.2 tog., * k.1, p.9, k.1, sl.1, k.2 tog., p.s.s.o.; repeat from * to last 21 sts., k.1, p.9, k.1, k.2 tog., k.8.

11th row: K.8, p.2, * k.2, w.fwd., k.5, w.fwd., k.2, p.3; repeat from * to last 19 sts., k.2, w.fwd., k.5, w.fwd., k.2, p.2, k.8.

12th row: K.8, k.2 tog., * p.11, w.t.b., sl.1, k.2 tog., p.s.s.o.; repeat from * to last 21 sts., p.11, k.2 tog., k.8.

These 12 rows form the pattern; repeat them 14 times more.

K.12 rows.

Cast off.

Pin out and press using a warm iron over a damp cloth.

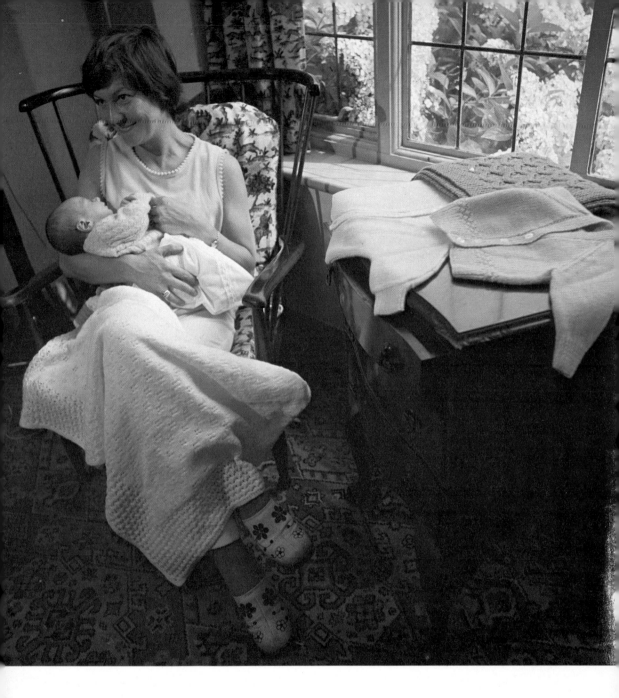

Shawl in quickerknit nylon (pattern p. 22); reversible pram cover in blue (pattern p. 27); first-size cardigans (patterns pp. 116–119).

Carrying Cape

Cape has detachable hood and is worked in stocking stitch with simple lacy panels

Materials

Eleven 25-gramme balls of Patons Baby Wool Quickerknit; a pair of long No. 9 knitting needles or a circular knitting needle No. 9.

Tension and Size

Worked at a tension of 1 repeat of the 13-stitch pattern to $2\frac{1}{4}$ inches in width and 8 rows to 1 inch in depth the cape will measure 50 inches all round hem and 20 inches from neck to lower edge.

Abbreviations

K., knit; p., purl; st., stitch; tog., together; sl., slip; dec., decrease (by working 2 sts. tog.); s.k.p.o., sl.1, k.1, pass slipped st.over; k.1, 2 or 3 sts.b., k.1, 2 or 3 sts. through back of loop; w.fwd., wool forward to make a st.; w.r.n., wool round needle to make a st.; st.st., stocking st. (k. on right side and p. on wrong side); single rib is k.1 and p.1 alternately.

● *Instructions in brackets must be worked the number of times stated after second bracket.*

To Make

With No. 9 needles – or for easier working use a circular needle and work backwards and forwards in rows – cast on 298 sts.

Foundation row (wrong side): P.1, k.1, p.1, k.1, p.1 for ribbed border, * k.2, p.11; repeat from * to last 7 sts., k.2, p.1, k.1, p.1, k.1, p.1.

Now work in pattern as follows:

1st row: K.1, p.1, k.1, p.1, k.1 for ribbed border, p.2, * s.k.p.o., k.3b., w.fwd., k.1, w.fwd., k.3b., k.2 tog., p.2; repeat from * to last 5 sts., k.1, p.1, k.1, p.1, k.1.

2nd, 4th and 6th rows: Rib 5, k.2, * p.11, k.2; repeat from * to last 5 sts., rib 5.

3rd row: Rib 5, p.2, * s.k.p.o., k.2b., w.fwd., k.1, w.fwd., s.k.p.o., w.fwd., k.2b., k.2 tog., p.2; repeat from * to last 5 sts., rib 5.

5th row: Rib 5, p.2, * s.k.p.o., k.1b., w.fwd., k.1 (w.fwd., s.k.p.o.) twice, w.fwd., k.1b., k.2 tog., p.2; repeat from * to last 5 sts., rib 5.

7th row: Rib 5, p.2, * s.k.p.o., w.fwd., k.1 (w.fwd., s.k.p.o.) 3 times, w.fwd., k.2 tog., p.2; repeat from * to last 5 sts., rib 5.

8th row: As 2nd row.

These 8 rows form the border pattern; repeat them twice more.

Now work in st.st. with pattern panels and shape as follows:

1st row: Rib 5, p.2, * s.k.p.o., k.3b., w.fwd., k.1, w.fwd., k.3b., k.2 tog., p.2, ** s.k.p.o., k.20, k.2 tog., p.2, *; repeat from * to * 6 times more, work from * to ** once, rib 5.

2nd, 4th and 6th rows: Rib 5, k.2, * p.11, k.2, **, p.22, k.2, *; repeat from * to * 6 times more, work from * to ** once, rib 5.

3rd row: Rib 5, p.2, * s.k.p.o., k.2b., w.fwd., k.1, w.fwd., s.k.p.o., w.fwd., k.2b., k.2 tog., p.2 ** k.22, p.2, *; repeat from * to * 6 times more, work from * to ** once, rib 5.

5th row: Rib 5, p.2, * s.k.p.o., k.1b., w.fwd., k.1 (w.fwd., s.k.p.o.) twice, w.fwd., k.1b., k.2 tog., p.2, ** k.22, p.2, *; repeat from * to * 6 times more, work from * to ** once, rib 5.

7th row: Rib 5, p.2, * s.k.p.o., w.fwd., k.1 (w.fwd., s.k.p.o.) 3 times, w.fwd., k.2 tog., p.2, ** k.22, p.2, *; repeat from * to * 6 times more, work from * to ** once, rib 5.

8th row: As 2nd row.

These 8 rows form the 8 pattern panels. Continuing in pattern as now set work a further 8 rows straight – that is omitting the decrease at each side of the st.st. panels on the 1st row.

Dec. 1 st. at each side of the st.st. panels, as before, on the next row and every following 16th row until the 6th dec. row has been worked – there are now 12 sts. in each st.st. panel.

Work 7 rows straight, then dec. 1 st. at each side of st.st. panels, as before, on the next row and every following 8th row until a further 5 dec. rows have been worked – there are now 2 sts. in each st.st. panel.

Now work as follows:

1st row: Rib 5, * k.2, p.11, k.2, p.2; repeat from * to last 20 sts., k.2, p.11, k.2, rib 5 – 144 sts.

2nd row: Rib 5, * p.2, pattern 11, p.2, s.k.p.o.; repeat from * to last 20 sts., p.2, pattern 11, p.2, rib 5 – 137 sts.

3rd row: Rib 5, * k.2, p.11, k.2, p.1; repeat from * to last 20 sts., k.2, p.11, k.2, rib 5.

4th row: Rib 5, * p.2 tog., pattern 11, p.2 tog., k.1; repeat from * to last 20 sts., p.2 tog., pattern 11, p.2 tog., rib 5 – 121 sts.

5th row: Rib 5, * k.1, p.11, k.1, p.1; repeat from * to last 18 sts., k.1, p.11, k.1, rib 5.

6th row: Rib 5, * p.1, pattern 11, p.1, k.1; repeat from * to last 18 sts., p.1, pattern 11, p.1, rib 5.

7th row: Rib 5, * k.1, p.11, k.1, p.1; repeat from * to last 18 sts., k.1, p.11, k.1, rib 5.

8th row: K.1, * p.1, k.1; repeat from * to end.

Work 3 rows in single rib.

Next (slot) row: K.1, p.1, * w.r.n., p.2 tog., k.1, p.1; repeat from * to last 3 sts., w.r.n., p.2 tog., k.1.

Work 3 rows in single rib.

Cast off loosely in rib.

The Hood

With No. 9 needles cast on 93 sts.

Foundation row (wrong side): K.2, * p.11, k.2; repeat from * to end.

Now work in pattern as follows:

1st row: P.2, * s.k.p.o., k.3b., w.fwd., k.1, w.fwd., k.3b., k.2 tog., p.2; repeat from * to end.

30

2nd, 4th and 6th rows: K.2, * p.11, k.2;
repeat from * to end.

3rd row: P.2, * s.k.p.o., k.2b., w.fwd., k.1,
w.fwd., s.k.p.o., w.fwd., k.2b., k.2 tog.,p.2;
repeat from * to end.

5th row: P.2, * s.k.p.o., k.1b., w.fwd., k.1
(w.fwd., s.k.p.o.) twice, w.fwd., k.1b.,
k.2 tog., p.2; repeat from * to end.

7th row: P.2, * s.k.p.o., w.fwd., k.1 (w.fwd.,
s.k.p.o.) 3 times, w.fwd., k.2 tog., p.2;
repeat from * to end.

8th row: As 2nd row.

These 8 rows form the border pattern;
repeat them twice more.

Now work in pattern with centre st.st.
panel as follows:

1st row: P.2, * s.k.p.o., k.3b., w.fwd., k.1,
w.fwd., k.3b., k.2 tog., p.2 * work from * to
* once, s.k.p.o., k.33, k.2 tog., p.2, work
from * to * twice.

2nd, 4th and 6th rows: K.2, p.11, k.2, p.11,
k.2, p.35, k.2, p.11, k.2, p.11, k.2.

3rd row: P.2, * s.k.p.o., k.2b., w.fwd., k.1,
w.fwd., s.k.p.o., w.fwd., k.2b., k.2 tog.,
p.2, * work from * to * once, k.35, p.2,
work from * to * twice.

5th row: P.2, * s.k.p.o., k.1b., w.fwd., k.1
(w.fwd., s.k.p.o.) twice, w.fwd., k.1b.,
k.2 tog., p.2, * work from * to * once, k.35,
p.2, work from * to * twice.

7th row: P.2, * s.k.p.o., w.fwd., k.1 (w.fwd.,
s.k.p.o.) 3 times, w.fwd., k.2 tog., p.2, *
work from * to * once, k.35, p.2, work from
* to * twice.

8th row: As 2nd row.

These 8 rows set the st.st. panel in centre.
Keeping continuity of the 2 pattern panels

at each side, dec. 1 st. at each side of the
st.st. panel, as before, on the next row and
following 10 right-side rows   60 sts.

Next row: K.2, p.11, k.2, p.11, k.2, p.13,
k.2, p.11, k.2, p.11, k.2.

To shape the back: Next row: Cast off
27 sts., k. to end.

Next row: Cast off 27 sts., p. to end.

On the remaining 15 sts., st.st. 16 rows.

Dec. 1 st. at each end of next row and the
3 following 4th rows – 7 sts.

P.1 row.

Cast off.

The Neck Edging: First join row ends of
back section to the sts. cast off at each side.

With right side of work facing, rejoin wool
to neck edge and pick up and k.65 sts.
evenly along neck edge.

Beginning wrong-side rows with p.1 and
right-side rows with k.1, work 3 rows in
single rib.

Work the slot row as given for cape.

Rib a further 3 rows.

Cast off loosely in rib.

To Make Up The Cape

Press on wrong side using a warm iron
over a damp cloth.

Make two lengths of twisted cord. With
neck edge of hood inside neck edge of cape,
beginning at centre back and, working out-
wards towards fronts, thread the cord
through both sets of holes to attach hood to
cape.

Tie ends of cords at centre back and trim
front ends with tassels.

Sleeping Bag

Materials

Ten 20-gramme balls of Sirdar Wonderland Courtelle Quick Knit in main colour and one ball in a contrast colour; a pair each of No. 8 and No. 10 knitting needles; 16 buttons.

Tension and Size

Worked at a tension of 14 stitches and 16 rows to 2 inches, over the pattern, using No. 8 needles, the bag will measure, when fastened. All round at underarms 27 inches; length $23\frac{1}{2}$ inches.

Abbreviations

K., knit; p., purl; st., stitch; tog., together; dec., decrease (by working 2 sts.tog.); inc., increase (by working twice into same st.); tw.2., twist 2 (k. into front of 2nd st. on left-hand needle, then k. into front of 1st st. and slip both sts. off needle tog.); y.fwd., yarn forward to make a st.; single rib is k.1 and p.1 alternately.

To Make

Begin at flap edge by casting on 96 sts. with No. 10 needles and main and k.6 rows.

Next (buttonhole) row: K.14, * y.fwd., k.2 tog., k.9; repeat from * 5 times more, y.fwd., k.2 tog., k.14.

K.5 rows.

Change to No. 8 needles and work in pattern as follows:

1st row: All k.

2nd row: K.8, p. to last 8 sts., k.8.

3rd row: K.8, p.1, * tw.2, p.2; repeat from * to last 11 sts., tw.2, p.1, k.8.

4th row: K.9, p.2, * k.2, p.2; repeat from * to last 9 sts., k.9.

5th row: As 3rd row.

6th row: As 4th row.

7th row: All k.

8th row: K.8, p. to last 8 sts., k.8.

9th row: K.8, p.3, * tw.2, p.2; repeat from * to last 13 sts., tw.2, p.3, k.8.

10th row: K.11, * p.2, k.2; repeat from * to last 13 sts., p.2, k.11.

11th row: As 9th row.

12th row: As 10th row.

Repeat these 12 rows once more.

Sleeping bag (pattern above); cot blanket in Courtelle (pattern p. 24).

Next row: Cast on 43 sts., k. to end.

Next row: Cast on 43 sts., k.2, p. to last 2 sts., k.2 – 182 sts.

Now continue as follows:

1st row: K.2, * p.2, tw.2; repeat from * to last 4 sts., p.2, k.2.

2nd row: K.4, * p.2, k.2; repeat from * to last 6 sts., p.2, k.4.

3rd row: As 1st row.

4th row: As 2nd row.

5th row: All k.

6th row: K.2, p. to last 2 sts., k.2.

7th row: K.2, * tw.2, p.2; repeat from * to last 4 sts., tw.2, k.2.

8th row: K.2, * p.2, k.2; repeat from * to end.

9th row: As 7th row.

10th row: As 8th row.

11th row: All k.

12th row: K.2, p. to last 2 sts., k.2.

Repeat these 12 rows 11 times more.

Sleeping suit (pattern p. 35).

Now divide sts. for back and fronts.

Next row: Pattern 40 for right front, cast off 6 for armhole – 1 st. left on right-hand needle – pattern next 89 sts. these 90 sts. are for back, cast off 6, pattern to end and work on these 40 sts. for left front.

The left front: Work 1 row back to armhole edge, then dec. 1 st. at armhole edge on next and following 15 right-side rows – 24 sts.

To shape the neck:

1st row: Cast off 4, pattern to end.

2nd row: K.3 tog., pattern to last 2 sts., k.2 tog.

3rd row: Work in pattern.

Repeat 2nd and 3rd rows 5 times more – 2 sts.

Take these 2 sts. tog. and fasten off.

The back: With wrong side of work facing, rejoin yarn to the 90 sts. and work 1 row.

Dec. 1 st. at each end of next and following 14 right-side rows – 60 sts.

Next row: Work in pattern.

Next row: K.3 tog., pattern to last 3 sts., k.3 tog.

Repeat last 2 rows 6 times more – 32 sts.

Work 1 row.

Cast off.

The right front: With wrong side of work facing, rejoin yarn to remaining 40 sts.

Work 1 row, then dec. 1 st. at armhole edge on next and following 14 right-side rows – 25 sts.

Work 1 row back to front edge.

To shape the neck:

1st row: Cast off 4, pattern to last 2 sts., k.2 tog.

2nd row: Work in pattern.

3rd row: K.2 tog., pattern to last 3 sts., k.3 tog.

Repeat 2nd and 3rd rows 5 times more – 2 sts.

Take these 2 sts. tog. and fasten off.

The Sleeves (both alike)

With No. 10 needles and main cast on 42 sts. and work 12 rows in single rib.

Change to No. 8 needles and work in pattern as follows:

1st row: All k.

2nd row: All p.

3rd row: P.2, * tw.2, p.2; repeat from * to end.

4th row: K.2, * p.2, k.2; repeat from * to end.

5th row: As 3rd row.

6th row: As 4th row.

7th row: All k.

8th row: All p.

9th row: Tw.2, * p.2, tw.2; repeat from * to end.

10th row: P.2, * k.2, p.2; repeat from * to end.

11th row: As 9th row.

12th row: As 10th row.

Keeping continuity of the pattern, inc. 1 st. at each end of next and every following 4th row until the 8th inc. row has been worked – 58 sts.

Work 13 rows straight.

To shape the raglan sleeve top: Cast off 3 sts. at beginning of next 2 rows, then dec. 1 st. at each end of next and following

21 right-side rows – 8 sts.

Work 1 row, then cast off.

The Neck Band

First join raglan seams. With right side of work facing, rejoin main to neck edge of left front and, using No. 10 needles, pick up and k.16 sts. from shaped edge, 6 sts. from left sleeve, 29 sts. across back, 6 sts. from right sleeve and 16 sts. from shaped edge of right front – 73 sts.

Beginning first row with p.1, work 7 rows in single rib.

Cast off.

The Button Band

With No. 10 needles and contrast colour cast on 9 sts. and k. 266 rows.

Cast off.

Join main colour to side at cast-on edge and, using No. 10 needles pick up and k. 132 sts. along side edge – that is 1 st. from each ridge – and 9 sts. along cast-off edge, turn and cast off these sts.

Work along other side and short edge in the same way.

The Buttonhole Band

With No. 10 needles and contrast colour cast on 9 sts. and k. 26 rows.

Next (buttonhole) row: K.4, y.fwd., k.2 tog., k.3.

K.25 rows.

Repeat last 26 rows 8 times more, then work buttonhole row again.

K.5 rows.

Cast off.

Work main colour edging as given for button band.

To Make Up The Bag

Do not press. Join sleeve seams. Sew bands to fronts on right side of work taking the sts. through the knitting inside the main coloured edgings. Sew on buttons. Turn up flap and sew 3 buttons to each front to correspond with buttonholes and secure centre to button on front band.

Sleeping Suit

(see illustration p. 33)

**The bootees are detachable when baby is
ready to wear shoes**

Materials

Seven 25-gramme balls of Sirdar
Random Courtelle; a pair each of
No. 9 and No. 10 knitting needles;
8 small buttons.

Tension and Size

Worked at a tension of 13 stitches and 16
rows to 2 inches, over the stocking stitch,
using No. 9 needles, the suit will fit baby
aged six to twelve months.

Abbreviations

K., knit; p., purl; st., stitch; tog., together;
k. or p.2 tog.b., k. or p.2 sts. tog. through
back of loops; dec., decrease (by working
2 sts.tog.); inc., increase (by working twice
into same st.); y.fwd., yarn forward to make
a st.; st.st., stocking st. (k. on right side and
p. on wrong side); single rib is k.1 and p.1
alternately; up 1 (pick up the thread which
lies between the needles and k. into back of
it, thus making a st.).

The Suit

The Back

First Leg: With No. 10 needles cast on
20 sts. and work 6 rows in single rib.
Next (slot) row: K.1, * y.fwd., k.2 tog.;
repeat from * to last st., k.1.
Rib 5 rows.
Change to No. 9 needles.
Next (inc.) row: K.2, * inc. in next st., k.4;
repeat from * twice more, inc. in next st.,
k.2 – 24 sts.
Beginning with a p. row, st.st. 5 rows **.
Inc. 1 st. at *beginning* of next row and
every following 8th row until the 6th inc. row
has been worked – 30 sts.
St.st. 3 rows, then inc. 1 st. at beginning
of next and following 3 right-side rows – 34
sts.
P.1 row.
Cast on 2 sts. at beginning of next row.
P.1 row.
Break off yarn and leave these 36 sts. on
a spare needle.
Second Leg: Work as given for first leg
to **.

Inc. 1 st. at *end* of next row and every
following 8th row until the 6th inc. row has
been worked – 30 sts.
St.st. 3 rows ending with a p. row, then
inc. 1 st. at end of next row and following
3 right-side rows – 34 sts.
P.1 row and k.1 row.
Next row: Cast on 2, p. to end. Do not
break off yarn.
Join legs together thus:
Next row: K. the 36 sts. of second leg,
turn, cast on 3 sts., turn and onto same
needle k. the 36 sts. of first leg – 75 sts ***.
Beginning with a p. row, st.st. 54 rows.
Next (dec.) row: P.5, * p.2 tog., p.7;
repeat from * 6 times more, p.2 tog., p.5 –
67 sts.
Change to No. 10 needles and, beginning
right-side rows with k.1 and wrong-side
rows with p.1, work 10 rows in single rib.
Change back to No. 9 needles and st.st.
20 rows, ending with a p. row.
To shape the raglan armholes: Cast
off 4 sts. at beginning of next 2 rows, then

dec. 1 st. at each end of the next row and following 17 right-side rows – 23 sts.

P.1 row, then break off yarn and leave sts. on a spare needle.

The Front

Work as given for back to ***.

Beginning with a p. row, st.st. 14 rows.

Now divide sts. for front opening.

Next row: P.34 and leave these sts. on a spare needle for right-half front, p. next 7 sts. and leave these on a safety-pin for buttonhole band, p. to end and work on these 34 sts. for the left-half front.

The left-half front: St.st. 39 rows.

Next (dec.) row: P.2, * p.2 tog., p.7; repeat from * twice, p.2 tog., p.3 – 30 sts.

Change to No. 10 needles and work 10 rows in single rib.

Change back to No. 9 needles and st.st. 20 rows (work 21 rows here on right-half front).

To shape the raglan armhole: Cast off 4 sts. at beginning of the next row; work 1 row, then dec. 1 st. at armhole edge on the next row and following 10 alternate rows, ending at front edge – 15 sts.

To shape the neck: Cast off 2 sts. at beginning of the next row, then dec. 1 st. at each end of the next row and following 3 alternate rows – 5 sts.

Work 1 row, then dec. 1 st. at armhole edge only on the next row and following 2 alternate rows.

Take remaining 2 sts. tog. and fasten off.

The right-half front: With right side of work facing, rejoin yarn to the 34 sts. left on spare needle and work as given for left-half front noting the extra row to be worked before shaping the armhole.

The Sleeves (both alike)

With No. 10 needles cast on 38 sts. and work 10 rows in single rib.

Change to No. 9 needles and, beginning with a k. row, st.st. 4 rows.

Inc. 1 st. at each end of the next row and every following 6th row until the 6th inc. row has been worked – 50 sts.

St.st. 9 rows.

To shape the raglan sleeve top: Work

as given for raglan armhole shaping on back when 6 sts. will remain.

Break off yarn and leave sts. on a safety-pin.

The Button Band

With No. 10 needles cast on 7 sts.

1st row: K.1, * p.1, k.1; repeat from * twice.

2nd row: K.2, p.1, k.1, p.1, k.2.

Repeat these 2 rows 48 times more.

Break off yarn and leave sts. on a safety-pin.

The Buttonhole Band

Slip the 7 sts. left at front onto No. 10 needle and work 4 rows in rib as given for button band.

Next (buttonhole) row: K.1, p.1, k.1, y.fwd., k.2 tog., p.1, k.1.

Rib 13 rows.

Repeat last 14 rows 5 times more, then work the buttonhole row again.

Rib 9 rows.

Break off yarn and leave sts. on a safety-pin.

The Neck Band

First join raglan seams and sew front bands to respective fronts.

With right side of work facing, slip the sts. of right-front band onto No. 10 needle with point to inner edge, rejoin yarn and pick up and k.14 sts. from right front neck edge, k. the 6 sts. of right sleeve, k. across the 23 sts. at back, k. the 6 sts. of left sleeve, pick up and k.14 sts. from left front neck edge and, finally, rib across the 7 sts. of left-front band – 77 sts.

Work 3 rows in single rib.

Work a buttonhole on the next row, then rib a further 3 rows.

Cast off loosely in rib.

To Make Up The Suit

Press on wrong side using a COOL iron over a DRY cloth. Join sleeve, side and inner leg seams. Neaten lower edge of front bands. Sew on buttons.

36

Opposite – Dolman sleeved romp (pattern p. 38).

The Bootees

With No. 9 needles cast on 40 sts. and p.1 row.

To shape the sole:

1st row: Inc. in 1st st., k.18, up 1, k.2, up 1, k.18, inc. in last st.

2nd, 4th and 6th rows: All p.

3rd row: Inc., k.20, up 1, k.2, up 1, k.20, inc.

5th row: Inc., k.22, up 1, k.2, up 1, k.22, inc. − 52 sts.

7th row (right side): All p.

Beginning with a p. row, st.st. 7 rows.

To shape the instep:

1st row: K.23, k.2 tog., k.2, k.2 tog.b., k.23.

2nd row: P.22, p.2 tog.b., p.2, p.2 tog., p.22.

3rd row: K.21, k.2 tog., k.2, k.2 tog.b., k.21.

4th row: P.20, p.2 tog.b., p.2, p.2 tog., p.20.

5th row: K.19, k.2 tog., k.2, k.2 tog.b., k. 19.

6th row: P.18, p.2 tog.b., p.2, p.2 tog., p. 18.

7th row: K.17, k.2 tog., k.2, k.2 tog.b., k.17 − 38 sts.

8th row: All p.

Change to No. 10 needles and work 2 rows in single rib.

Next (slot) row: K.1, * y.fwd., k.2 tog.; repeat from * to last st., k.1.

Rib 3 rows.

Cast off loosely in rib.

To Make Up The Bootees

Join back and underfoot seam. Make a length of twisted cord and with slot row at lower edge of suit in line with holes on bootees, thread cord through both sets of holes.

Dolman Sleeved Romper

(see illustration p. 37)

Materials

Six 20-gramme balls of Sirdar Wonderland Courtelle Quick Knit; a pair of No. 10 knitting needles; 9 buttons.

Tension and Size

Worked at a tension of 8 stitches and 10 rows to 1 inch unstretched, using No. 10 needles, the romper will fit baby aged six to twelve months.

Abbreviations

K., knit; p., purl; st., stitch; tog., together; dec., decrease (by working 2 sts. tog.); y.fwd., yarn forward to make a st.; single rib is k.1 and p.1 alternately.

The Back

With No. 10 needles cast on 27 sts.
1st row: K.3, * p.1, k.3; repeat from * to end.
2nd row: K.1, p.1, * k.3, p.1; repeat from * to last st., k.1.
These two rows form the ribbed pattern; repeat them 4 times more.
Keeping continuity of the pattern, cast on 2 sts. at beginning of each of next 28 rows – 83 sts.
Work 54 rows straight.
Next row: P.1, * k.1, p.1; repeat from * to end.
Next row: K.1, * p.1, k.1; repeat from * to end.
Repeat these 2 rows twice more.
Next (slot) row: P.1, k.1, * y.fwd., k.2 tog., p.1, k.1; repeat from * to last st., p.1. Rib 5 rows **.
Now work the 2 ribbed pattern rows 15 times.
To shape for sleeves: Cast on 2 sts. at beginning of next 10 rows; 3 sts. on next 4 rows and 8 sts. on next 2 rows – 131 sts.

Work 32 rows straight.
To shape top of sleeve and shoulder: Cast off 8 sts. at beginning of next 6 rows and 12 sts. on next 4 rows.
Cast off remaining 35 sts.

The Front

Work as back to **.
Work the 2 ribbed pattern rows 3 times, then work 1st row again.
Now divide sts. for front opening.
Next row: Pattern 38 and leave these sts. on a spare needle for right side, pattern next 7 sts. and leave on a safety-pin for buttonhole band, pattern to end and work on these 38 sts. for left side.
The left side: Work 22 rows straight.
To shape for sleeve: Cast on 2 sts. at beginning of next and following 4 alternate rows; 3 sts. on the next 2 alternate rows and 8 sts. on following alternate row – 62 sts.
Work 22 rows straight, ending at front edge.

To shape the neck: Cast off 4 sts. at beginning of next row, then dec. 1 st. at neck edge on next 10 rows – 48 sts.

To shape top of sleeve and shoulder: Cast off 8 sts. at beginning of next and following 2 alternate rows and 12 sts. on next alternate row – 12 sts.

Work 1 row, then cast off.

The right side: With right side of work facing, rejoin yarn to 38 sts. on spare needle and pattern to end of row.

Now work as given for left side to end.

The Sleeve Borders (both alike)

First join upper sleeve seams.

With right side of work facing, rejoin yarn to lower edge of sleeve and, using No. 10 needles, pick up and k.56 sts. along edge.

Work 7 rows in single rib.

Cast off loosely in rib.

The Neck Band

With right side of work facing, rejoin yarn to neck edge and, using No. 10 needles, pick up and k.20 sts. along shaped edge, 33 sts. across back, 20 sts. from shaped edge – 73 sts.

Beginning wrong-side rows with p.1 and right-side rows with k.1, work 7 rows in single rib.

Cast off in rib.

The Leg Borders (both alike)

First join side and sleeve seams.

With right side of work facing, rejoin yarn to leg edge and, using No. 10 needles, pick up and k.80 sts. along entire leg edge.

Work 7 rows in single rib.

Cast off in rib.

The Lower Edge Button Border

With right side of work facing, rejoin yarn to lower edge of back and, using No. 10 needles, pick up and k.38 sts. along edge including leg bands.

Work 9 rows in single rib.

Cast off in rib.

The Lower Edge Buttonhole Border

With right side of work facing, rejoin yarn to lower edge of front and, using No. 10 needles, pick up and k.38 sts.

Work 5 rows in single rib.

Next (buttonhole) row: Rib 6, * y.fwd., k.2 tog., rib 6; repeat from * 3 times.

Rib 3 rows.

Cast off in rib.

The Front Button Band

With No. 10 needles cast on 7 sts. and k.68 rows.

Cast off.

The Front Buttonhole Band

Rejoin yarn to 7 sts. left at front and, using No. 10 needles, k.14 rows.

Next (buttonhole) row: K.3, y.fwd., k.2 tog., k.2.

K.11 rows.

Repeat last 12 rows 3 times more; work buttonhole row, then k.5 rows.

Cast off.

To Make Up The Romper

Do not press. Sew bands to respective fronts and neaten lower edge.

Sew on buttons. Make length of twisted cord for waist.

Dressing Gown

**Generous wrap-over style will see the
children through 3 or 4 winters**

Materials

Fourteen 25-gramme balls of Emu
Scotch Superwash Double Knitting
Wool for 1st size; sixteen balls for 2nd
size. For either size: a pair each of
No. 8 and No. 9 knitting needles; small
motif.

Tension

Work at a tension of 11 stitches and 15
rows to 2 inches, over the stocking stitch,
using No. 8 needles, to obtain the following
measurements:

Measurements

	INCHES	
	1st size	2nd size
All round at underarms-		
fastened	27	29
Side seam	17¼	19¼
Length	22¼	24¼
Sleeve seam	8½	9½

Abbreviations

K., knit; p., purl; st., stitch; tog., together;
inc., increase (by working twice into same
st.); k.2 tog.b., k.2 sts. tog. through back of
loops; w.t.f., wool to front; w.t.b., wool to
back; sl., slip; st.st., stocking st. (k. on
right side and p. on wrong side); m.st.,
moss st. (k.1 and p.1 alternately and on
subsequent rows the sts. are reversed).

● *The instructions are given for 1st size.
Where they vary, work figures in brackets for
2nd size.*

The Back

With No. 9 needles cast on 103 (109) sts.
M.st. row: K.1, * p.1, k.1; repeat from * to
end.
Repeat this row 11 times more.
Change to No. 8 needles and, beginning
with a k. row, st.st. 18 (20) rows.
Now shape as follows:
1st (shaping) row: * K.19 (20), k.2 tog.b.,
repeat from * once, k.19 (21), ** k.2 tog.,
k.19 (20); repeat from ** once.
St.st. 13 (15) rows.

2nd (shaping) row: * K.18 (19), k.2 tog.b.;
repeat from * once, k.19 (21), ** k.2 tog.,
k.18 (19); repeat from ** once.
St.st. 13 (15) rows.
3rd (shaping) row: * K.17 (18), k.2 tog.b.;
repeat from * once, k.19 (21), ** k.2 tog.,
k.17 (18); repeat from ** once.
St.st. 13 (15) rows.
4th (shaping) row: * K.16 (17), k.2 tog.b.;
repeat from * once, k.19 (21), ** k.2 tog.,
k.16 (17); repeat from ** once.
St.st. 13 (15) rows.

5th (shaping) row: * K.15 (16), k.2 tog.b.; repeat from * once, k.19 (21), ** k.2 tog., k.15 (16); repeat from ** once.
St.st. 13 (15) rows.

6th (shaping) row: * K.14 (15), k.2 tog.b.; repeat from * once, k.19 (21), ** k.2 tog., k.14 (15); repeat from ** once.
St.st. 13 (15) rows.

7th (shaping) row: * K.13 (14), k.2 tog.b.; repeat from * once, k.19 (21), ** k.2 tog., k.13 (14); repeat from ** once – 75 (81) sts.
St.st., 19 (21) rows.

To shape the armholes:

1st and 2nd rows: Cast off 6 (7) sts. at beginning of each row.

3rd row: K.1, k.2 tog.b., k. to last 3 sts., k.2 tog., k.1.

4th row: K.1, p. to last st., k.1.

Repeat 3rd and 4th rows twice more, then work 3rd row again – 55 (59) sts.
St.st. 29 (31) rows.

To slope the shoulders: Cast off 5 sts. at beginning of next 2 rows; 5 (6) sts. on following 2 rows and 6 sts. on next 2 rows.
Cast off remaining 23 (25) sts.

The Left Front

With No. 9 needles cast on 75 (77) sts. and work 12 rows in m.st. as given for back.
Change to No. 8 needles.

1st row: K. to last 8 sts., m.st. 8.

2nd row: M.st. 8, p. to end.
Repeat these 2 rows 8 (9) times more.
Keeping continuity of the m.st. border, shape as follows:

1st (shaping) row: K.19 (20), k.2 tog.b., k.19 (20), k.2 tog.b., work to end.
Work 13 (15) rows.

2nd (shaping) row: K.18 (19), k.2 tog.b., k.18 (19), k.2 tog.b., work to end.
Work 13 (15) rows.

3rd (shaping) row: K.17 (18), k.2 tog.b., k.17 (18), k.2 tog.b., work to end.
Work 13 (15) rows.

4th (shaping) row: K.16 (17), k.2 tog.b., k.16 (17), k.2 tog.b., work to end.
Work 13 (15) rows.

5th (shaping) row: K.15 (16), k.2 tog.b., k.15 (16), k.2 tog.b., work to end.
Work 13 (15) rows.

6th (shaping) row: K.14 (15), k.2 tog.b., k.14 (15), k.2 tog.b., work to end.

Work 13 (15) rows.

7th (shaping) row: K.13 (14), k.2 tog.b., k.13 (14), k.2 tog.b., work to end – 61 (63) sts.
Work 1 (5) row(s).

To slope front edge:

1st row: K. to last 10 sts., k.2 tog., m.st.8.

2nd row: M.st.8, p. to end.
Repeat these 2 rows 8 (7) times more – 52 (55) sts.

To shape the armhole and continue sloping front edge:

1st row: Cast off 6 (7) sts., k. to last 10 sts., k.2 tog., m.st.8.

2nd row: M.st.8, p. to last st., k.1.

3rd row: K.1, k.2 tog.b., k. to last 10 sts., k.2 tog., m.st.8.
Repeat 2nd and 3rd rows 3 times more – 37 (39) sts. This completes armhole shaping.
Continue to slope front edge as follows:

1st row: M.st.8, p. to last st., k.1.

2nd row: K. to last 10 sts., k.2 tog., m.st.8.
Repeat these 2 rows 12 (13) times more – 24 (25) sts.
Work 3 rows straight, ending at armhole edge.

To slope the shoulder: Cast off 5 sts. at beginning of next row; 5 (6) sts. on following alternate row and 6 sts. on next alternate row.
On remaining 8 sts. work 19 (20) rows in m.st. for front band extension.
Cast off.

The Right Front

With No. 9 needles cast on 75 (77) sts. and work 12 rows in m.st. as given for back.
Change to No. 8 needles.

1st row: M.st.8, k. to end.

2nd row: P. to last 8 sts., m.st.8.
Repeat these 2 rows 8 (9) times more.
Keeping continuity of m.st. border shape as follows:

1st (shaping) row: M.st.8, k.25, k.2 tog., k.19 (20), k.2 tog., k.19 (20).
Work 13 (15) rows.

2nd (shaping) row: M.st.8, k.25, k.2 tog., k.18 (19), k.2 tog., k.18 (19).
Work 13 (15) rows.

3rd (shaping) row: M.st.8, k.25, k.2 tog., k.17 (18), k.2 tog., k.17 (18).
Work 13 (15) rows.

4th (shaping) row: M.st.8, k.25, k.2 tog., k.16 (17), k.2 tog., k.16 (17).
Work 13 (15) rows.
5th (shaping) row: M.st.8, k.25, k.2 tog., k.15 (16), k.2 tog., k.15 (16).
Work 13 (15) rows.
6th (shaping) row: M.st.8, k.25, k.2 tog., k.14 (15), k.2 tog., k.14 (15).
Work 13 (15) rows.
7th (shaping) row: M.st.8, k.25, k.2 tog., k.13 (14), k.2 tog., k.13 (14) – 61 (63) sts.
Work 1 (5) row(s).
To slope front edge:
1st row: M.st.8, k.2 tog.b., k. to end.
2nd row: P. to last 8 sts., m.st.8.
Repeat these 2 rows 8 (7) times more, then work 1st row again – 51 (54) sts.
To shape the armhole:
1st row: Cast off 6 (7) sts., p. to last 8 sts., m.st.8.
2nd row: M.st.8, k.2 tog.b., k. to last 3 sts., k.2 tog., k.1.
3rd row: K.1, p. to last 8 sts., m.st.8.
Repeat 2nd and 3rd rows twice more, then work 2nd row again – 37 (39) sts.
This completes armhole shaping.
Continue to slope front edge as follows:
1st row: K.1, p. to last 8 sts., m.st.8.
2nd row: M.st.8, k.2 tog.b., k. to end.
Repeat these 2 rows 12 (13) times more – 24 (25) sts.
Work 4 rows, ending at armhole edge.
To slope the shoulder: Cast off 5 sts. at beginning of next row; 5 (6) sts. on following alternate row and 6 sts. on next alternate row.
On remaining 8 sts. work 19 (20) rows in m.st. for front band extension.
Cast off.

The Sleeves (both alike)

With No. 9 needles cast on 37 (39) sts. and work 10 rows in m.st. as given for back.
Change to No. 8 needles and, beginning with a k. row, st.st. 4 rows.

Inc. 1 st. at each end of next and every following 4th row until the 12th inc. row has been worked – 61 (63) sts.
St.st. 9 (15) rows.
Work 6 (8) rows in m.st.
To shape the sleeve top:
1st row: K.1, k.2 tog.b., k. to last 3 sts., k.2 tog., k.1.
2nd row: K.1, p. to last st., k.1.
Repeat these 2 rows 3 times more.
Cast off.

The Pocket

With No. 8 needles cast on 19 sts. and, beginning with a k. row, st.st. 22 rows.
Change to No. 9 needles and m.st. 4 rows.
Cast off.

The Belt

With No. 8 needles cast on 6 sts.
Rouleau row: * K.1, w.t.f., sl.1, w.t.b.; repeat from * twice.
This row produces tubular knitting; repeat until belt measures 45 inches.
Next row: K.2 tog., k.2 tog., k.2 tog.
Cast off remaining 3 sts.

The Belt Loops (make 2)

With No. 9 needles cast on 11 sts. and work 3 rows in m.st.
Cast off.

To Make Up The Dressing Gown

Press on wrong side, using a warm iron over a damp cloth. Join shoulder and side seams. Join sleeve seams as far as m.st. band, then set in sleeves sewing the free row-ends to the sts. cast off for armholes on back and fronts. Join cast-off edges of front band extensions together and sew in place across back neck. Sew belt loops to side seams. Sew on pocket. Trim belt with tassels. Add motif.

Siren Suit

Trimmed with loop stitch in a contrast colour for girls. For boys, pick up the stitches as given in the instructions, then cast them off for a plain edge

Materials

Fifteen 25-gramme balls of Bairnswear Pleasure Double Knitting Wool for 1st size; sixteen balls for 2nd size. For either size: two 25-gramme balls of Bairnswear Pleasure 4-ply Wool in a contrast colour; a pair each of No. 8 and No. 10 knitting needles; a 12-inch zip.

Tension

Work at a tension of 11 stitches and 15 rows to 2 inches, over the stocking stitch, using No. 8 needles, to obtain the following measurements:

Measurements

	INCHES	
	1st size	2nd size
All round at underarms	$24\frac{1}{2}$	$25\frac{1}{2}$
Sleeve seam	$8\frac{1}{2}$	$9\frac{1}{4}$
Inside leg seam	12	$12\frac{1}{2}$
Outside leg to waist ribbing	18	19

Abbreviations

K., knit; p., purl; st., stitch; tog., together; dec., decrease (by working 2 sts. tog.); inc., increase (by working twice into same st.); up 1 (pick up the thread which lies between the needles and k. into back of it, thus making a st.); single rib is k.1 and p.1 alternately; st.st., stocking st. (k. on right side and p. on wrong side).

● *The instructions are given for 1st size. Where they vary, work figures in brackets for 2nd size.*

44

The Left Leg

With No. 10 needles cast on 46 (48) sts. and work 18 rows in single rib.

Change to No. 8 needles and, beginning with a k. row, st.st. 2 (6) rows.

Next (shaping) row: Inc. in 1st st., k.21 (22), up 1, k.2 and mark these 2 sts. with a coloured thread for centre, up 1, k.20 (21), inc. in next st., k.1.

St.st. 5 rows.

Inc. 1 st. at each end and work 'up 1' at each side of centre 2 sts. as before, on next row and every following 6th row until the 7th shaping row has been worked – 74 (76) sts.

St.st. 3 rows, then inc. 1 st. at *each end only* on next row and every following 4th row until a further 8 inc. rows have been completed – 90 (92) sts.

St.st. 3 rows ending with a p. row – work 4 rows here when working right leg to end with a k. row.

To shape the crotch: Cast off 4 sts. at beginning of next 2 rows and 3 sts. on following 2 rows – 76 (78) sts.

Next row: Cast off 3, work to end.

Next row: Dec., work to end.

Next row: Dec., work to end – 71 (73) sts.

Dec. 1 st. at beginning of next row and following alternate row – 69 (71) sts.

St.st. 30 (34) rows ending with a p. row – end with a k. row here when working right leg **.

To shape for extra length on back:

1st and 2nd (turning) rows: K.30 for 1st row, turn and p. to end for 2nd row.

3rd and 4th rows: K.23, turn and p. to end.

5th and 6th rows: K.16, turn and p. to end.

Break off wool and leave sts. on spare needle.

The Right Leg

Work as given for left leg to ** noting the variation in the number of rows to be worked where indicated to reverse the crotch shaping.

To shape for extra length on back:

1st and 2nd (turning) rows: P.30, turn and k. to end.

3rd and 4th rows: P.23, turn and k. to end.

5th and 6th rows: P.16, turn and k. to end.

Do not break off wool, but join legs together thus:

Next (joining) row: Onto the needle holding the sts. of right leg k. the 69 (71) sts. of left leg picking up a thread at each point where work was turned and taking this together with next st. to avoid a gap in the knitting.

P.1 row across all sts. closing gaps across right leg – 138 (142) sts.

Change to No. 10 needles and work 8 rows in single rib decreasing 3 (1) st.(s). evenly across last row – 135 (141) sts.

Change back to No. 8 needles and work in pattern for top as follows:

1st row: K.3, * p.3, k.3; repeat from * to end.

2nd row: P.3, * k.3, p.3; repeat from * to end.

3rd row: As 1st row.

4th row: As 1st row.

5th row: As 2nd row.

6th row: As 1st row.

These 6 rows form the basket st. pattern; repeat them 3 (4) times more, then work first 4 rows again.

Now divide sts. for back and fronts.

Next row: Pattern 34 (35) turn and, leaving remaining 101 (106) sts. on a spare needle, work on these sts. for right front.

The right front: To shape the raglan armhole: Cast off 4 sts. at beginning of next row, then dec. 1 st. at armhole edge on next and following 12 (13) alternate rows – 17 sts.

Work 1 row to end at front edge.

To shape the neck: Cast off 6 sts. at beginning and dec. 1 st. at end of next row, then dec. 1 st. at each end of following 4 alternate rows.

Work 1 row, then take remaining 2 sts. tog. and fasten off.

The Back: With right side of work facing, rejoin wool to sts. on spare needle, cast off 4 – 1 st. left on right-hand needle not included in next item, pattern 62 (66) turn and work on these 63 (67) sts. for back.

Next row: Cast off 4, pattern to end.

Dec. 1 st. at each end of next and following 17 (18) alternate rows – 23 (25) sts.

Work 1 row, then break off wool and leave sts. on spare needle.

The left front: With right side of work facing, rejoin wool to the 34 (35) sts. and work as given for right front to end.

The Sleeves (both alike)

With No. 10 needles cast on 42 sts. and work 16 rows in single rib increasing 3 sts. evenly across last row — 45 sts.

Change to No. 8 needles and work the 6 pattern rows of basket st. once.

Keeping continuity of pattern, inc. 1 st. at each end of next and every following 6th row until the 6th (7th) inc. row has been worked — 57 (59) sts.

Work 19 rows straight.

To shape the raglan sleeve top: Cast off 4 sts. at beginning of next 2 rows, then dec. 1 st. at each end of next and following 17 (18) alternate rows — 13 sts.

Work 1 row, then break off wool and leave sts. on safety-pin.

The Hood

First join raglan seams. With right side of work facing, rejoin wool to neck edge of right front and, using No. 10 needles, pick up and k.16 sts. from shaped edge, k.13 sts. of right sleeve, 23 (25) sts. across back, 13 sts. of left sleeve and, finally, pick up and k.16 sts. from left front neck edge — 81 (83) sts.

1st row: P.1, * k.1, p.1; repeat from * to end.

2nd row: K.1, * p.1, k.1; repeat from * to end.

Repeat these 2 rows 3 times more.

Cast off 6 sts. at beginning of next 2 rows — 69 (71) sts.

Next (increase) row: K.2, * up 1, k.2; repeat from * once (6 times), ** up 1, k.3; repeat from ** 18 (12) times, *** up 1, k.2; repeat from *** twice (7 times) — 93 (99) sts.

Change to No. 8 needles.

Work the 6 pattern rows of basket st. pattern 6 (7) times.

To shape the top: Cast off 3 sts. at beginning of next 8 (10) rows and 21 sts. on next 2 rows — 27 sts.

Work 6 rows, then inc. 1 st. at each end of next and every following 6th row until the 6th (7th) inc. row has been worked — 39 (41) sts.

Work 9 rows straight.

Cast off.

The Trimming

Front edges: With right side of work facing, using Double Knitting and No. 10 needles, pick up and k.62 (70) sts. along front edge from top of neck ribbing to 1 inch below waist ribbing, Break off wool and secure each end.

With wrong side facing, join on 2 strands of 4-ply and, using No. 10 needles, work loop st. as follows:

Loop st. row: * Insert needle into st., wind wool clockwise twice round needle and first finger of left hand, then round needle only, draw loops through onto right-hand needle, slip them back onto left-hand needle and k. them together through back of loops; repeat from * in every st. to end of row.

K.1 row.

Cast off.

The Hood Edging: First join row ends of top section to cast-off edges of side sections.

Work as given for front edgings picking up 86 (96) sts. all round face edge.

To Make Up The Suit

Press on wrong side, avoiding the ribbing, using a warm iron over a damp cloth. Join inner leg, front, back and sleeve seams. Insert zip.

Ribbed Pram Set

(see illustration p. 49)

Make it in Double Knitting Wool or Tricel

Materials

Sixteen 25-gramme balls Emu Scotch Superwash Double Knitting Wool or fourteen 20-gramme balls of Emu Tricel Nylon Double Knitting; a pair each of No. 8 and No. 10 knitting needles; 4 buttons for coat; 1 button for cap; 1 yard of 1-inch wide ribbon for bonnet; 1 yard of narrow ribbon for girl's mitts and waist length of elastic for girl's leggings.

Abbreviations

K., knit; p., purl; st., stitch; tog., together; dec., decrease (by working 2 sts. tog.); inc., increase (by working twice into same st.); s.k.p.o., slip 1, k.1, pass slipped st. over; k.1b., k.1 through back of loop; y.fwd., yarn forward to make a st.; st.st., stocking st. (k. on right side and p. on wrong side); single rib is k.1 and p.1 alternately; up 1 (pick up the thread which lies between the needles and k. into back of it, thus making a st.).

Tension and Size

Worked at a tension 11 stitches and 15 rows to 2 inches, over the stocking stitch, using No. 8 needles, the set will fit baby aged three to six months.

The Jacket

The Back

With No. 8 needles cast on 67 sts.

1st row: K.1, p.1, * k.1b., p.1; repeat from * to last st., k.1.

2nd row: K.2, * p.1, k.1; repeat from * ending last repeat with k.2.

3rd row: As 1st row.

4th row: K.1, p. to last st., k.1.

5th row: K.1, * k.1b., p.1; repeat from * to last 2 sts., k.1b., k.1.

6th row: K.1, * p.1, k.1; repeat from * to end.

7th row: As 5th row.

8th row: K.1, p. to last st., k.1.

These 8 rows form the pattern; repeat them 5 times more, then work first 4 rows again **

To shape the raglan armholes:

1st row: Cast off 4, pattern to end.

2nd row: Cast off 4, pattern to end.

3rd row: K.2, s.k.p.o., pattern to last 4 sts., k.2 tog., k.2.

4th row: K.2, p.1, pattern to last 3 sts., p.1, k.2.

Repeat 3rd and 4th rows 18 times more – 21 sts.

Cast off.

The Left Front

With No. 8 needles cast on 35 sts. and work as back to **.
To shape the raglan armhole:
1st row: Cast off 4, pattern to end.
2nd row: Work in pattern.
3rd row: K.2, s.k.p.o., pattern to end.
4th row: Pattern to last 3 sts., p.1, k.2.
Repeat 3rd and 4th rows 10 times more, then work 3rd row again – 19 sts.
To shape the neck:
1st row: Cast off 6, pattern to end.
2nd row: K.2, s.k.p.o., pattern to last 2 sts., k.2 tog.
3rd row: Pattern to last 3 sts., p.1, k.2.
Repeat 2nd and 3rd rows 3 times more – 5 sts.
Next row: K.2, s.k.p.o., k.1.
Next row: P.2, k.2.
Next row: K.2, s.k.p.o.
Next row: P.1, k.2.
Next row: K.1, s.k.p.o.
Next row: P.2.
Take remaining 2 sts. tog. and fasten off.

The Right Front

With No. 8 needles cast on 35 sts. and work as back to **.
Work 1 row more to finish at side edge.
To shape the raglan armhole:
1st row: Cast off 4, pattern to end.
2nd row: Pattern to last 4 sts., k.2 tog., k.2.
3rd row: K.2, p.1, pattern to end.
Repeat 2nd and 3rd rows 11 times more – 19 sts.
To shape the neck:
1st row: Cast off 6, pattern to last 4 sts., k.2 tog., k.2.
2nd row: Work in pattern.
3rd row: K.2 tog., pattern to last 4 sts., k.2 tog., k.2.
Repeat 2nd and 3rd rows 3 times more – 4 sts.
Next row: K.2, p.2.
Next row: K.2 tog., k.2.
Next row: K.2, p.1.
Next row: K.2 tog., k.1.
Next row: P.2.
Take remaining 2 sts. tog. and fasten off.

The Sleeves (both alike)

With No. 10 needles cast on 37 sts. and, beginning right-side rows with k.1 and wrong-side rows with p.1, work 12 rows in single rib.
Change to No. 8 needles and work the first 4 rows of pattern as given for back.
Keeping continuity of the pattern, inc. 1 st. at each end of next row and every following 4th row until the 8th inc. row has been worked – 53 sts.
Work 11 rows straight.
To shape the raglan sleeve top: Work exactly as given for raglan armhole shaping on back when 7 sts. will remain.
Cast off.

The Collar

With No. 8 needles cast on 65 sts. and work the 8 pattern rows as given for back twice, then work first 4 rows again.
Cast off loosely.

The Buttonhole Band

With No. 10 needles cast on 7 sts. and work 40 rows in single rib as given for sleeves.
Next (buttonhole) row: Rib 2, k.2 tog., y.fwd., rib 3.
Rib 11 rows.
Repeat last 12 rows twice more, then work buttonhole row again.
Rib 3 rows.
Cast off.

The Button Band

With No. 10 needles cast on 7 sts. and work 80 rows in rib as given for sleeves.
Cast off.

To Make Up The Jacket

Pin out and press with a warm iron over a damp cloth (cool iron and dry cloth for Tricel). Join raglan seams, then join sleeve and side seams. Sew bands to fronts. Beginning and ending in centre of front bands, sew cast-on edge of collar evenly to neck edge. Sew on buttons.

The Leggings

The Right Leg

With No. 10 needles cast on 56 sts. and work 6 rows in single rib.

Next (slot) row: Rib 3, * y.fwd., k.2 tog., rib 2; repeat from * ending rib 3.

Rib 3 rows.

Change to No. 8 needles.

To shape for extra length on back:

1st and 2nd (turning) rows: K.12 for 1st row, turn and p. to end for 2nd row.

3rd and 4th rows: K.23, turn and p. to end.

5th and 6th rows: K.34, turn and p. to end.

7th and 8th rows: K.45, turn and p. to end.

Next row: K. across all sts. picking up a thread at each point where work was turned and taking this together with next st. to avoid a gap in the knitting.

Beginning with a p. row, st.st. 17 rows.

** Inc. 1 st. at each end of next row and every following 6th row until the 4th inc. row has been worked – 64 sts.

St.st. 5 rows.

Inc. 1 st. at each end of next 5 rows – 74 sts.

P.1 row.

To shape the leg: Dec. 1 st. at each end of next and following 2 alternate rows – 68 sts.

St.st. 3 rows.

Dec. 1 st. at each end of next and every following 3rd row until the 18th dec. row has been worked – 32 sts. – ending with a p. row.

Change to No. 10 needles and work 8 rows in single rib **.

Now divide sts. for instep.

Next row: K.26, turn and p.10.

On these 10 sts., st.st. 14 rows for instep. Break off yarn.

With right side of work facing, rejoin yarn to inner edge of 16 sts. at right-hand side and pick up and k.13 sts. along row ends of instep, k. the 10 sts. of instep, pick up and k.13 sts. along other side and k. the 6 sts. at left-hand side – 58 sts.

K.11 rows.

To shape the foot:

1st row: K.3, s.k.p.o., k.2 tog., k.25, s.k.p.o., k.2 tog., k.22.

2nd row: All k.

3rd row: K.2, s.k.p.o., k.2 tog., k.23, s.k.p.o., k.2 tog., k.21.

4th row: All k.

5th row: K.1, s.k.p.o.. k.2 tog., k.21, s.k.p.o., k.2 tog., k.20.

Cast off remaining 46 sts.

The Left Leg

With No. 10 needles cast on 56 sts. and work 6 rows in single rib.

Next (slot) row: Rib 3, * y.fwd., k.2 tog., rib 2; repeat from * ending rib 3.

Rib 3 rows.

Change to No. 8 needles.

To shape for extra length on back:

1st and 2nd (turning) rows: P.12 for 1st row, turn and k. to end for 2nd row.

3rd and 4th rows: P.23, turn and k. to end.

5th and 6th rows: P.34, turn and k. to end.

7th and 8th rows: P.45, turn and k. to end.

Next row: P. across all sts. closing gaps.

Beginning with a k. row, st.st. 18 rows.

Now work as given for right leg from ** to **.

Divide sts. for instep.

Next row: K.16, turn and p.10.

On these 10 sts., st.st. 14 rows for instep. Break off yarn.

With right side of work facing, rejoin yarn to inner edge of 6 sts. at right-hand side and pick up and k.13 sts. along row ends of instep, k. the 10 sts. of instep, pick up and k.13 sts. along other side of instep and k. the 16 sts. at left-hand side – 58 sts.

K.11 rows.

To shape the foot:

1st row: K.22, s.k.p.o., k.2 tog., k.25, s.k.p.o., k.2 tog., k.3.

2nd row: All k.

3rd row: K.21, s.k.p.o., k.2 tog., k.23, s.k.p.o., k.2 tog., k.2.

4th row: All k.

5th row: K.20, s.k.p.o., k.2 tog., k.21, s.k.p.o., k.2 tog., k.1.
Cast off remaining 46 sts.

To Make Up The Leggings

Press as given for jacket. Join inner leg and underfoot seams, then join front and back seams. Make a length of twisted cord and thread through holes at waist. Trim with tassles. (For girl's set, add elastic.)

The Cap

First Ear Piece

With No. 10 needles cast on 6 sts. and k.6 rows.
Next (buttonhole) row: K.1, k.2 tog., y.fwd., k.3.
K.11 rows.
* Now shape as follows:
1st row: K.3, up 1, k.3.
2nd row: K.3, p.1, k.3.
3rd row: K.3, up 1, k.1, up 1, k.3.
4th row: K.3, p.3, k.3.
5th row: K.3, up 1, k. to last 3 sts., up 1, k.3.
6th row: K.3, p. to last 3 sts., k.3.
Repeat 5th and 6th rows 4 times more, then work 5th row again – 21 sts *.
Next row: K.3, p. to last 3 sts., k.3.
Next row: All k.
Repeat last 2 rows once more, then work first of these rows again.
Next row: Cast on 8, k. to end.
Next row: K.3, p. to last 11 sts., k.11.
Next row: All k.
Repeat last 2 rows once more. Break off yarn and leave sts. on spare needle.

Second Ear Piece

With No. 10 needles cast on 6 sts. and k.18 rows.
Work from * to * of first ear piece.
Next row: K.3, p. to last 3 sts., k.3.
Next row: All k.
Repeat these 2 rows once more.
Next row: Cast on 8, k. these 8 sts., then k.3, p. to last 3 sts., k.3.
Next row: All k.

Next row: K.11, p. to last 3 sts., k.3.
Repeat last 2 rows once more.
Next row: All k.
Now join the two pieces together as follows:
Next row: P.29, turn, cast on 25, turn and, onto same needle, p. the 29 sts. of first ear piece – 83 sts.
Continue as follows:
1st row: K.29, p.1, * k.1, p.1; repeat from * 11 times, k. 29.
2nd row: P.29, k.1, * p.1, k.1; repeat from * 11 times, p. 29.
Repeat these 2 rows once more.
Change to No. 8 needles and, beginning with a k. row, st.st. 22 rows.
To shape the crown:
1st row: K.5, s.k.p.o., k.1, k.2 tog., k.17, s.k.p.o., k.1, k.2 tog., k.19, s.k.p.o., k.1, k.2 tog., k.17, s.k.p.o., k.1, k.2 tog., k.5.
2nd and every alternate row: All k.
3rd row: K.4, s.k.p.o., k.1, k.2 tog., k.15, s.k.p.o., k.1, k.2 tog., k.17, s.k.p.o., k.1, k.2 tog., k.15, s.k.p.o., k.1, k.2 tog., k.4.
5th row: K.3, s.k.p.o., k.1, k.2 tog., k.13, s.k.p.o., k.1, k.2 tog., k.15, s.k.p.o., k.1, k.2 tog., k.13, s.k.p.o., k.1, k.2 tog., k.3.
7th row: K.2, s.k.p.o., k.1, k.2 tog., k.11, s.k.p.o., k.1, k.2 tog., k.13, s.k.p.o., k.1, k.2 tog., k.11, s.k.p.o., k.1, k.2 tog., k.2.
9th row: K.1, s.k.p.o., k.1, k.2 tog., k.9, s.k.p.o., k.1, k.2 tog., k.11, s.k.p.o., k.1, k.2 tog., k.9, s.k.p.o., k.1, k.2 tog., k.1.
11th row: S.k.p.o., k.1, k.2 tog., k.7, s.k.p.o., k.1, k.2 tog., k.9, s.k.p.o., k.1, k.2 tog., k.7, s.k.p.o., k.1, k.2 tog.
12th row: All k. – 35 sts.

13th row: K.1, * k.2 tog.; repeat from * to end – 18 sts.

14th row: * K.2 tog.; repeat from * to end – 9 sts.

Break off yarn; run end through remaining sts., draw up and fasten off securely, then join row ends to form back seam.

To Make Up The Cap

Press as given for jacket. Sew on button.

The Bonnet

To Make

With No. 10 needles cast on 78 sts. and work 16 rows in single rib.

Change to No. 8 needles and, beginning with a k. row, st.st. 26 rows.

To shape the crown:

1st row: K.3, * s.k.p.o., k.14, k.2 tog.; repeat from * 3 times, k.3.

2nd and every alternate row: All k.

3rd row: K.3, * s.k.p.o., k.12, k.2 tog.; repeat from * 3 times, k.3.

5th row: K.3, * s.k.p.o., k.10, k.2 tog.; repeat from * 3 times, k.3.

7th row: K.3, * s.k.p.o., k.8, k.2 tog.; repeat from * 3 times, k.3.

9th row: K.3, * s.k.p.o., k.6, k.2 tog.; repeat from * 3 times, k.3.

11th row: K.3, * s.k.p.o., k.4, k.2 tog.; repeat from * 3 times, k.3 – 30 sts.

13th row: * K.2 tog.; repeat from * to end.

15th row: K.1, * k.2 tog.; repeat from * to end – 8 sts.

Break off yarn; run end through remaining sts., draw up and fasten off securely, then join row ends along crown and 1 inch of the st.st. section to form back seam.

To Make Up The Bonnet

Press as given for jacket. Turn back ribbed edge and trim with ribbon.

The Mitts

To Make (both alike)

With No. 8 needles cast on 33 sts. and work the 8 pattern rows given for back of jacket once, then work first 4 rows again.

Next (slot) row: K.1, * y.fwd., k.2 tog., k.2; repeat from * to end.

Next (dec.) row: P.4, * p.2 tog., p.2; repeat from * ending last repeat with p.3 – 26 sts.

Beginning with a k. row, st.st. 18 rows.

To shape the top:

1st row: K.2, * k.2 tog., k.2; repeat from * to end.

2nd row: All p.

3rd row: K.2, * k.2 tog., k.1; repeat from * to end.

4th row: * P.2 tog.; repeat from * to end.

Break off yarn; run end through remaining 7 sts., draw up and fasten off securely, then join row ends.

To Make Up The Mitts

Press as given for jacket. Make a length of twisted cord and thread through holes at wrist. (For girl's set add ribbon.)

Pram Set
in Courtelle

Materials

Eight 22.68 gramme balls of Emu Courtelle Baby Quickerknit; a pair of No. 8 knitting needles; 3 buttons; 1½ yards of narrow ribbon; 1 yard of 1-inch wide ribbon; a waist length of elastic.

Tension

Work at a tension of 6 stitches and 8 rows to 1 inch, over the stocking stitch, using No. 8 needles, to obtain the following measurements:

Measurements

	INCHES
The Jacket	
All round at underarms	20
Side seam	6¼
Length	11¼
Sleeve seam	6¾
The Leggings	
All round at widest part	26
Inside leg seam	8

Abbreviations

K., knit; p., purl; st., stitch; tog., together; dec., decrease (by working 2 sts. tog.); inc., increase (by working twice into same st.); sl., slip; y.t.b., yarn to back; p.s.s.o., pass slipped st. over; k.2 tog.b., k.2 sts. tog. through back of loops; y.o.n., yarn over needle to make a st.; y.r.n., yarn round needle to make a st.; y.fwd., yarn forward to make a st.; st.st., stocking st. (k. on right side and p. on wrong side); single rib is k.1 and p.1 alternately.

The Jacket

The Back

With No. 8 needles cast on 94 sts.
1st row: P.3, * k.3, p.2; repeat from * ending last repeat with p.3.
2nd row: K.3, * p.3, k.2; repeat from * ending last repeat with k.3.
3rd row: P.3, * y.o.n., sl.1, k.2 tog., p.s.s.o., y.r.n., p.2; repeat from * ending last repeat with p.3.
4th row: K.3, * p.3, k.2; repeat from * ending last repeat with k.3.
These 4 rows form the pattern; repeat them 11 times more, then work first two rows again.
Next (dec.) row: P.3, * y.t.b., sl.1, k.2 tog., p.s.s.o., p.2; repeat from * ending last repeat with p.3 — 58 sts.
Next row: K.3, * p.1, k.2; repeat from * ending last repeat with k.3.
To shape the raglan armholes:
1st row: K.2 tog., k. to last 2 sts., k.2 tog.
2nd row: All p.
3rd row: All k.
4th row: All p.
5th row: K.2 tog., k. to last 2 sts., k.2 tog.
6th row: All p.
Repeat 5th and 6th rows 17 times more — 20 sts.
Cast off.

The Left Front

With No. 8 needles cast on 52 sts.
1st row: P.3, * k.3, p.2; repeat from * to last 4 sts., k.4.
2nd row: K.6, * p.3, k.2; repeat from * ending last repeat with k.3.
3rd row: P.3, * y.o.n., sl.1, k.2 tog., p.s.s.o., y.r.n., p.2; repeat from * to last 4 sts., k.4.
4th row: K.6, * p.3, k.2; repeat from * ending last repeat with k.3.

These 4 rows form the pattern; repeat them 11 times more, then work first 2 rows again.
Next (dec.) row: P.3, * y.t.b., sl.1, k.2 tog., p.s.s.o., p.2; repeat from * to last 4 sts., k.4 — 34 sts.
Next row: K.6, * p.1, k.2; repeat from * ending last repeat with k.3.
To shape the raglan armhole:
1st row: K.2 tog., k. to end.
2nd row: K.4, p. to end.
3rd row: All k.
4th row: K.4, p. to end.
5th row: K.2 tog., k. to end.
6th row: K.4, p. to end.
Repeat 5th and 6th rows 9 times more, then work 5th row again — 22 sts.
To shape the neck:
Next row: Cast off 7 sts., p. to end.
Now work 6 rows decreasing 1 st. at neck edge on each row and 1 st. at armhole edge on each right-side row — 6 sts.
Dec. 1 st. at armhole edge only on next and following 3 right-side rows.
Next row: P.2, then take these 2 sts. tog., and fasten off.

The Right Front

With No. 8 needles cast on 52 sts.
1st row: K.4, * p.2, k.3; repeat from * to last 3 sts., p.3.
2nd row: K.3, * p.3, k.2; repeat from * ending last repeat with k.6.
3rd row: K.4, * p.2, y.o.n., sl.1, k.2 tog., p.s.s.o., y.r.n.; repeat from * to last 3 sts., p.3.
4th row: K.3, * p.3, k.2; repeat from * ending last repeat with k.6.
These 4 rows form the pattern; repeat them 11 times more, then work first 2 rows again.

Next (dec.) row: K.4, * p.2, y.t.b., sl.1, k.2 tog., p.s.s.o.; repeat from * to last 3 sts., p.3 – 34 sts.

Next row: K.3, " p.1, k.2; repeat from " ending last repeat with k.6.

To shape the raglan armhole:

1st row: K. to last 2 sts., k.2 tog.

2nd row: P. to last 4 sts., k.4.

3rd (buttonhole) row: K.2, y.fwd., k.2 tog., k. to end.

4th row: P. to last 4 sts., k.4.

5th row: K. to last 2 sts., k.2 tog.

6th row: P. to last 4 sts., k.4.

Repeat 5th and 6th rows 10 times more working buttonholes, as before, on the 4th and 9th repeats of the 5th row – 22 sts.

To shape the neck:

Next row: Cast off 7 sts., k. to last 2 sts., k.2 tog.

Now work 6 rows decreasing 1 st. at neck edge on each row and 1 st. at armhole edge on each right-side row – 5 sts.

Work 1 row, then dec. 1 st. at armhole edge only on next and following 2 right-side rows.

Next row: P.2, then take these 2 sts. tog. and fasten off.

The Sleeves (both alike)

With No. 8 needles cast on 34 sts. and work the 4 pattern rows given for back 3 times.

Beginning with a k. row, st.st. 4 rows.

Inc. 1 st. at each end of next and every following 6th row until the 6th inc. row has been worked – 46 sts.

St.st. 7 rows.

To shape the raglan sleeve top: Work exactly as given for raglan armhole shaping on back when 8 sts. will remain.

Cast off.

The Collar

With No. 8 needles cast on 74 sts. and work the 4 pattern rows given for back 4 times.

Cast off.

To Make Up The Jacket

Press very lightly with a cool iron over a dry cloth. Join raglan seams, then join sleeve and side seams. Sew cast-off edge of collar evenly to neck edge. Sew on buttons.

The Leggings

The Right Leg

With No. 8 needles cast on 66 sts. and work 4 rows in single rib.

Next (slot) row: Rib 2, * y.o.n., k.2 tog., rib 2; repeat from * to end.

Work 3 rows in single rib increasing 1 st. at each end of last row – 68 sts. **

To shape for extra length on back:

1st and 2nd (turning) rows: K.49 for 1st row, turn and p. to end for 2nd row.

3rd and 4th rows: K.43, turn and p. to end.

5th and 6th rows: K.37, turn and p. to end.

7th and 8th rows: K.31, turn and p. to end.

9th and 10th rows: K.25, turn and p. to end.

11th and 12th rows: K.19, turn and p. to end.

13th and 14th rows: K.13, turn and p. to end.

Next row: K. across all sts. picking up a thread at each point where work was turned and taking this together with next st. to avoid a gap in the knitting – 68 sts.

St.st. 9 rows.

*** Inc. 1 st. at each end of next and every following 10th row until the 5th inc. row has been worked – 78 sts.

St.st. 7 rows.

To shape the leg: Dec. 1 st. at each end of next and following 7 right-side rows – 62 sts.

St.st. 2 rows.

Dec. 1 st. at each end of next and every following 3rd row until a further 13 dec. rows have been worked – 36 sts.

St.st. 2 rows, ending with a p. row ***.

Now divide sts. for instep and work foot as follows:

Next row: K.29, turn and p. 13.

On these 13 sts. work 16 rows in st.st. Break off yarn.

With right side of work facing, rejoin yarn to inner edge of the 16 sts. at right-hand side and pick up and k.10 sts. along row-ends of instep, then work k.6, k.2 tog., k.5 across instep sts., pick up and k.10 sts. from other side of instep and finally k. across the 7 sts. at left-hand side – 55 sts.

Beginning with a p. row, st.st. 5 rows.

To shape the foot:

1st row: K.3, k.2 tog., k.2 tog., k.23, k.2 tog., k.2 tog., k.21.

2nd row: All p.

3rd row: K.2, k.2 tog., k.2 tog., k.21, k.2 tog., k.2 tog., k.20.

4th row: All p.

5th row: K.1, k.2 tog., k.2 tog., k.19, k.2 tog., k.2 tog., k. 19.

Cast off.

The Left Leg

Work as given for right leg to **.

K.1 row, then shape for extra length on back as given for right leg but read p. for k. and k. for p. to reverse shapings and end with p.1 row across all sts.

St.st. 8 rows then work as given for right leg from *** to ***.

Now divide sts. for instep and work foot as follows:

Next row: K.20, turn and p.13.

On these 13 sts., work 16 rows in st.st. Break off yarn.

With right side of work facing, rejoin yarn to inner edge of 7 sts. at right-hand side and pick up and k.10 sts. along row-ends of instep, k.6, k.2 tog., k.5 across instep sts., pick up and k.10 sts. from other side of instep and finally k. the 16 sts. at left-hand side – 55 sts.

Beginning with a p. row, st.st. 5 rows.

To shape the foot:

1st row: K.21, k.2 tog., k.2 tog., k.23, k.2 tog., k.2 tog., k.3.

2nd row: All p.

3rd row: K.20, k.2 tog., k.2 tog., k.21, k.2 tog., k.2 tog., k.2.

4th row: All p.

5th row: K.19, k.2 tog., k.2 tog., k.19, k.2 tog., k.2 tog., k.1.

Cast off.

To Make Up The Leggings

Join underfoot and inner leg seams, then join front and back seams.

Thread elastic through holes at waist.

The Bonnet

To Make

With No. 8 needles cast on 89 sts. and work the 4 pattern rows given for back of jacket 8 times.

To shape the crown:

1st row: * K.6, k.2 tog.; repeat from * 10 times, k.1.

2nd and every alternate row: All p.

3rd row: * K.5, k.2 tog.; repeat from * 10 times, k.1.

5th row: * K.4, k.2 tog.; repeat from * 10 times, k.1.

7th row: * K.3, k.2 tog.; repeat from * 10 times, k.1.

9th row: * K.2, k.2 tog.; repeat from * 10 times, k.1.

11th row: * K.1, k.2 tog.; repeat from * 10 times, k.1.

13th row: * K.2 tog.; repeat from * 10 times, k.1.

Break off yarn; run end through remaining 12 sts., draw up and fasten securely, then join row-ends of crown section and 1 inch of patterned section to form back seam. Add ribbon.

The Mitts

To Make (both alike)

With No. 8 needles cast on 34 sts. and work the 4 pattern rows given for back of jacket 3 times.

Beginning with a k. row, st.st. 20 rows.

To shape the top:

1st row: * K.1, k.2 tog.b., k.11, k.2 tog., k.1; repeat from * once.

2nd row: All p.

3rd row: * K.1, k.2 tog.b., k.9, k.2 tog., k.1; repeat from * once.

4th row: All p.

5th row: * K.1, k.2 tog.b., k.7, k.2 tog., k.1; repeat from * once.

Cast off remaining 22 sts.

To Make Up The Mitts

Fold in half and join side and top seam. Thread ribbon through holes in pattern.

Pram Set
in 4-ply

Eleven 25-gramme balls of Wendy 4-ply Nylonised in main colour and two balls in a contrast colour; a pair each of No. 10, No. 11 and No. 12 knitting needles; a waist length of elastic; 3 buttons for coat; 1 button for helmet; 1 yard of 1-inch wide ribbon for bonnet; 3 yards of narrow ribbon for girl's leggings, coat and mitts.

Tension and Size

Worked at a tension of 7 stitches and 9 rows to 1 inch, over the stocking stitch, using No. 10 needles, the set will be suitable for baby aged six to twelve months.

Abbreviations

K., knit; p., purl; st., stitch; tog., together; dec., decrease (by working 2 sts. tog.); inc., increase (by working twice into same st.); k.2 tog.b., k.2 sts. tog. through back of loops; y.fwd., yarn forward to make a st.; sl., slip; st.st., stocking st. (k. on right side and p. on wrong side); garter st. is k. on every row; single rib is k.1 and p.1 alternately; m., main colour; c., contrast colour; up 1 (pick up the thread which lies between the needles and k. into back of it, thus making a st.).

The Coat

The Back

With No. 11 needles and c., cast on 105 sts. and slipping first st. on every row, k. 8 rows.

Break off c., join on m., change to No. 10 needles and p.1 row.

Now work in pattern as follows:

1st row (right side): K.1, * p.7, k.1; repeat from * to end.

2nd row: K.8, * p.1, k.7; repeat from * ending last repeat with k.8.

3rd row: As 1st row.

4th row: K.1, p. to last st., k.1.

5th row: K.1, p.3, * k.1, p.7; repeat from * to last 5 sts., k.1, p.3, k.1.

6th row: K.4, * p.1, k.7; repeat from * ending last repeat with k.4.

7th row: As 5th row.

8th row: K.1, p. to last st., k.1.

These 8 rows form the brick pattern; repeat them 8 times more **.

Next (dec.) row: * K.2, k.2 tog.; repeat from * to last st., k.1 – 79 sts.

Next row (wrong side): All k.

Next (slot) row: K.1, * y.fwd., k.2 tog., k.1.; repeat from * to end.

Next row (wrong side): All k.

K.1 row and p.1 row.

To shape the raglan armholes:

1st row: Cast off 4, k. to end.

2nd row: Cast off 4, p. to end.

3rd row: K.1, k.2 tog., k. to last 3 sts., k.2 tog.b., k.1.

4th row: K.1, p. to last st., k.1.

Repeat 3rd and 4th rows 18 times more – 33 sts.

Cast off.

The Left Front

With No. 11 needles and c., cast on 57 sts., and work as given for back to **.

Next (dec.) row: K.4, * k.2 tog., k.1; repeat from * to last 5 sts., k.2 tog., k.3 – 40 sts.

Next row (wrong side): All k.

Next (slot) row: K.1, * y.fwd., k.2 tog., k.1; repeat from * to end.

Next row (wrong side): All k.

K.1 row and p.1 row.

To shape the raglan armhole:

1st row: Cast off 4, k. to end.

2nd row: All p.

3rd row: K.1, k.2 tog., k. to end.

4th row: P. to last st., k.1.

Repeat 3rd and 4th rows 12 times more, then work 3rd row again – 22 sts.

To shape the neck:

Next row: Cast off 4, p. to last st., k.1.

Work 10 rows decreasing 1 st. at armhole edge on each right-side row and, at the same time, dec. 1 st. at neck edge on each of these rows.

Take remaining 3 sts. tog. and fasten off.

The Right Front

With No. 11 needles and c., cast on 57 sts. and work as given for back to **.

Next (dec.) row: K.3, * k.2 tog., k.1; repeat from * to last 6 sts., k.2 tog., k.4 – 40 sts.

Next row (wrong side): All k.

Next (slot) row: K.1, * y.fwd., k.2 tog., k.1; repeat from * to end.

Next row (wrong side): All k.

Beginning with a k. row, st.st. 3 rows.

To shape the armhole:

1st row: Cast off 4, p. to end.

2nd row: K. to last 3 sts., k.2 tog.b., k.1.

3rd row: K.1, p. to end.

Repeat 2nd and 3rd rows 13 times more – 22 sts.

To shape the neck:

Next row: Cast off 4, k. to last 3 sts., k.2 tog.b., k.1.

Next row: K.1, p. to end.

Work 9 rows decreasing 1 st. at armhole edge on each right-side row and, at the same time, dec. 1 st. at neck edge on each of these rows.

Take remaining 3 sts. tog. and fasten off.

The Sleeves (both alike)

With No. 12 needles and c., cast on 39 sts.

and k.8 rows as given for back.

Break off c., join on m., change to No. 10 needles and p.1 row.

Next (inc.) row: * K.2, inc. in next st.; repeat from * to last 3 sts., k.3 – 51 sts.

Beginning with a p. row, st.st. 51 rows.

To shape the raglan sleeve top: Work exactly as given for raglan armhole shaping on back when 5 sts. will remain.

Cast off.

The Button Band

With No. 11 needles and c., cast on 6 sts. and work 134 rows in garter st. as given for back.

Break off yarn and leave sts. on a safety-pin.

The Buttonhole Band

With No. 11 needles and c., cast on 6 sts. and work 90 rows in garter st.

Next (buttonhole) row: Sl.1, k.2, y.fwd., k.2 tog., k.1.

K.23 rows.

Repeat buttonhole row, then k.19 rows.

Break off wool and leave sts. on safety-pin.

The Neck Band

First join raglan seams.

With right side of work facing slip the sts. of right front band onto No. 12 needle with point to inner edge and, onto this needle, using c., pick up and k.15 sts. from neck edge of right front, 4 sts. from top of sleeve, 31 sts. across back, 4 sts. from sleeve top and 15 sts. from neck edge of left front, then k. the 6 sts. of left front band – 81 sts.

K.3 rows, work a buttonhole on next row, then k. a further 3 rows.

Cast off.

To Make Up The Coat

Press on wrong side using a warm iron over a damp cloth. Join sleeve and side seams. Sew front bands in place. Sew on buttons. Trim with ribbon or twisted cord as shewn in photograph.

The Leggings

The Right Leg

With No. 12 needles cast on 90 sts. and work 6 rows in single rib.

Next (slot) row: K.1, * y.fwd., k.2 tog., p.1, k.1; repeat from * to last st., p.1.

Rib 5 rows **.

Change to No. 10 needles and k.1 row and p.1 row.

To shape for extra length on back:

1st and 2nd (turning) rows: K.75 for 1st row, turn and p. to end for 2nd row.

3rd and 4th rows: K.60, turn and p. to end.

5th and 6th rows: K.45, turn and p. to end.

7th and 8th rows: K.30, turn and p. to end.

9th and 10th rows: K.15, turn and p. to end.

Next row: K. across all sts. picking up a thread at each point where work was turned and taking this together with the next st. to avoid a gap in the knitting.

Next row: All p.

*** Continuing in st.st., inc. 1 st. at beginning – back seam edge – (inc. 1 st. at end here when working left leg) on the next row and every following 10th row until the 6th inc. row has been worked – 96 sts.

St.st. 9 rows.

To shape the leg: Dec. 1 st. at each end of the next row and following 18 alternate rows – 58 sts.

St.st. 3 rows.

Dec. 1 st. at each end of next row and every following 3rd row until a further 7 dec. rows have been worked – 44 sts.

St.st. 16 rows, ending with a k. row.

Next row (wrong side): All k.

Next (slot) row: * K.1, y.fwd., k.2 tog.; repeat from * to last 2 sts., k.2.

Next row (wrong side): All k. ***.

Change to No. 12 needles and divide sts. for instep as follows:

Next row: K.36, turn and p.16.

On these 16 sts., st.st. 20 rows for instep.

Break off yarn.

With right side of work facing, rejoin yarn to base of instep at inner edge of 20 sts. at right-hand side and pick up and k.16 sts. along row ends of instep, k. the 16 instep sts., then pick up and k.16 sts. along other side of instep and finally, k. the 8 sts. at left-hand side – 76 sts.

K.9 rows.

To shape the foot:

1st row: K.3, k.2 tog., k.2, k.2 tog., k.27, k.3 tog., k.10, k.3 tog., k.24 – 70 sts.

2nd and 4th rows: All k.

3rd row: K.2, k.2 tog., k.2, k.2 tog., k.26, k.3 tog., k.6, k.3 tog., k.24 – 64 sts.

5th row: K.1, k.2 tog., k.2, k.2 tog., k.25, k.3 tog., k.2, k.3 tog., k.24 – 58 sts.

6th row: All k.

Cast off.

The Left Leg

Work as given for right leg to **.

Change to No. 10 needles and, beginning with a k. row, st.st. 3 rows.

To shape for extra length on back:

1st and 2nd (turning) rows: P.75 for 1st row, turn and k. to end for 2nd row.

3rd and 4th rows: P.60, turn and k. to end.

5th and 6th rows: P.45, turn and k. to end.

7th and 8th rows: P.30, turn and k. to end.

9th and 10th rows: P.15, turn and k. to end.

Next row: P. across all sts. closing gaps.

Now work as given for right leg from *** to *** noting that first set of increases are worked at end of row where indicated.

Change to No. 12 needles and divide sts. for instep as follows:

Next row: K.24, turn and p.16.

On these 16 sts., st.st. 20 rows for instep. Break off yarn.

With right side of work facing, rejoin yarn to base of instep at inner edge of the 8 sts. at right-hand side and pick up and k.16 sts. along row ends of instep, k. the 16 instep sts., pick up and k.16 sts. from other side of instep and k. the 20 sts. at left-hand side – 76 sts.

K.9 rows.

To shape the foot:

1st row: K.24, k.3 tog., k.10, k.3 tog., k.27, k.2 tog., k.2, k.2 tog., k.3 – 70 sts.

2nd and 4th rows: All k.

3rd row: K.24, k.3 tog., k.6, k.3 tog., k.26, k.2 tog., k.2, k.2 tog., k.2 – 64 sts.

5th row: K.24, k.3 tog., k.2, k.3 tog., k.25, k.2 tog., k.2, k.2 tog., k.1 – 58 sts.

6th row: All k.

Cast off.

To Make Up The Leggings

Press as given for coat. Join underfoot and inner leg seams, then join front and back seams. Insert elastic. Add ribbon or cord at ankles.

The Bonnet

The Frill

With No. 12 needles and c., cast on 208 sts. and k.7 rows as given for coat.

Next (dec.) row: K.1, * k.2 tog.; repeat from * to last st., k.1 – 105 sts.

Break off yarn and leave sts. on needle.

The Main Part

With No. 12 needles and m., cast on 105 sts. and k.7 rows.

With the needle holding the sts. of frill in front of the needle holding sts. of main part, using No. 10 needle and m., k.1 st. from front needle together with 1 st. from back needle to end of row, thus joining frill to main part.

Still using No. 10 needles, k.1 row.

Work the 8 pattern rows given for coat 4 times, then work the first 4 rows again.

Change to No. 12 needles and k.1 row and p.1 row.

To shape the crown:

1st (shaping) row: * K.6, k.2 tog.; repeat from * to last st., k.1.

St.st. 3 rows.

2nd (shaping) row: * K.5, k.2 tog.; repeat from * to last st., k.1.

St.st. 3 rows.

3rd (shaping) row: * K.4, k.2 tog.; repeat

from * to last st., k.1.
St.st. 3 rows.

4th (shaping) row: * K.3, k.2 tog.; repeat from * to last st., k.1.
St.st. 3 rows.

5th (shaping) row: * K.2, k.2 tog.; repeat from * to last st., k.1.
St.st. 3 rows.

6th (shaping) row: * K.1, k.2 tog.; repeat from * to last st., k.1.

7th (shaping) row: * K.2 tog.; repeat from * to last st., k.1.

Next row: All p.

Break off yarn; run end through remaining 14 sts., draw up and fasten securely.

To Make Up The Bonnet

Press as given for coat. Join row ends of st.st. section plus 8 rows of pattern section to form back seam.

To neaten neck edge: With right side of work facing, rejoin m. and using No. 12 needles, pick up and k.41 sts. along neck edge, then cast off.

Add ribbon.

The Helmet

To Make

With No. 11 needles and c., cast on 106 sts. and k.4 rows.

Break off c. join on m.

Change to No. 10 needles.

1st (shaping) row: K.2, up 1, k.17, k.2 tog., k.2 tog., k.17, up 1, k.2, up 1, k.9, k.2 tog., k.2 tog., k.9, up 1, k.2, up 1, k.17, k.2 tog., k.2 tog., k.16, up 1, k.3.

2nd row: All p. – 106 sts.

Repeat these 2 rows 16 times more.

To shape the top:

1st row: K.1, k.2 tog., k.16, * k.2 tog., k.2 tog., k.28; repeat from * once, k.2 tog., k.2 tog., k.16, k.2 tog., k.1 – 98 sts.

2nd row: All p.

3rd row: K.17, k.2 tog., k.2 tog., k.26, k.2 tog., k.2 tog., k.26, k.2 tog., k.2 tog., k.17 – 92 sts.

4th row: All p.

5th row: K.1, k.2 tog., k.13, * k.2 tog., k.2 tog., k.24; repeat from * once, k.2 tog., k.2 tog., k.13, k.2 tog., k.1 – 84 sts.

6th row: P.14, * p.2 tog., p.2 tog., p.22; repeat from * once, p.2 tog., p.2 tog., p.14 – 78 sts.

7th row: K.13, * k.2 tog., k.2 tog., k.20; repeat from * once, k.2 tog., k.2 tog., k.13.

8th row: P.12, * p.2 tog., p.2 tog., p.18; repeat from * once, p.2 tog., p.2 tog., p.12.

9th row: K.1, k.2 tog., k.8, * k.2 tog., k.2 tog., k.16; repeat from * once, k.2 tog., k.2 tog., k.8, k.2 tog., k.1 – 58 sts.

10th row: P.9, * p.2 tog., p.2 tog., p.14; repeat from * once, p.2 tog., p.2 tog., p.9 – 52 sts.

11th row: K.1, k.2 tog., k.5, * k.2 tog., k.2 tog., k.12; repeat from * once, k.2 tog., k.2 tog., k.5, k.2 tog., k.1.

12th row: P.6, * p.2 tog., p.2 tog., p.10; repeat from * once, p.2 tog., p.2 tog., p.6.

13th row: K.5, * k.2 tog., k.2 tog., k.8; repeat from * once, k.2 tog., k.2 tog., k.5.

14th row: P.4, * p.2 tog., p.2 tog., p.6; repeat from * once, p.2 tog., p.2 tog., p.4.

Break off yarn; run end through remaining 26 sts. draw up and fasten securely.

The Strap

With No. 11 needles and c., cast on 6 sts. and k.56 rows.

Next (buttonhole) row: K.2, y.fwd., k.2 tog., k.2.

K.4 rows.

Cast off.

To Make Up The Helmet

Press as given for coat.

Join back seam. Sew on strap. Add button.

The Mitts

To Make (both alike)

With No. 11 needles and c., cast on 41 sts. and k.4 rows.

Break off c., join on m.

Change to No. 10 needles and p.1 row.

Work the 8 pattern rows given for back of coat twice.

Next 2 rows: All k.

Next (slot) row: * K.1, y.fwd., k.2 tog.; repeat from * to last 2 sts., k.2.

Next row: All k.

Change to No. 12 needles and, beginning with a k. row, st.st. 20 rows.

To shape the top:

1st row: K.1, * k.2 tog., k.15, k.2 tog.b., k.1; repeat from * once.

2nd and every alternate row: All p.

3rd row: K.1, * k.2 tog., k.13, k.2 tog.b., k.1; repeat from * once.

5th row: K.1, * k.2 tog., k.11, k.2 tog.b., k.1; repeat from * once.

7th row: K.1, * k.2 tog., k.9, k.2 tog.b., k.1; repeat from * once.

8th row: All p.

Cast off remaining 25 sts.

To Make Up The Mitts

Press as given for coat. Fold in half and join top and side seams.

Add ribbon or twisted cord.

Pram Set
with Flared Trousers
(see illustration p. 69)

Contributed by Grace Paull

Materials

Eighteen 25-gramme balls of Hayfield Gaylon Double Knitting for 1st size; twenty balls for 2nd size. For either size; a pair each of No. 9 and No. 10 knitting needles; 4 buttons for jacket; 1 button for bonnet; a waist length of elastic for trousers.

Measurements

	INCHES	
	1st size	2nd size
The Jacket		
All round at underarms	22	24
Side seam	$7\frac{1}{4}$	$8\frac{1}{4}$
Length	$11\frac{1}{2}$	13
Sleeve seam	$6\frac{1}{2}$	$7\frac{1}{2}$
The Trousers		
All round at widest part	26	28
Inside Leg	$9\frac{1}{2}$	$10\frac{1}{2}$
Outside Leg	18	$19\frac{1}{2}$
The Bonnet		
All round face edge	15	16
The Cap		
All round head edge	17	18
The Mitts		
All round palm	5	$5\frac{1}{2}$
Length	$4\frac{3}{4}$	$5\frac{1}{2}$

Tension

Work at a tension of 6 stitches and 8 rows to 1 inch, over the stocking stitch, using No. 9 needles, to obtain the following measurements:

Abbreviations

K., knit; p., purl; st., stitch; tog., together; dec., decrease (by working 2 sts. tog.); inc., increase (by working twice into same st.); st.st., stocking st. (k. on right side and p. on wrong side); y.fwd., yarn forward to make a st.

● *The instructions are given for 1st size. Where they vary, work figures in brackets for 2nd size.*

The Jacket

The Back

With No. 10 needles cast on 79 (85) sts. and k.5 rows.

Change to No. 9 needles and work in pattern as follows:

1st row (right side): All k.
2nd row: All p.
3rd row: K.1, * p.2, k.1; repeat from * to end.
4th row: All p.

These 4 rows form the pattern; repeat them twice more.

Keeping continuity of pattern dec. 1 st. at each end of next and every following 8th (10th) row until the 6th dec. row has been worked – 67 (73) sts.

Work 7 (5) rows.

To shape the armholes: Cast off 3 (4) sts. at beginning of next 2 rows, then dec. 1 st. at each end of next and following 4 right-side rows – 51 (55) sts.

Work 21 (25) rows.

To slope the shoulders: Cast off 8 sts. at beginning of next 2 rows, and 8 (9) sts. on following 2 rows.

Cast off remaining 19 (21) sts.

The Left Front

With No. 10 needles cast on 37 (40) sts. and k.5 rows.

Change to No. 9 needles and work the 4 pattern rows given for back 3 times.

Dec. 1 st. at beginning – read end here on right front – on next row and every following 8th (10th) row until the 6th dec. row has been worked – 31 (34) sts.

Work 7 (5) rows – work 8 (6) rows here on right front.

To shape the armhole: Cast off 3 (4) sts. at beginning of next row; work 1 row, then dec. 1 st. at armhole edge on next and following 4 alternate rows – 23 (25) sts.

Work 10 (14) rows.

To shape the neck: Cast off 2 (3) sts. at beginning of next row, then dec. 1 st. at neck edge on next 5 rows – 16 (17) sts.

Work 5 rows.

To slope the shoulder: Cast off 8 sts. at beginning of next row; work 1 row, then cast off remaining 8 (9) sts.

The Right Front

With No. 10 needles cast on 37 (40) sts. and work as given for left front noting that the decreases are worked at end of right-side rows and the extra row to be worked before shaping the armhole.

The Sleeves (both alike)

With No. 10 needles cast on 31 (34) sts. and k.5 rows.

Change to No. 9 needles and work the 4 pattern rows given for back, once. Keeping continuity of pattern and, taking the extra sts. into the pattern as they occur, inc. 1 st. at each end of next and every following 6th row until the 8th (9th) inc. row has been worked – 47 (52) sts.

Work 5 (7) rows.

To shape the sleeve top: Cast off 3 (4) sts. at beginning of next 2 rows, then dec. 1 st. at each end of next and following 4 right-side rows – 31 (34) sts.

P.1 row, then cast off 2 sts. at beginning of next 2 (4) rows and 4 sts. on following 4 rows.

Cast off remaining 11 (10) sts.

The Button Band

With No. 10 needles cast on 6 sts. and k.102 (114) rows.

Cast off.

The Buttonhole Band

With No. 10 needles cast on 6 sts. and k.44 (50) rows.

1st (buttonhole) row: K.2, cast off 2, k. to end.

2nd (buttonhole) row: K.2, turn, cast on 2, turn, k.2.

K.16 (18) rows.

Repeat last 18 (20) rows twice more, then work the 2 buttonhole rows again.

K.2 rows.

Cast off.

The Collar

With No. 10 needles cast on 15 (16) sts. and k.5 (7) rows.

Shape as follows:

1st and 2nd (turning) rows: K.11 (12) turn and k. to end.

3rd to 12th rows: All k.

Repeat these 12 rows 8 times more, then work the first 8 (10) rows again.

Cast off.

To Make Up The Coat

Press on wrong side using a warm iron over a damp cloth. Join shoulder seams, set in sleeves, then join sleeve and side seams. Sew front bands in place. Beginning and ending in centre of front bands, sew the short edge of collar evenly to neck edge. Sew on buttons.

The Trousers

The Right Leg

With No. 10 needles cast on 76 (80) sts. and, beginning with a k. row, st.st. 7 rows.
Next row: All k. on wrong side to mark hemline.

Change to No. 9 needles and, beginning with a k. row, st.st. 8 rows.

Dec. 1 st. at each end of next and every following 6th (8th) row until the 5th dec. row has been worked – 66 (70) sts.

Work 11 (9) rows.

Inc. 1 st. at each end of next and every following 4th row until the 5th inc. row has been worked – 76 (80) sts.

Work 1 row, then inc. 1 st. at each end of next 1 (2) right-side row(s) – 78 (84) sts.**.

Work 3 rows. Mark end of last row with a coloured thread to denote front seam edge.

Dec. 1 st. at each end of next row – 76 (82) sts.

Now dec. 1 st. at beginning – front seam edge – on every following 6th row and 1 st. at end – back seam edge– on every following 8th row until a further 9 (10) front-edge decreases and a further 6 (7) back-edge decreases have been worked – 61 (65) sts.

Work 4 (2) rows ending with a k. row. Work 3 (1) row(s) here on left leg.
To shape for extra length on back:
1st and 2nd (turning) rows: P.47 (49), for 1st row, turn and k. to end for 2nd row.
3rd and 4th rows: P.37 (39), turn and k. to end.
5th and 6th rows: P.27 (29), turn and k. to end.
7th and 8th rows: P.17 (19), turn and k. to end.
K.1 row across all sts. to mark fold line.

Change to No. 10 needles and, beginning with a k. row, st.st. 6 rows.
Cast off.

The Left Leg

Work as right leg to **.

Work 3 rows. Mark beginning of last row to denote front seam edge.

Dec. 1 st. at each end of next row – 76 (82) sts.

Now dec. 1 st. at end – front seam edge – on every following 6th row and 1 st. at beginning – back seam edge – on every following 8th row until a further 9 (10) front-edge decreases and a further 6 (7) back-edge decreases have been worked – 61 (65) sts.

Work 3 (1) row(s), ending with a p. row.
To shape for extra length on back:
1st and 2nd (turning) rows: K.47 (49), turn and p. to end.
3rd and 4th rows: K.37 (39), turn and p. to end.
5th and 6th rows: K.27 (29), turn and p. to end.
7th and 8th rows: K.17 (19), turn and p. to end.
P.1 row across all sts. to mark hemline.

Change to No. 10 needles and, beginning with a p. row, st.st. 6 rows.
Cast off.

To Make Up The Trousers

Press as given for jacket. Join inner leg and front and back seams. Turn up hems and slip st. in place. Fold at waist and sew in place leaving a small opening. Insert elastic and close seam.

The Bonnet

To Make

With No. 10 needles cast on 91 (97) sts. and k.3 rows.

Change to No. 9 needles and work 17 rows in pattern as given for jacket.

Beginning with a k. row on wrong side to reverse brim, st.st. 34 (36) rows. decreasing 3 (1) st.(s) evenly across last row – 88 (96) sts.

To shape the crown:

Next (shaping) row: * K.9 (10), k.2 tog.; repeat from * to end.

Next row: All p.

Repeat these 2 rows 8 (9) times more working 1 st. less between the decreases on each repeat – 16 sts.

Next row: * K.2 tog.; repeat from * to end.

Break off yarn; run end through remaining 8 sts. draw up and fasten securely, then join row ends for 3 inches to form back seam.

The Strap

With No. 10 needles cast on 6 sts. and k.4 rows.

Make a buttonhole over next 2 rows as given for front band.

K.44 rows.

Cast off.

To Make Up The Bonnet

Press as given for jacket. Turn back brim and catch in place. Sew on strap. Add button.

The Cap

To Make   (*Not illustrated*)

With No. 10 needles cast on 103 (109) sts. and k.3 rows.

Change to No. 9 needles and work 17 rows in pattern as given for jacket.

Beginning with a k. row on wrong side to reverse brim, st.st. 18 (22) rows.

To shape the top:

Decrease row: * K.19 (8), k.2 tog.; repeat from * 3 (9) times, k.19 (9) – 99 sts.

St.st. 3 rows.

Next (shaping) row: * K.7, k.2 tog.; repeat from * to end.

St.st. 3 rows.

Repeat last 4 rows 5 times more, working 1 st. less between the decreases on each repeat, then work the shaping row again – 22 sts.

P.1 row.

Next row: * K.2 tog.; repeat from * to end.

Break off yarn; run end through remaining 11 sts. draw up and fasten securely, then join row ends to form back seam.

To Make Up The Cap

Press as given for jacket. Turn back brim and catch in place. Make and add pom-pon.

The Mitts

The Left Mitt

With No. 10 needles cast on 34 (37) sts. and k. 3 rows.

Change to No. 9 needles and work 10 rows in pattern as given for jacket decreasing 2 (1) st.(s) evenly in last row – 32 (36) sts.

Next (slot) row: K.2 (1), * y.fwd., k.2 tog., k.1; repeat from * to end (to last 2 sts., y.fwd., k.2 tog.).

Beginning with a p. row, st.st. 5 (7) rows. **

Now divide sts. for thumb.

Next row: K.16 (18), turn, cast on 3 sts., turn.

Next row: P.10, turn, cast on 3 sts., turn.

On these 13 sts., st.st. 8 (10) rows for thumb.

To shape the top:

1st row: K.1, * k.2 tog., k.1; repeat from * to end.

2nd row: All p.

66

3rd row: * K.2 tog.; repeat from * 3 times, k.1.

Break off yarn; run end through remaining 5 sts., draw up and fasten securely, then join seam.

The Palm: With right side of work facing, rejoin yarn to base of thumb at inner edge of the 9 (11) sts. at right-hand side and pick up and k.7 sts. from cast-on edge of thumb, then k. across the 16 (18) sts. at left-hand side – 32 (36) sts.

*** Dec. 1 st. at each end of next row – 30 (34) sts.

Beginning with a k. row, st.st. 10 (14) rows.

To shape the top:

1st row: K.2 tog., * k.2, k.2 tog.; repeat from * to end.

2nd row: All p.

3rd row: K.2 tog., * k.2 tog., k.1; repeat from * to last 2 sts., k. 2 tog.

4th row: All p.

5th row: * K.2 tog.; repeat from * to end – 7 (8) sts.

Break off yarn and complete as given for thumb.

The Right Mitt

Work as given for left mitt to **.

Now divide sts. for thumb.

Next row: K.23 (25), turn, cast on 3 sts., turn.

Next row: P.10, turn, cast on 3 sts., turn.

On these 13 sts., work thumb as given for left mitt.

The Palm: With right side of work facing, rejoin yarn to base of thumb at inner edge of the 16 (18) sts. at right-hand side and pick up and k.7 sts. from cast-on edge of thumb, then k. the 9 (11) sts. at left-hand side – 32 (36) sts.

Now work as given for left mitt from *** to end.

To Make Up The Mitts

Press as given for jacket. Make 2 lengths of cord and thread through holes at wrist.

Pram Set
Cardigan Style

Contributed by Grace Paull

Materials

Twelve ounces of Hayfield Beaulon Double Knitting in main colour and three ounces in a contrast colour for 1st size; fourteen ounces in main and four ounces in contrast for 2nd size. For either size: a pair each of No. 9 and No. 11 knitting needles; 6 buttons for jacket; 1 button for bonnet; 1 button for cap; a waist length of elastic for trousers.

Tension

Work at a tension of 6 stitches and 8 rows to 2 inches, over the stocking stitch, using No. 9 needles, to obtain the following measurements:

● *The instructions are given for 1st size. Where they vary, work figures in brackets for 2nd size.*

Measurements

	INCHES	
	1st size	2nd size
The Jacket		
All round at underarms	22	24
Side seam	$7\frac{1}{2}$	$8\frac{1}{4}$
Length	$12\frac{1}{2}$	14
Sleeve seam	$7\frac{1}{4}$	$8\frac{1}{2}$
The Trousers		
All round at widest part	$26\frac{1}{2}$	$28\frac{1}{2}$
Inside Leg	$9\frac{1}{2}$	$10\frac{1}{2}$
Outside Leg	$18\frac{1}{2}$	20
The Bonnet		
All round face edge	15	16
The Cap		
All round head	$16\frac{1}{2}$	$17\frac{1}{2}$
The Mitts		
All round palm	5	$5\frac{1}{2}$
Length	$4\frac{3}{4}$	$5\frac{1}{2}$

Abbreviations

K., knit; p., purl; st., stitch; tog., together; dec., decrease (by working 2 sts. tog.); increase (by working twice into same st.); sl., slip; st.st., stocking st. (k. on right side and p. on wrong side); single rib is k.1 and p.1 alternately; m., main colour; c., contrast colour.

The Jacket

The Back

With No. 11 needles and m., cast on 72 (78) sts. and work 13 rows in single rib increasing 3 (5) sts. evenly across last row — 75 (83) sts.

Change to No. 9 needles and p.1 row.

Join on c. and work in pattern as follows:

1st row: With c., k.3, * sl.1 p.wise, k.3; repeat from * to end.

2nd row: With c., p.3, * sl.1 p.wise, p.3; repeat from * to end.

3rd row: With m., k.1, * sl.1 p.wise, k.3; repeat from * to last 2 sts., sl.1 p.wise, k.1.

4th row: With m., p.1, * sl.1 p.wise, p.3; repeat from * to last 2 sts., sl.1 p.wise, p.1.

Opposite — Pram set with fla trousers in yellow (pattern p. cardigan style pram set in blue.

These 4 rows form the pattern; repeat them 14 (16) times more, then work first 2 rows again.

To shape the raglan armholes: Cast off 4 sts. at beginning of next 2 rows, then dec. 1 st. at each end of next and following 21 (24) right-side rows – 23 (25) sts.

Work 1 row.

Cast off.

The Left Front

With No. 11 needles and m., cast on 33 (37) sts. and, beginning right-side rows with k.1 and wrong side rows with p.1, work 13 rows in single rib increasing 2 sts. evenly across last row – 35 (39) sts.

Change to No. 9 needles and p.1 row.

Join on c. and work the 4 pattern rows given for back 15 (17) times, then work first 2 rows again **.

To shape the raglan armhole: Cast off 4 sts. at beginning of next row; work I row, then dec. 1 st. at armhole edge on next and following 16 (19) right-side rows – 14 (15) sts.

To shape the neck: Cast off 2 (3) sts. at beginning of next row, then dec. 1 st. at each end of next and following 4 right-side rows – 2 sts.

Next row: P.2.

Take 2 sts. tog. and fasten off.

The Right Front

Work as given for left front to **.

Work 1 row more to finish at side edge.

To shape the raglan armhole: Cast off 4 sts. at beginning of next row, then dec. 1 st. at armhole edge on next and following 15 (18) right-side rows – 15 (16) sts.

Work 1 row back to front edge.

To shape the neck:

Next row: Cast off 2 (3) sts., pattern to last 2 sts., dec.

Work 1 row, then dec. 1 st. at each end of next and following 4 right-side rows – 2 sts.

Next row: P.2.

Take 2 sts. tog. and fasten off.

The Sleeves (both alike)

With No. 11 needles and m., cast on 36 (38) sts. and work 13 rows in single rib

increasing 3 (5) sts. evenly across last row – 39 (43) sts.

Change to No. 9 needles and p.1 row.

Join on c. and work the 4 pattern rows given for jacket twice.

Keeping continuity of pattern and, taking the extra sts. into the pattern as they occur, inc. 1 st. at each end of next and every following 6th row until the 8th (10th) inc. row has been worked – 55 (63) sts.

Work 7 rows.

To shape the raglan sleeve top: Cast off 4 sts. at beginning of next 2 rows, then dec. 1 st. at each end of next and every following 4th row until the 3rd dec. row has been worked – 41 (49) sts.

Work 1 row, then dec. 1 st. at each end of next and following 16 (19) right-side rows – 7 (9) sts.

Work 1 row.

Cast off.

The Button Band

With No. 11 needles and m., cast on 9 sts.

1st row: K.1, * p.1, k.1; repeat from * to end.

2nd row: K.2, * p.1, k.1; repeat from * ending last repeat with k.2.

Repeat these 2 rows 44 (49) times more.

Break off yarn and leave sts. on safety-pin.

The Buttonhole Band

With No. 11 needles and m., cast on 9 sts. and work 4 rows in rib as given for button band.

1st (buttonhole) row: Rib 3, cast off 3, rib to end.

2nd (buttonhole) row: Rib 3, turn, cast on 3, turn, rib 3.

Rib 16 (18) rows.

Repeat last 18 (20) rows 3 times more, then work 2 buttonhole rows again.

Rib 12 (14) rows.

Break off yarn and leave sts. on safety-pin.

The Neck Band

First join raglan seams. Slip 9 sts. of right front band onto No. 11 needle and with right side of work facing, rejoin m. yarn to neck edge and pick up and k.11 sts. from right front neck edge, 5 (7) sts. from right sleeve, 21 (23) sts. across back, 5 (7) sts. from left sloovo, 11 otc. from nock edge of left front and finally rib across the 9 sts. of left front band – 71 (77) sts.

Rib 3 rows.

Work a buttonhole over next 2 rows.

Rib 4 rows.

Cast off.

To Make Up The Jacket

Press on wrong side using a cool iron over a dry cloth. Join sleeve and side seams. Sew front bands in place. Sew on buttons.

The Trousers

The Left Leg

With No. 11 needles and m., cast on 60 (64) sts. for waist edge and, beginning with a k. row, st.st. 7 rows.

Next row: All k. on wrong side to mark fold line **.

Change to No. 9 needles.

Beginning with a k. row, st.st. 7 rows.

To shape for extra length on back:

1st and 2nd (turning) rows: P.50 (52) for 1st row, turn and k. to end for 2nd row.

3rd and 4th rows: P.42 (44), turn and k. to end.

5th and 6th rows: P.34 (36), turn and k. to end.

7th and 8th rows: P.26 (28), turn and k. to end.

Next row: P. across all sts. picking up a thread at each point where work was turned and taking this together with next st. to avoid a gap in the knitting.

Beginning with a k. row, st.st. 6 rows.

*** Inc. 1 st. at each end of next and every following 8th row until the 5th inc. row has been worked – 70 (74) sts.

Work 3 rows, then inc. 1 st. at each end of next and every following 4th row until a further 5 (6) inc. rows have been completed – 80 (86) sts.

P.1 row.

To shape the leg: Dec. 1 st. at each end of next and following 11 (12) alternate rows – 56 (60) sts.

Work 7 rows, then dec. 1 st. at each end of next and every following 8th row until a further 2 (3) dec. rows have been worked – 52 (54) sts.

Work 11 (9) rows.

Change to No. 11 needles and work 18 rows in single rib.

Cast off.

The Right Leg

Work as given for left leg to **.

Change to No. 9 needles.

Beginning with a k. row, st.st. 8 rows.

To shape for extra length on back:

1st and 2nd (turning) rows: K.50 (52), turn and p. to end.

3rd and 4th rows: K.42 (44), turn and p. to end.

5th and 6th rows: K.34 (36), turn and p. to end.

7th and 8th rows: K.26 (28), turn and p. to end.

K.1 row across all sts. closing gaps.

Beginning with a p. row, st.st. 5 rows.

Now work as given for left leg from *** to end.

To Make Up The Trousers

Press as given for jacket. Join inside leg and front and back seams. Fold at hemline and slip stitch in place leaving small opening. Insert elastic. Close seam.

The Bonnet

To Make

With No. 11 needles and m., cast on 94 (100) sts. and work 5 rows in single rib increasing 1 (3) st.(s) evenly across last row – 95 (103) sts.

Change to No. 9 needles and p.1 row.

Join on c. and work 14 rows in pattern as given for jacket.

Break off c.

Next (dec.) **row**: * K.9 (8), k.2 tog.; repeat from * to last 7 (3) sts., k.7 (3) – 87 (93) sts.

Beginning with a k. row on wrong side to reverse brim, st.st. 28 (32) rows.

To shape the back: Cast off 8 sts. at beginning of next 2 (6) rows and 7 sts. on next 6 (2) rows – 29 (31) sts.

St.st. 4 (6) rows.

Dec. 1 st. at each end of next and every following 6th row until the 6th dec. row has been worked – 17 (19) sts.

St.st. 3 (5) rows.

Cast off.

The Neck Edging

First join row ends of back section to the sts. cast off at each side. Turn back brim and catch in place.

With right side of work facing, rejoin m. to neck edge and, using No. 11 needles, working through both thicknesses of brim, pick up and k.66 (70) sts. along neck edge, turn and cast on 24 sts. for strap – 90 (94) sts.

Work 3 rows in single rib.

1st (buttonhole) row: Rib to last 6 sts., cast off 3, rib to end.

2nd (buttonhole) row: Rib 3, turn, cast on 3, turn, rib to end.

Rib 3 rows.

Cast off.

To Make Up The Bonnet

Press and add button.

The Cap

To Make (*Not illustrated*)

With No. 11 needles and m., cast on 102 (108) sts. and work 5 rows in single rib increasing 1 (3) st.(s) evenly across last row – 103 (111) sts.

Change to No. 9 needles and p.1 row.

Join on c. and work the 4 pattern rows given for jacket 8 (9) times, then work first 2 rows again.

Break off c.

Next (dec.) **row**: * K.11 (12), k.2 tog.; repeat from * to last 12 (13) sts., k.12 (13) – 96 (104) sts.

Next row: All p.

To shape the crown:

1st row: * K.10 (11), k.2 tog.; repeat from * to end.

2nd row: All p.

Repeat these 2 rows 9 (10) times more working 1 st. less between the decreases on each repeat – 16 sts.

Next row: * K.2 tog.; repeat from * to end – 8 sts.

Break off yarn; run end through remaining sts. draw up and fasten securely, then join row ends to form back seam.

The Right Ear Flap

With right side of work facing, rejoin m. to the 12th st. from back seam and, using No. 11 needles, pick up and k.19 (21) sts. along cast-on edge.

Beginning 1st row with p.1, work 11 rows in single rib.

Dec. 1 st. at each end of next and following 4 (5) alternate rows – 9 sts. **.

Rib 19 (21) rows.

Dec. 1 st. at each end of next 3 rows.

K.3 tog. and fasten off.

The Left Ear Flap

With right side of work facing, rejoin m. to the 31st (33rd) st. from other side of back seam and work as given for right flap to **.

Rib 17 (19) rows.

Work a buttonhole over next 2 rows as given for buttonhole band.

Dec. 1 st. at each end of next 3 rows.

K.3 tog. and fasten off.

To Make Up The Cap

Press. Sew on button. Make and add pom-pon to top.

Opposite – Three pairs of boot (pattern p. 74).

The Mitts

The Left Mitt

With No. 11 needles and m., cast on 36 (38) sts. and work 13 rows in single rib increasing 3 (5) sts. evenly across last row — 39 (43) sts.

Change to No. 9 needles and p.1 row.

Join on c. and work 10 rows in pattern as given for jacket **.

Now divide sts. for thumb.

Next row: Pattern 20 (22) turn and cast on 3 sts.

Next row: With m., p.11, turn and cast on 3 sts.

On these 14 sts., with m., st.st. 8 (10) rows.

To shape the top:

1st row: K.2 tog., * k.1, k.2 tog.; repeat from * to end.

2nd row: All p.

3rd row: * K.2 tog.; repeat from * 3 times, k.1.

Break off yarn; run end through remaining 5 sts. draw up and fasten securely, then join thumb seam.

The Palm: With right side of work facing, rejoin m. to base of thumb at inner edge of the 12 (14) sts. at right-hand side and pick up and k.8 sts. from cast-on edge of thumb, then pattern across the 19 (21) sts. at left-hand side — 39 (43) sts.

Work 15 (17) rows in pattern.

Break off c.

To shape the top:

1st row: * K.2 tog., k.2; repeat from * ending last repeat with k.1 — 29 (32) sts.

2nd and 4th rows: All p.

3rd row: K.2 tog., * k.1, k.2 tog.; repeat from * to end — 19 (21) sts.

5th row: K.3 tog., * k.2 tog.; repeat from * to end — 9 (10) sts.

Break off yarn; run end through remaining sts., draw up and fasten securely, then join side seam.

The Right Mitt

Work as given for left mitt to **.

Now divide sts. for thumb.

Next row: Pattern 27 (29) turn, cast on 3 sts., turn.

Next row: With m., p.11, turn, cast on 3 sts., turn.

On these 14 sts., with rn., work thumb as given for left mitt.

The Palm: With right side of work facing, rejoin m. to base of thumb at inner edge of the 19 (21) sts. at right-hand side and, pick up and k.8 sts. from cast-on edge of thumb, then pattern across the 12 (14) sts. at left-hand side — 39 (43) sts.

Complete as given for left mitt.

Three Pairs of Bootees

(see illustration p. 73)

**Snug fitting boots, dainty shoes and shoe
and sock style**

Materials

The Pink Bootees: One ounce of Double Knitting Wool; a pair of No. 10 knitting needles.

The Blue Shoes: One ounce of 4-ply wool; a pair of No. 10 knitting needles; 2 small buttons.

The Two-colour Bootees: Oddments of Courtelle Quick Knit in 2 colours; a pair of No. 10 knitting needles; 2 small buttons.

Abbreviations

K., knit; p., purl; st., stitch; tog., together; inc., increase (by working twice into same st.); up 1 (pick up the thread which lies between the needles and k. into back of it thus making a st.); k. or p.2 tog.b., k. or p.2 sts. tog. through back of loops; sl., slip; p.s.s.o., pass slipped st. over; y.fwd., yarn forward to make a st.; single rib is k.1 and p.1 alternately; st.st., stocking st. (k. on right side and p. on wrong side); m., main colour; c., contrast colour.

The Pink Bootees

To Make (both alike)

With No. 10 needles cast on 38 sts. and p.1 row.

To shape the sole:

1st row: Inc. in 1st st., k.17, up 1, k.2, up 1, k.17, inc. in last st.

2nd row: All p.

3rd row: Inc., k.19, up 1, k.2, up 1, k.19, inc.

4th row: All p.

5th row: Inc., k.21, up 1, k.2, up 1, k.21, inc.

6th row: All p. – 50 sts.

7th row (right side): All p.

Beginning with a p. row, st.st. 7 rows.

To shape the instep:

1st row: K.22, k.2 tog., k.2, k.2 tog.b., k.22.

2nd row: P.21, p.2 tog.b., p.2, p.2 tog., p.21.

3rd row: K.20, k.2 tog., k.2, k.2 tog.b., k.20.

4th row: P.19, p.2 tog.b., p.2, p.2 tog., p. 19.

5th row: K.18, k.2 tog., k.2, k.2 tog.b., k. 18.

6th row: P.17, p.2 tog.b., p.2, p.2 tog., p. 17.

7th row: K.16, k.2 tog., k.2, k.2 tog.b., k.16 – 36 sts.

Next row: All p.

Next row: K.15, k.2 tog., k.2, k.2 tog.b., k.15 – 34 sts.

Next row: All p.

Work 12 rows in single rib.

Cast off loosely in rib.

To Make Up The Bootees

Join back and underfoot seam. Fold ribbed top to right side.

The Blue Shoes

To Make (both alike)

With No. 10 needles cast on 32 sts. and k.1 row.

To shape the side:

1st row: K.1, up 1, k.14, up 1, k.2, up 1, k.14, up 1, k.1.

2nd and every alternate row: All k.

3rd row: K.1, up 1, k.16, up 1, k.2, up 1, k.16, up 1, k.1.

5th row: K.1, up 1, k.18, up 1, k.2, up 1, k.18, up 1, k.1.

7th row: K.1, up 1, k.20, up 1, k.2, up 1, k.20, up 1, k.1.

9th row: K.1, up 1, k.22, up 1, k.2, up 1, k.22, up 1, k.1.

11th row: K.1, up 1, k.24, up 1, k.2, up 1, k.24, up 1, k.1 – 56 sts.

12th row: K.1, * y.fwd., k.2 tog.; repeat from * to last st., k.1.

K.3 rows.

Beginning with a p. row, st.st. 9 rows.

To shape the instep:

1st row: K.31, sl.1, k.2 tog., p.s.s.o., turn.

2nd row: P.7, p.3 tog., turn.

3rd row: K.7, sl.1, k.2 tog., p.s.s.o., turn.

Repeat 2nd and 3rd rows twice more, then work 2nd row again.

Next row: K.8, then k. across the 16 sts. at left-hand side.

Next row: K. across all sts. – 40 sts.

K.1 row.

Next row: K.1, * y.fwd., k.2 tog.; repeat from * to last st., k.1.

K.1 row.

Cast off.

The Strap

With No. 10 needles cast on 38 sts. and k.2 rows.

Next (buttonhole) row: K.3, y.fwd., k.2 tog., k. to end.

K.1 row.

Cast off.

To Make Up The Shoes

Join back and underfoot seam. Catch centre of strap to centre back. Sew on button.

The Two-Colour Bootees

To Make (both alike)

With No. 10 needles and m., cast on 38 sts. and work 20 rows in single rib.

Now divide sts. for instep.

Next row: Join on c. and taking m. across back of work k.14 sts. with c. then with m., k.10 turn, and with m. p.10.

On these centre 10 sts., with m., beginning with a k. row, st.st. 14 rows. Break off m., join in a length of c. and st.st. 4 rows. This completes instep.

With right side of work facing, take up c. at inner edge of the 14 sts. at right-hand side and pick up and k.10 sts. along row ends of instep, k. the 10 sts. at centre, pick up and k.10 sts. along other side of instep and k. the 14 sts. at left-hand side – 58 sts.

Work 7 rows in st.st.

To shape the foot:

1st row: K.2 tog., k.22, k.2 tog.b., k.6, k.2 tog., k.22, k.2 tog.

2nd, 4th and 6th rows: All p.

3rd row: K.2 tog., k.21, k.2 tog.b., k.4, k.2 tog., k.21, k.2 tog.

5th row: K.2 tog., k.20, k.2 tog.b., k.2, k.2 tog., k.20, k.2 tog.

7th row: K.2 tog., k.19, k.2 tog.b., k.2 tog., k.19, k.2 tog.

Cast off remaining 42 sts.

The Strap

With No. 10 needles and c., cast on 38 sts. and k.2 rows.

Next (buttonhole) row: K.3, y.fwd., k.2 tog., k. to end.

K.1 row.

Cast off.

To Make Up The Bootees

Join back and underfoot seam. Sew centre of strap to centre back. Sew on button.

White Matinee Set

Worked in a dainty pattern in fine wool,
this set takes only a small amount, but lots
of time

Materials

Four 25-gramme balls of Patons Beehive Baby Wool 3-ply, a pair each of No. 11 and No. 12 knitting needles; 2 small buttons; 1 yard of 1-inch wide ribbon; 1½ yards of narrow ribbon.

Tension and Size

Worked at a tension of 17 stitches and 22 rows to 2 inches, over the stocking stitch, using No. 11 needles, the set will fit baby aged birth to 3 months.

Abbreviations

K., knit; p., purl; st., stitch; tog., together; dec., decrease (by working 2 sts. tog.), inc., increase (by working twice into same st.); w.fwd., wool forward to make a st.; sl., slip; p.s.s.o., pass slipped st. over; st.st., stocking st. (k. on right side and p. on wrong side).

The Jacket

The Main Part (worked in one piece to armholes)

With No. 11 needles cast on 205 sts. and k.2 rows.

Now work in pattern as follows:

1st row: K.8, * w.fwd., k.3, sl.1, k.2 tog., p.s.s.o., k.3, w.fwd., k.1; repeat from * to last 7 sts., k.7 more.

2nd row: K.7, p. to last 7 sts., k.7.

3rd row: K.9, * w.fwd., k.2, sl.1, k.2 tog., p.s.s.o., k.2, w.fwd., k.3; repeat from * to last 6 sts., k.6 more.

4th row: K.7, p. to last 7 sts., k.7.

5th row: K.7, k.2 tog., * w.fwd., k.1, w.fwd., k.1, sl.1, k.2 tog., p.s.s.o., k.1, w.fwd., k.1, w.fwd., sl.1, k.2 tog., p.s.s.o.; repeat from * to last 16 sts., w.fwd., k.1, w.fwd., k.1, sl.1, k.2 tog., p.s.s.o., k.1, w.fwd., k.1, w.fwd., k.2 tog., k.7.

6th row: K.7, p. to last 7 sts., k.7.

These 6 rows form the pattern; repeat them 11 times more.

Next (dec.) row: K.10, * k.2 tog., k.3; repeat from * 6 times more, k.2 tog., k.16, ** k.2 tog., k.4; repeat from ** 12 times more, k.2 tog., k.15, *** k.2 tog., k.3; repeat from *** 6 times more, k.2 tog., k.10 – 175 sts.

Next row: K.7, p. to last 7 sts., k.7.

Now divide sts. for back and fronts.

Next row: K.43 for right front, cast off next 8 sts. for armhole – 1 st. left on right-hand needle – k. next 72 sts., these 73 sts. are for back, cast off 8, k. to end and work on these 43 sts. for left front.

The left front: To shape the raglan armhole:

1st row: K.7, p. to end.

2nd row: K.2 tog., k. to end.

Repeat these 2 rows 14 times more, ending at front edge – 28 sts.

To shape the neck:

1st row: Cast off 10, p. to end.

2nd row: K.2 tog., k. to last 2 sts., k.2 tog.

3rd row: Cast off 2, p. to end.

4th row: K.2 tog., k. to last 2 sts., k.2 tog.

Repeat 3rd and 4th rows twice more – 4 sts.

Next row: P.4.

Next row: K.2 tog., k.2 tog.

Next row: P.2.

Take remaining 2 sts. tog. and fasten off.

The Back: With wrong side of work facing, rejoin wool to 73 sts. and p.1 row.

To shape the raglan armholes:

1st row: K.2 tog., k. to last 2 sts., k.2 tog.

2nd row: All p.

Repeat these 2 rows 19 times more.

Cast off remaining 33 sts.

The right front: With wrong side of work facing, rejoin wool to the 43 sts., p. to last 7 sts., k.7.

To shape the raglan armhole:

1st row: K. to last 2 sts., k.2 tog.

2nd row: P. to last 7 sts., k.7.

Repeat these 2 rows 5 times more – 37 sts.

Next (buttonhole) row: K.3, w.fwd., k.2 tog., k. to last 2 sts., k.2 tog.

Work 2nd row, then work 1st and 2nd rows 6 times more – 30 sts.

Repeat buttonhole row; work 2nd row,

then work 1st and 2nd rows once more —
28 sts.

To shape the neck:

1st row: Cast off 10, k. to last 2 sts., k.2 tog.

2nd row: P. to last 2 sts., p.2 tog.

3rd row: Cast off 2, k. to last 2 sts., k.2 tog.
Repeat 2nd and 3rd rows twice more, then work 2nd row again — 4 sts.

Next row: K.2 tog., k.2 tog.

Next row: P.2.
Take remaining 2 sts. tog. and fasten off.

The Sleeves (both alike)

With No. 12 needles cast on 45 sts.

1st row: K.1, * p.1, k.1 ; repeat from * to end.

2nd row: P.1, * k.1, p.1 ; repeat from * to end.
Repeat these 2 rows 5 times more.
Change to No. 11 needles and, beginning with a k. row, st.st. 6 rows.
Inc. 1 st. at each end of next and every following 8th row until the 5th inc. row has been worked — 55 sts.
St.st. 11 rows.

To shape the raglan sleeve top: Cast

off 4 sts. at beginning of next 2 rows, then dec. 1 st. at each end of next and following 19 right-side rows — 7 sts.
P.1 row.
Cast off.

The Collar

With No. 11 needles cast on 75 sts. and k.2 rows.
Work the 6 pattern rows given for main part 3 times.

Next row: K.7, * p.1, k.1 ; repeat from * to last 8 sts., p.1, k.7.

Next row: K.8, * p.1, k.1 ; repeat from * to last 9 sts., p.1, k.8.
Repeat these 2 rows twice more.
Cast off working in rib across centre.

To Make Up The Jacket

Press the st.st. parts only on wrong side, using a warm iron over a damp cloth. Join sleeve seams and set in sleeves. Beginning and ending in centre of front bands, sew the cast-off edge of collar evenly to neck edge. Sew on buttons.

The Bonnet

To Make

With No. 11 needles cast on 85 sts. and k.8 rows.
Work the 6 pattern rows given for jacket 8 times.

To shape the crown:

1st row: K.1, * k.2 tog., k.10 ; repeat from * to end.

2nd and every alternate row: All p.

3rd row: K.1, * k.2 tog., k.9 ; repeat from * to end.

5th row: K.1, * k.2 tog., k.8 ; repeat from * to end.

7th row: K.1, * k.2 tog., k.7 ; repeat from * to end.

9th row: K.1, * k.2 tog., k.6 ; repeat from * to end.

11th row: K.1, * k.2 tog., k.5 ; repeat from * to end.

13th row: K.1, * k.2 tog., k.4 ; repeat from * to end.

15th row: K.1, * k.2 tog., k.3 ; repeat from * to end.
Break off wool ; run end through remaining 29 sts., draw up and fasten securely, then join row-ends to within 2½ inches of cast-on edge.
Press and attach ribbon.

The Bootees

To Make (both alike)

With No. 11 needles cast on 43 sts. and k.2 rows.

1st row: K.2, * w.fwd., k.3, sl.1, k.2 tog., p.s.s.o., k.3, w.fwd., k.1; repeat from * ending last repeat with k.2.

2nd row: All p.

3rd row: K.3, * w.fwd., k.2, sl.1, k.2 tog., p.s.s.o., k.2, w.fwd., k.3; repeat from * to end.

4th row: All p.

5th row: K.1, k.2 tog., * w.fwd., k.1, w.fwd., k.1, sl.1, k.2 tog., p.s.s.o., k.1, w.fwd., k.1, w.fwd., sl.1, k.2 tog., p.s.s.o.; repeat from * to last 10 sts., w.fwd., k.1, w.fwd., k.1, sl.1, k.2 tog., p.s.s.o., k.1, w.fwd., k.1, w.fwd., k.2 tog., k.1.

6th row: All p. **.

Repeat these 6 rows 3 times more.

Next (dec.) row: K.13, k.2 tog., k.13, k.2 tog., k.13 – 41 sts.

Next row: All k.

Next (slot) row: K.1, * w.fwd., k.2 tog.; repeat from * to end.

Next row: All k.

Now divide sts. for foot.

Next row: K.27, turn and p.13 for instep, turn.

St.st. 18 rows on these centre 13 sts. for instep.

Break off wool. With right side of work facing, rejoin wool to inner edge of the 14 sts. at right-hand side and pick up and k.11 sts. along row-ends of instep, k. across centre 13 sts., pick up and k.11 sts. from other side of instep and k. across the 14 sts. at left-hand side – 63 sts.

Beginning with a p. row, st.st. 9 rows.

To shape heel and toe:

1st row: K.2 tog., k.23, k.2 tog., k.9, k.2 tog., k.23, k.2 tog.

2nd row: P.2 tog., p.22, p.2 tog., p.7, p.2 tog., p.22, p.2 tog.

3rd row: K.2 tog., k.21, k.2 tog., k.5, k.2 tog., k.21, k.2 tog.

4th row: P.2 tog., p.20, p.2 tog., p.3, p.2 tog., p.20, p.2 tog.

5th row: K.2 tog., k.19, k.2 tog., k.1, k.2 tog., k.19, k.2 tog.

6th row: P.2 tog., p.18, sl.1, p.2 tog., p.s.s.o., p.18, p.2 tog.

Cast off remaining 39 sts.

To Make Up The Bootees

Press. Join back and underfoot seam. Thread with ribbon.

The Mitts

To Make (both alike)

With No. 11 needles, cast on 43 sts. and work as given for bootees to **.

Repeat these 6 rows twice more.

Next (dec.) row: K.6, * k.2 tog., k.4; repeat from * 4 times more, k.2 tog., k.5 – 37 sts.

Next row: All k.

Next (slot) row: K.1, * w.fwd., k.2 tog.; repeat from * to end.

Next row: All k.

Beginning with a k. row, st.st. 18 rows.

To shape the top:

1st row: K.1, * k.2 tog., k.4; repeat from * to end.

2nd row: * P.3, p.2 tog.; repeat from * to last st., p.1.

3rd row: K.1, * k.2 tog., k.2; repeat from * to end.

4th row: * P.1, p.2 tog.; repeat from * to last st., p.1.

5th row: * K.2 tog.; repeat from * to last st., k.1.

Break off wool, run end through remaining 7 sts., draw up and fasten securely, then join side seam.

Press and thread with ribbon.

Turquoise or Girl's Matinee Set

Jacket, Bonnet, Bootees and Mitts

Materials

Six 20-gramme balls of Sirdar Wonderland Courtelle Quick Knit; a pair each of No. 9 and No. 10 knitting needles; 3 buttons; 1 yard of 1-inch wide ribbon; 1½ yards of narrow ribbon.

Tension and Size

Worked at a tension of 13 stitches and 16 rows to 2 inches, over the stocking stitch, using No. 9 needles, the jacket will measure 21½ inches all round at underarms and be suitable for baby aged three to six months.

Abbreviations

K., knit; p., purl; st., stitch; tog., together; dec., decrease (by working 2 sts. tog.); inc., increase (by working twice into same st.); sl., slip; s.k.p.o. sl.1, k.1, pass slipped st. over; y.fwd., yarn forward to make a st.; p.s.s.o., pass slipped st. over; st.st., stocking st. (k. on right side and p. on wrong side); single rib is k.1 and p.1 alternately; garter st. is k. on every row.

The Jacket

The Back

With No. 10 needles cast on 99 sts. and k.5 rows.

Change to No. 9 needles and work in pattern as follows:

1st row: K.7, * p.1, k.5; repeat from * to last 2 sts., k.2 more.

2nd row: P.7, * k.1, p.5; repeat from * to last 2 sts., p.2 more.

3rd row: K.2, * y.fwd., s.k.p.o., p.1, k.2 tog., y.fwd., k.1; repeat from * to last st., k.1 more.

4th row: P.4, * k.1, p.5; repeat from * ending last repeat with p.4.

5th row: K.4, * p.1, k.5; repeat from * ending last repeat with k.4.

6th row: P.4, * k.1, p.5; repeat from * ending last repeat with p.4.

7th row: K.2, * k.2 tog., y.fwd., k.1, y.fwd., s.k.p.o., p.1; repeat from * to last 7 sts., k.2 tog., y.fwd., k.1, y.fwd., s.k.p.o., k.2.

8th row: P.7, * k.1, p.5; repeat from * ending last repeat with p.7.

Repeat these 8 rows 6 times more.

Next (dec.) row: K.3, * sl.1, k.2 tog., p.s.s.o., k.1, p.1, k.1; repeat from * to last 6 sts., s.k.p.o., k.4 – 68 sts.

Next row (wrong side): All k.

Break off yarn and leave sts. on a spare needle.

The Sleeves (both alike)

With No. 10 needles cast on 32 sts. and work 8 rows in single rib.

Change to No. 9 needles and, beginning with a k. row, st.st. 4 rows.

Inc. 1 st. at each end of the next row and every following 4th row until the 7th inc. row has been worked – 46 sts.

St.st. 11 rows.

Break off yarn and leave sts. on a spare needle.

The Left Front

With No. 10 needles cast on 50 sts. and, slipping first st. on every row, k.5 rows.

Change to No. 9 needles and work in pattern as follows:

1st row: K.7, * p.1, k.5; repeat from * to last 7 sts., k.7 more.

2nd row: Sl.1, k.4, p.7, * k.1, p.5; repeat from * to last 2 sts., p.2 more.

3rd row: K.2, * y.fwd., s.k.p.o., p.1, k.2 tog., y.fwd., k.1; repeat from * to last 12 sts., y.fwd., s.k.p.o., p.1, k.2 tog., y.fwd., k.7.

4th row: Sl.1, k.4, p.4, * k.1, p.5; repeat from * ending last repeat with p.4.

5th row: K.4, * p.1, k.5; repeat from * ending last repeat with k.9.

6th row: Sl.1, k.4, p.4, * k.1, p.5; repeat from * ending last repeat with p.4.

7th row: K.2, * k.2 tog., y.fwd., k.1, y.fwd., s.k.p.o., p.1; repeat from * to last 12 sts., k.2 tog., y.fwd., k.1, y.fwd., s.k.p.o., k.7.

8th row: Sl.1, k.4, p.7, * k.1, p.5; repeat from * to last 2 sts., p.2 more.

Repeat these 8 rows 6 times more.

Next (dec.) row: K.3, * sl.1, k.2 tog., p.s.s.o., k.1, p.1, k.1; repeat from * to last 11 sts., sl.1, k.2 tog., p.s.s.o., k.8 – 36 sts.

Next row (wrong side): Sl.1, k. to end.

Break off yarn and leave sts. on a spare needle.

The Right Front

With No. 10 needles cast on 50 sts. and slipping 1st st. on every row, k. 5 rows.

Change to No. 9 needles and work in pattern as follows:

1st row: Sl.1, k.11, * p.1, k.5; repeat from * to last 2 sts., k.2 more.

2nd row: P.7, k.1, * p.5, k.1; repeat from * to last 12 sts., p.7, k.5.

3rd row: Sl.1, k.6, * y.fwd., s.k.p.o., p.1, k.2 tog., y.fwd., k.1; repeat from * to last st., k.1 more.

4th row: P.4, * k.1, p.5; repeat from * to last 10 sts., k.1, p.4, k.5.

5th row: Sl.1, k.8, * p.1, k.5; repeat from * ending last repeat with k.4.

6th row: P.4, * k.1, p.5; repeat from * to last 10 sts., k.1, p.4, k.5.

7th row: Sl.1, k.6, * k.2 tog., y.fwd., k.1, y.fwd., s.k.p.o., p.1; repeat from * to last 7 sts., k.2 tog., y.fwd., k.1, y.fwd., s.k.p.o., k.2.

8th row: P.7, * k.1, p.5; repeat from * to last 7 sts., p.2, k.5.

Repeat these 8 rows 6 times more.

osite – **Girl's and boy's matinee sets (see p. 84).**

Next (dec.) row: Sl.1, k.7, * sl.1, k.2 tog., p.s.s.o., k.1, p.1, k.1; repeat from * to last 6 sts., sl.1, k.2 tog., p.s.s.o., k.3 – 36 sts.

Next row (wrong side): All k.

Do not break off yarn; join all pieces together for yoke as follows:

Next (joining) row: Sl.1, k.35 across sts. of right front then, onto same needle, k.46 sts. of one sleeve, 68 sts. of back, 46 sts. of other sleeve and 36 sts. of left front – 232 sts.

Next row: Sl.1, k.4, p. to last 5 sts., k.5.

To shape the yoke:

1st (buttonhole) row: Sl.1, k.2 tog., yfwd., k.29, k.3 tog., k.2, sl.1, k.2 tog., p.s.s.o., k.38, k.3 tog., k.2, sl.1, k.2 tog., p.s.s.o., k.60, k.3 tog., k.2, sl.1, k.2 tog., p.s.s.o., k.38, k.3 tog., k.2, sl.1, k.2 tog., p.s.s.o., k. to end – 216 sts.

2nd row: Sl.1, k.4, p. to last 5 sts., k.5.

3rd row: Sl.1, k.29, k.3 tog., k.2, sl.1, k.2 tog., p.s.s.o., k.34, k.3 tog., k.2, sl.1, k.2 tog., p.s.s.o., k.56, k.3 tog., k.2, sl.1, k.2 tog., p.s.s.o., k.34, k.3 tog., k.2, sl.1, k.2 tog., p.s.s.o., k. to end – 200 sts.

Repeat 2nd and 3rd rows 5 times more working 2 sts. less at each end and 4 sts. less between the decreases on each successive repeat – 120 sts.

Keeping garter st. borders work 7 rows more in st.st. making a buttonhole on the 2nd of these rows.

Now decrease as follows:

1st (dec.) row: Sl.1, k.6, k.2 tog., * k.2, k.2 tog.; repeat from * to last 7 sts., k.7 – 93 sts.

Next row (wrong side): Sl.1, k. to end. Keeping garter st. borders, st.st. 4 rows.

2nd (dec.) row: Sl.1, k.4, k.2 tog., * k.1, k.2 tog.; repeat from * to last 5 sts., k.5 – 65 sts.

Next row (wrong side): Sl.1, k. to end. Keeping garter st. borders, st.st. 2 rows. Change to No. 10 needles.

The Neck Band

1st (buttonhole) row: Sl.1, k.2 tog., y.fwd., k.2, * p.1, k.1; repeat from * to last 6 sts., p.1, k.5.

2nd row: Sl.1, k.5, p.1, * k.1, p.1; repeat from * to last 6 sts., k.6.

Work a further 2 rows in rib and garter st. Cast off.

To Make Up The Jacket

Do not press. Join sleeve and side seams. Sew on buttons.

The Bonnet

The Main Part

With No. 10 needles cast on 75 sts., and k.5 rows.

Change to No. 9 needles and work the 8 pattern rows given for back of jacket 4 times.

To shape the back: Cast off 24 sts. at beginning of each of the next 2 rows.

The back section: On remaining 27 sts., work 3rd to 8th pattern rows.

Work the 8 pattern rows 3 times more. Cast off.

The Neck Band: First join cast-off edges of main part to the row ends of back section. With right side of work facing, rejoin yarn to neck edge and, using No. 10 needles, pick up and k.23 sts. along row ends of main part, 25 sts. across back and 23 sts. along other side of main part – 71 sts.

Beginning wrong-side rows with p.1 and right-side rows with k.1, work 5 rows in single rib.

Cast off.

Add ribbon.

The Bootees

To Make (both alike)

With No. 10 needles cast on 39 sts. and work 4 rows in single rib as given for bonnet.

Change to No. 9 needles and work the 8 pattern rows given for back of jacket twice.

Next row: All k.

Next row (wrong side): All k.

Next (slot) row: K.2, * y.fwd., k.2 tog.; repeat from * to last st., k.1.

Next (wrong side) row: All k.

Now divide sts. for instep.

Next row: K.26, turn and p.13.

On these centre 13 sts., beginning with a k. row, st.st. 12 rows for instep.

Break off yarn.

With right side of work facing, rejoin yarn to inner edge of the 13 sts. at right-hand side at base of instep and pick up and k.14 sts. along row ends of instep, k.6, k.2 tog., k.5 across the centre 13 sts., then pick up and k.14 sts. from other side of instep and, finally k.13 sts. at left-hand side – 66 sts.

St.st. 5 rows.

To shape the foot:

1st row: K.2 tog., k.23, k.3 tog., k.10, sl.1, k.2 tog., p.s.s.o., k.23, k.2 tog.

2nd row: All p.

3rd row: K.2 tog., k.21, k.3 tog., k.8, sl.1, k.2 tog., p.s.s.o., k.21, k.2 tog.

4th row: All p.

5th row: K.2 tog., k.19, k.3 tog., k.6, sl.1, k.2 tog., p.s.s.o., k.19, k.2 tog.

6th row: All p.

Cast off remaining 48 sts.

To Make Up The Bootees

Join back and underfoot seam. Add ribbon.

The Mitts

To Make (both alike)

With No. 10 needles cast on 39 sts. and work 4 rows in single rib as given for bonnet.

Change to No. 9 needles and work the 8 pattern rows given for back of jacket once, then work first 4 rows again.

Next row: All k.

Next row (wrong side): All k.

Next (slot) row: K.2, * y.fwd., k.2 tog.; repeat from * to last st., k.1.

Next (dec.) row: K.4, * k.2 tog., k.5; repeat from * to end – 34 sts.

Beginning with a k. row, st.st. 16 rows.

To shape the top:

1st row: K.1, s.k.p.o., k.11, k.2 tog., k.2, s.k.p.o., k.11, k.2 tog., k.1.

2nd and 4th rows: All p.

3rd row: K.1, s.k.p.o., k.9, k.2 tog., k.2, s.k.p.o., k.9, k.2 tog., k.1.

5th row: K.1, s.k.p.o., k.7, k.2 tog., k.2, s.k.p.o., k.7, k.2 tog., k.1.

6th row: All p.

Cast off remaining 22 sts.

To Make Up The Mitts

Fold in half and join top and side seam. Add ribbon.

Orange or Boy's Matinee Set

Jacket, Helmet, Bootees and Mitts

(see illustration p. 80)

Materials

Six 20-gramme balls of Sirdar Wonderland Courtelle Quick Knit; a pair each of No. 9 and No. 10 knitting needles; 3 buttons; 1½ yards of narrow ribbon.

Tension and Size

Worked at a tension of 13 stitches and 16 rows to 2 inches, over the stocking stitch, using No. 9 needles, the jacket will measure 21½ inches all round at underarms and be suitable for baby aged three to six months.

Abbreviations

K., knit; p., purl; st., stitch; tog., together; dec., decrease (by working 2 sts. tog.); inc., increase (by working twice into same st.); sl., slip; s.k.p.o., sl.1, k.1, pass slipped st. over; p.s.s.o., pass slipped st. over; y.fwd., yarn forward to make a st.; st.st., stocking st. (k. on right side and p. on wrong side); single rib is k.1 and p.1 alternately; garter st. is k. on every row; up 1 (pick up the thread which lies between the needles and k. into back of it, thus making a st.).

The Jacket

The Back

With No. 10 needles cast on 99 sts. and k.5 rows.

Change to No. 9 needles and work in pattern as follows:

1st row: K.2, * k.2 tog., y.fwd., k.1, y.fwd., s.k.p.o., k.1; repeat from * to last st., k.1 more.

2nd, 4th and 6th rows: All p.

3rd row: K.1, k.2 tog., * y.fwd., k.3, y.fwd., sl.1, k.2 tog., p.s.s.o.; repeat from * to last 6 sts., y.fwd., k.3, y.fwd., s.k.p.o., k.1.

5th row: K.2, * y.fwd., s.k.p.o., k.1, k.2 tog., y.fwd., k.1; repeat from * to last st., k.1 more.

7th row: K.3, * y.fwd., sl.1, k.2 tog., p.s.s.o., y.fwd., k.3; repeat from * to end.

8th row: All p.

Repeat these 8 rows 6 times more.

Next (dec.) row: K.6, * sl.1, k.2 tog., p.s.s.o., k.3; repeat from * to last 3 sts., k.3 more – 69 sts.

Next row (wrong side): K.33, k.2 tog., k.34 – 68 sts.

Break off yarn and leave sts. on a spare needle.

The Sleeves (both alike)

With No. 10 needles cast on 32 sts. and work 8 rows in single rib.

Change to No. 9 needles and, beginning with a k. row, st.st. 4 rows.

Inc. 1 st. at each end of the next row and every following 4th row until the 7th inc. row has been worked – 46 sts.

St.st. 11 rows.

Break off yarn and leave sts. on a spare needle.

The Left Front

With No. 10 needles cast on 50 sts. and, slipping first st. on every row, k.5 rows.

Change to No. 9 needles and work in pattern with garter st. border as follows:

1st row: K.2, * k.2 tog., y.fwd., k.1, y.fwd., s.k.p.o., k.1; repeat from * to last 6 sts., k.6 more.

2nd, 4th and 6th rows: Sl.1, k.4, p. to end.

3rd row: K.1, k.2 tog., * y.fwd., k.3, y.fwd., sl.1, k.2 tog., p.s.s.o.; repeat from * to last 11 sts., y.fwd., k.3, y.fwd., s.k.p.o., k.6.

5th row: K.2, * y.fwd., s.k.p.o., k.1, k.2 tog., y.fwd., k.1; repeat from * to last 6 sts., k.6 more.

7th row: K.3, * y.fwd., sl.1, k.2 tog., p.s.s.o., y.fwd., k.3; repeat from * to last 5 sts., k.5 more.

8th row: Sl.1, k.4, p. to end.

Repeat these 8 rows 6 times more.

Next (dec.) row: K.6, * sl.1, k.2 tog., p.s.s.o., k.3; repeat from * to last 8 sts., sl.1, k.2 tog., p.s.s.o., k.5 – 36 sts.

Next row (wrong side): Sl.1, k. to end.

Break off yarn and leave sts. on a spare needle.

The Right Front

With No. 10 needles cast on 50 sts. and, slipping first st. on every row, k.5 rows.

Change to No. 9 needles and work in pattern with garter st. border as follows:

1st row: Sl.1, k.6, * k.2 tog., y.fwd., k.1, y.fwd., s.k.p.o., k.1; repeat from * to last st., k.1 more.

2nd, 4th and 6th rows: P. to last 5 sts., k.5.

3rd row: Sl.1, k.5, s.k.p.o., * y.fwd., k.3, y.fwd., sl.1, k.2 tog., p.s.s.o.; repeat from * to last 6 sts., y.fwd., k.3, y.fwd., s.k.p.o., k.1.

5th row: Sl.1, k.6, * y.fwd., s.k.p.o., k.1, k.2 tog., y.fwd., k.1; repeat from * to last st., k.1 more.

7th row: Sl.1, k.7, * y.fwd., sl.1, k.2 tog., p.s.s.o., y.fwd., k.3; repeat from * to end.

8th row: P. to last 5 sts., k.5.

Repeat these 8 rows 6 times more.

Next (dec.) row: Sl.1, k.4, * sl.1, k.2 tog., p.s.s.o., k.3; repeat from * to last 3 sts., k.3 more – 36 sts.

Next row (wrong side): All k.

Do not break off yarn.

Next (joining) row: Sl.1, k.35 across the sts. of right front then, with right side of each piece facing, onto same needle, k.46 sts. of one sleeve, 68 sts. of back, 46 sts. of other sleeve and 36 sts. of left front – 232 sts.

Next row: Sl.1, k.4, p. to last 5 sts., k.5.

The Yoke

1st (buttonhole) row: Sl.1, k.31, k.3 tog., k.2, sl.1, k.2 tog., p.s.s.o., k.30, k.3 tog., k.2, sl.1, k.2 tog., p.s.s.o., k.60, k.3 tog., k.2, sl.1, k.2 tog., p.s.s.o., k.38, k.3 tog., k.2, sl.1, k.2 tog., p.s.s.o., k. to last 3 sts., y.fwd., k.2 tog., k.1 – 216 sts.

2nd row: Sl.1, k.4, p. to last 5 sts., k.5.

3rd row: Sl.1, k.29, k.3 tog., k.2, sl.1, k.2 tog., p.s.s.o., k.34, k.3 tog., k.2, sl.1, k.2 tog., p.s.s.o., k.56, k.3 tog., k.2, sl.1, k.2 tog., p.s.s.o., k.34, k.3 tog., k.2, sl.1, k.2 tog., p.s.s.o., k. to end – 200 sts.

Repeat 2nd and 3rd rows 5 times more working 2 sts. less at each end and 4 sts. less between the decreases on each repeat – 120 sts.

Keeping garter st. borders as set, work 7 rows in st.st. making a buttonhole on the 2nd of these rows.

Now decrease as follows:

1st (dec.) row: Sl.1, k.6, k.2 tog., * k.2, k.2 tog.; repeat from * to last 7 sts., k.7 – 93 sts.

Next row (wrong side): Sl.1, k. to end.

Keeping garter st. borders, st.st. 4 rows.

2nd (dec.) row: Sl.1, k.4, k.2 tog., * k.1, k.2 tog.; repeat from * to last 5 sts., k.5 – 65 sts.

Next row (wrong side): Sl.1, k. to end.

Keeping garter st. borders, st.st. 2 rows.

Change to No. 10 needles.

The Neck Band

1st (buttonhole) row: Sl.1, k.4, p.1, * k.1, p.1; repeat from * to last 5 sts., k.2, y.fwd., k.2 tog., k.1.

2nd row: Sl.1, k.5, p.1, * k.1, p.1; repeat from * to last 6 sts., k.6.

Work a further 2 rows in rib and garter st. Cast off.

To Make Up The Jacket

Do not press. Join sleeve and side seams. Sew on buttons.

The Cap

The Ear Pieces (make 2)

With No. 10 needles cast on 4 sts. and work 46 rows in garter st.

Now shape as follows:

1st row: K.1, up 1, k.2, up 1, k.1.

2nd row: All k.

3rd row: K.2, up 1, k. to last 2 sts., up 1, k.2.

Repeat 2nd and 3rd rows 7 times more — 22 sts.

K.7 rows.

Break off yarn and leave sts. on a spare needle.

The Main Part

With No. 10 needles cast on 8 sts. then, onto same needle, k. the 22 sts. of one ear piece, turn, cast on 21 sts., turn and k. across the 22 sts. of second ear piece, turn and cast on 8 sts. — 81 sts.

K.7 rows.

Change to No. 9 needles and work the 8 pattern rows given for back of jacket 3 times.

To shape the crown:

1st row: * K.8, k.2 tog.; repeat from * to last st., k.1 — 73 sts.

2nd row (wrong side): All k.

3rd row: All k.

4th row: All p.

5th row: * K.7, k.2 tog.; repeat from * to last st., k.1.

6th row (wrong side): All k.

7th row: All k.

8th row: All p.

9th row: * K.6, k.2 tog.; repeat from * to last st., k.1 — 57 sts.

10th and every following alternate row: All p.

11th row: * K.5, k.2 tog.; repeat from * to last st., k.1.

13th row: * K.4, k.2 tog.; repeat from * to last st., k.1.

15th row: * K.3, k.2 tog.; repeat from * to last st., k.1.

17th row: * K.2, k.2 tog.; repeat from * to last st., k.1.

19th row: * K.1, k.2 tog.; repeat from * to last st., k.1.

Break off yarn; run end through remaining 17 sts., draw up and fasten securely, then join row ends to form back seam.

The Bootees

To Make (both alike)

With No. 10 needles cast on 39 sts. and, beginning right-side rows with k.1 and wrong-side rows with p.1, work 4 rows in single rib.

Change to No. 9 needles and work the 8 pattern rows given for back of jacket twice.

Next row: All k.

Next row (wrong side): All k.

Next (slot) row: K.2, * y.fwd., k.2 tog.; repeat from * to last st., k.1.

Next row (wrong side): All k.

Now divide sts. for instep.

Next row: K.26, turn and p.13.

On these centre 13 sts., beginning with a k. row, st.st. 12 rows for instep.

Break off yarn.

With right side of work facing rejoin yarn to base of instep at inner edge of 13 sts. at right-hand side and pick up and k.14 sts. along row ends of instep, then work k.6, k.2 tog., k.5 across 13 sts., pick up and k.14 sts. from other side of instep and finally k. the 13 sts. at left-hand side — 66 sts.

St.st. 5 rows.

To shape the foot:
1st row: K.2 tog., k.23, k.3 tog., k.10, sl.1, k.2 tog., p.s.s.o., k.23, k.2 tog.
2nd and 4th rows: All p.
3rd row: K.2 tog., k.21, k.3 tog., k.8, sl.1, k.2 tog., p.s.s.o., k.21, k.2 tog.
5th row: K.2 tog., k.19, k.3 tog., k.6, sl.1, k.2 tog., p.s.s.o., k.19, k.2 tog.

6th row: All p.
Cast off remaining 48 sts.

To Make Up The Bootees

Join back and underfoot seam. Add ribbon.

The Mitts

To Make (both alike)

With No. 10 needles cast on 39 sts. and work 4 rows in single rib as given for bootees.

Change to No. 9 needles and work the 8 pattern rows given for back of jacket once, then work first 4 rows again.

Next row: All k.
Next row (wrong side): All k.
Next (slot) row: K.2, * y.fwd., k.2 tog.; repeat from * to last st., k.1.
Next (dec.) row: K.4, * k.2 tog., k.5; repeat from * to end – 34 sts.
Beginning with a k. row, st.st. 16 rows.

To shape the top:
1st row: K.1, s.k.p.o., k.11, k.2 tog., k.2, s.k.p.o., k.11, k.2 tog., k.1.
2nd and 4th rows: All p.
3rd row: K.1, s.k.p.o., k.9, k.2 tog., k.2, s.k.p.o., k.9, k.2 tog., k.1.
5th row: K.1, s.k.p.o., k.7, k.2 tog., k.2, s.k.p.o., k.7, k.2 tog., k.1.
6th row: All p.
Cast off remaining 22 sts.

To Make Up The Mitts

Fold in half and join top and side seam. Add ribbon.

Nylon Matinee Set

Jacket, Bonnet, Bootees and Mitts

Materials

Seven 20-gramme balls of Sirdar Wonderland Nylon 4-ply; a pair each of No. 9 and No. 10 knitting needles; 1 yard of 1-inch wide ribbon; 1½ yards of narrow ribbon; 3 buttons.

Tension and Size

Worked at a tension of 7 stitches and 9 rows to 1 inch, over the stocking stitch, using No. 9 needles, the set will be suitable for baby aged birth to three months.

Abbreviations

K., knit; p., purl; st., stitch; tog., together; dec., decrease (by working 2 sts. tog.); inc., increase (by working twice into same st.); y.fwd., yarn forward to make a st.; sl., slip; p.s.s.o., pass slipped st. over; st.st., stocking st. (k. on right side and p. on wrong side); single rib is k.1 and p.1 alternately.

The Jacket

The Main Part (worked in one piece to armholes)

With No. 9 needles cast on 175 sts.

Foundation row: K.2, p.1, k.1, p.1 for border then, k.3, * p.3, k.3; repeat from * to last 5 sts., p.1, k.1, p.1, k.2.

Now work in pattern as follows:

1st row: K.1, p.1, k.1, p.1, k.1, p.3, * k.3, p.3; repeat from * to last 5 sts., k.1, p.1, k.1, p.1, k.1.

2nd row: K.2, p.1, k.1, p.1, k.3, * p.3, k.3; repeat from * to last 5 sts., p.1, k.1, p.1, k.2.

3rd row: K.1, p.1, k.1, p.1, k.4, * y.fwd., sl.1, k.2 tog., p.s.s.o., y.fwd., k.3; repeat from * to last 11 sts., y.fwd., sl.1, k.2 tog., p.s.s.o., y.fwd., k.4, p.1, k.1, p.1, k.1.

4th row: K.2, p.1, k.1, p.4, * k.3, p.3; repeat from * to last 11 sts., k.3, p.4, k.1, p.1, k.2.

5th row: K.1, p.1, k.1, p.1, k.4, * p.3, k.3; repeat from * to last 11 sts., p.3, k.4, p.1, k.1, p.1, k.1.

6th row: K.2, p.1, k.1, p.4, * k.3, p.3; repeat from * to last 11 sts., k.3, p.4, k.1, p.1, k.2.

7th row: K.1, p.1, k.1, p.1, k.2, k.2 tog., * y.fwd., k.3, y.fwd., sl.1, k.2 tog., p.s.s.o.; repeat from * to last 11 sts., y.fwd., k.3, y.fwd., sl.1, k.1, p.s.s.o., k.2, p.1, k.1, p.1, k.1.

8th row: K.2, p.1, k.1, p.1, k.3, * p.3, k.3; repeat from * to last 5 sts., p.1, k.1, p.1, k.2.

Repeat these 8 rows 7 times more.

Next (dec.) row: Rib 5, k.4, * k.2 tog., k.4; repeat from * 9 times more, ** k.2 tog., k.5; repeat from ** 4 times more, *** k.2 tog., k.4; repeat from *** 10 times more, rib 5 – 149 sts.

Now divide st. for back and fronts.

Next row: Rib 5, p.34 and leave these 39 sts. on a spare needle for left front, p. next 71 sts. and leave these on a spare needle for back, p. to last 5 sts., rib 5 and work on these 39 sts. for right front.

The right front: To shape the raglan armhole:

1st row: Rib 5, k. to end.

2nd row: Cast off 2, p. to last 5 sts., rib 5.

3rd (buttonhole) row: Rib 3, y.fwd., k.2 tog., k. to last 2 sts., dec.

4th row: P. to last 5 sts., rib 5.

5th row: Rib 5, k. to last 2 sts., dec.

Repeat 4th and 5th rows 6 times more, then work 4th row again – 29 sts.

Work the buttonhole row, then work 4th and 5th rows 5 times more and 4th row again – 23 sts. – ending at front edge.

To shape the neck:

1st row: Rib 5 and sl. these sts. onto safety-pin, k.2 tog., k. to last 2 sts., dec.

2nd row: P. to last 2 sts., dec.

3rd row: Dec., k. to last 2 sts., dec.

Repeat 2nd and 3rd rows 3 times more, then work 2nd row again – 3 sts.

Next row: K.1, k.2 tog.

Next row: P.2.

Take remaining 2 sts. tog. and fasten off.

The back: With right side of work facing, rejoin yarn to 71 sts. on spare needle.

1st row: Cast off 2, k. to end.

2nd row: Cast off 2, p. to end.

3rd row: Dec., k. to last 2 sts., dec.

4th row: All p.

Repeat 3rd and 4th rows 19 times more – 27 sts.

Break off yarn and leave sts. on a spare needle.

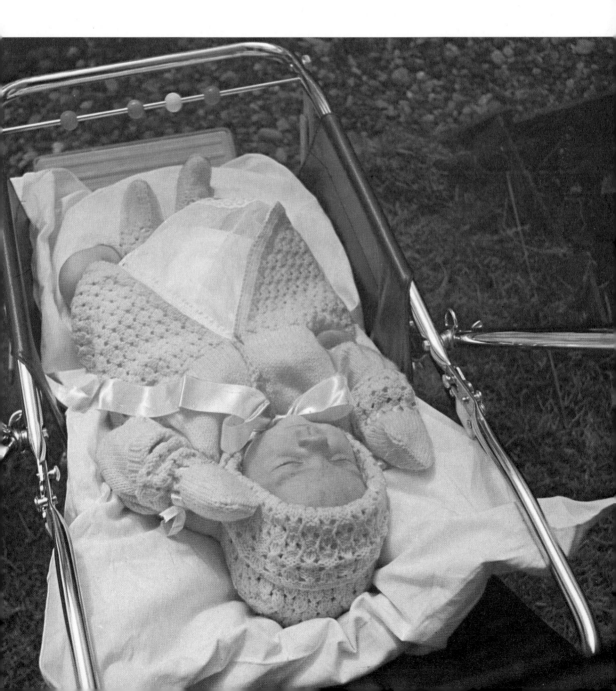

The left front: With right side of work facing, rejoin yarn to 39 sts. on stitch-holder.

1st row: Cast off 2, k. to last 5 sts., rib 5.

2nd row: Rib 5, p. to end.

3rd row: Dec., k. to last 5 sts., rib 5.

Repeat 2nd and 3rd rows 13 times more — 23 sts. — ending at front edge.

To shape the neck:

1st row: Rib 5 and sl. these onto safety-pin, p. 2 tog., p. to end.

2nd row: Dec., k. to last 2 sts., dec.

3rd row: Dec., p. to end.

Repeat 2nd and 3rd rows 4 times more — 2 sts.

Next row: K.2

Take remaining 2 sts. tog. and fasten off.

The Sleeves (both alike)

With No. 10 needles cast on 38 sts. and work 8 rows in single rib.

Change to No. 9 needles and, beginning with a k. row, st.st. 4 rows.

Inc. 1 st. at each end of next and every following 4th row until the 7th inc. row has been worked — 52 sts.

St.st. 19 rows.

To shape the raglan sleeve top: Work exactly as given for raglan armhole shaping on back when 8 sts. will remain.

Break off yarn and leave sts. on safety-pin.

The Neck Band

First join raglan seams. With right side of work facing, sl. the 5 sts. of right front band onto No. 10 needle with point to inner edge, rejoin yarn and pick up and k.12 sts. from right front edge, k.8 sts. of right sleeve, 27 sts. across back, 8 sts. of left sleeve and pick up and k.12 sts. from left front neck edge and rib the 5 sts. of left front band.

On these 77 sts., work 3 rows in single rib.

Work a buttonhole on next row, then rib a further 3 rows.

Cast off in rib.

To Make Up The Jacket

Press with a cool iron over a dry cloth. Join sleeve seams. Sew on buttons.

The Bonnet

To Make

With No. 9 needles cast on 87 sts.

Foundation row: K.3, * p.3, k.3; repeat from * to end.

Now work in pattern as follows:

1st row: P.3, * k.3, p.3; repeat from * to end.

2nd row: K.3, * p.3, k.3; repeat from * to end.

3rd row: K.3, * y.fwd., sl.1, k.2 tog., p.s.s.o., y.fwd., k.3; repeat from * to end.

4th row: P.3, * k.3, p.3; repeat from * to end.

5th row: K.3, * p.3, k.3; repeat from * to end.

6th row: P.3, * k.3, p.3; repeat from * to end.

7th row: K.1, k.2 tog., * y.fwd., k.3, y.fwd., sl.1, k.2 tog., p.s.s.o.; repeat from * to last 6 sts., y.fwd., k.3, y.fwd., sl.1, k.1, p.s.s.o., k.1.

8th row: K.3, * p.3, k.3; repeat from * to end **.

Work first 4 rows again; work the foundation row to reverse the pattern for turn-back, then work 1st to 8th rows 6 times more.

To shape the back: Cast off 30 sts. at beginning of next 2 rows.

On centre 27 sts., work a further 38 rows. Cast off.

To Make Up The Bonnet

Join row ends of back section to the cast-off groups at each side.

Turn back brim and catch in place.

To neaten neck edge: With right side of work facing, rejoin yarn to neck edge and, using No. 10 needles, working through both thicknesses of brim, pick up and k.66 sts. all round neck edge, then cast off these sts. Add ribbon.

The Bootees

To Make (both alike)

With No. 9 needles cast on 39 sts. and work as given for bonnet to **.

Repeat these 8 rows once more, then work first 5 rows again.

Next row: All k. on wrong side.

Next (slot) row: K.1, * y.fwd., k.2 tog.; repeat from * to end.

Next row (wrong side): All k.

Now divide sts. for instep.

Next row: K.26, turn and p.13.

On these centre 13 sts., beginning with a k. row, st.st. 16 rows. Break off yarn.

With right side of work facing, rejoin yarn to base of instep at inner edge of the 13 sts. at right-hand side and pick up and k.12 sts. along row ends of instep, k. the 13 instep sts., pick up and k.12 sts. from other side of instep and k. the 13 sts. at left-hand side — 63 sts.

Beginning with a p. row, st.st. 9 rows.

To shape the foot:

1st row: K.2 tog., k.23, k.2 tog., k.9, k.2 tog., k.23, k.2 tog.

2nd row: All p.

3rd row: K.2 tog., k.22, k.2 tog., k.7, k.2 tog., k.22, k.2 tog.

4th row: All p.

Cast off.

To Make Up the Bootees

Join back and underfoot seam. Thread with ribbon.

The Mitts

To Make (both alike)

With No. 9 needles cast on 39 sts. and work as given for bonnet to **.

Repeat these 8 rows once more, then work 1st row again.

Next row: All k. on wrong side.

Next (slot) row: K.1, * y.fwd., k.2 tog.; repeat from * to end.

Next (dec.) row: K.9, * k.2 tog., k.8; repeat from * twice — 36 sts.

Beginning with a k. row, st.st. 18 rows.

To shape the top:

1st row: K.2 tog., k.14, k.2 tog., k.2 tog., k.14, k.2 tog.

2nd row: P.2 tog., p.12, p.2 tog., p.2 tog., p.12, p.2 tog.

3rd row: K.2 tog., k.10, k.2 tog., k.2 tog., k.10, k.2 tog.

Cast off remaining 24 sts.

To Make Up The Mitts

Fold in half and join top and side seam. Thread with ribbon.

Crew and 'V' Neck Raglans

in 4-ply

Materials

For either size or style: Three 50-gramme balls of Patons Purple Heather 4-ply Wool; a pair each of No. 10 and No. 12 knitting needles; oddments of contrast colours if desired.

Tension

Work at a tension of 7 stitches and 9 rows to 1 inch, over the stocking stitch, using No. 10 needles, to obtain the following measurements:

Abbreviations

K., knit; p., purl; st., stitch; tog., together; dec., decrease (by working 2 sts. tog.); inc., increase (by working twice into same st.); k. or p.2 tog.b., k. or p.2 sts. tog. through back of loops; st.st., stocking st. (k. on right side and p. on wrong side); single rib is k.1 and p.1 alternately.

● *The instructions are given for 1st size. Where they vary, work figures in first brackets for 2nd size; work figures in second brackets for 3rd size.*

Measurements

	INCHES		
	1st size	2nd size	3rd size
All round at under-arms	$21\frac{1}{4}$	23	$24\frac{3}{4}$
Side seam	$6\frac{1}{2}$	$7\frac{1}{4}$	8
Length	12	13	14
Long sleeve seam	$8\frac{1}{4}$	9	$9\frac{1}{2}$
Short sleeve seam	$2\frac{1}{2}$	$2\frac{3}{4}$	$2\frac{3}{4}$

Crew Neck Style

The Back

With No. 12 needles cast on 68 (74) (80) sts. and work 15 rows in single rib.
Next (inc.) row: Rib 10, * inc. in next st., rib 7 (8) (9); repeat from * 5 times, inc. in next st., rib 9 – 75 (81) (87) sts.

Change to No. 10 needles and, beginning with a k. row, st.st. 46 (52) (58) rows.
To shape the raglan armholes:
1st row: Cast off 2 (3) (4), k. to end.
2nd row: Cast off 2 (3) (4), p. to end.

3rd row: K.2, k.2 tog.b., k. to last 4 sts., k.2 tog., k.2.

4th row: All p. **.

Repeat 3rd and 4th rows 18 (19) (20) times more, then work 3rd row again — 31 (33) (35) sts.

Now divide sts. for back neck.

Next row: P.6 and leave on safety-pin for left side, p. next 19 (21) (23) and leave on stitch-holder for neck band, p. to end and work on these 6 sts. for right side.

The right side:

1st row: K.2, k.2 tog.b., k.2.

2nd row: P.5.

3rd row: K.2, k.2 tog.b., k.1.

4th row: P.4.

5th row: K.2, k.2 tog.b.

6th row: P.3.

7th row: K.1, k.2 tog.b.

8th row: P.2.

Take these 2 sts. tog. and fasten off.

The left side: With right side of work facing, rejoin wool to 6 sts.

1st row: K.2, k.2 tog., k.2.

2nd row: P.5.

3rd row: K.1, k.2 tog., k.2.

4th row: P.4.

5th row: K.2 tog., k.2.

6th row: P.3.

7th row: K.2 tog., k.1.

8th row: P.2.

Take these 2 sts. tog. and fasten off.

The Front

Work as back to **.

Repeat 3rd and 4th rows 14 (15) (16) times more, then work 3rd row again — 39 (41) (43) sts.

Now divide sts. for front neck.

Next row: P.14 and leave these sts. on a spare needle for right side, p. next 11 (13) (15) sts. and leave on stitch-holder for neck band, p. to end and work on these 14 sts. for left side.

The left side:

1st row: K.2, k.2 tog.b., k. to last 2 sts., k.2 tog.

2nd row: All p.

Repeat these 2 rows 3 times more — 6 sts.

Dec. 1 st. at armhole edge on next and following 2 alternate rows — 3 sts.

Next row: P.3.

Next row: K.1, k.2 tog.b.

Next row: P.2.

Take these 2 sts. tog. and fasten off.

The right side: With right side of work facing, rejoin wool to the 14 sts. on spare needle.

1st row: K.2 tog., k. to last 4 sts., k.2 tog., k.2.

2nd row: All p.

Repeat these 2 rows 3 times more — 6 sts.

Dec. 1 st. at armhole edge on next and following 2 alternate rows — 3 sts.

Next row: P.3.

Next row: K.2 tog., k.1.

Next row: P.2.

Take these 2 sts. tog. and fasten off.

The Long Sleeves (both alike)

With No. 12 needles cast on 40 (40) (42) sts. and work 21 rows in single rib.

Next (inc.) row: Rib 1 (1) (2), * inc. in next st., rib 8; repeat from * 3 times more, inc. in next st., rib 2 (2) (3) — 45 (45) (47) sts.

Change to No. 10 needles and, beginning with a k. row, st.st. 8 (4) (4) rows.

Inc. 1 st. at each end of next and every following 6th row until the 7th (9th) (10th) inc. row has been worked — 59 (63) (67) sts.

St.st. 15 (11) (9) rows.

To shape the raglan sleeve top: Work the first 4 rows of raglan armhole shaping given for back, then work 3rd and 4th rows 23 (24) (25) times more — 7 sts.

Break off wool and leave sts. on safety-pin.

The Neck Band

First join right raglan seams, then join left sleeve to front only. With right side of work facing, rejoin wool to top of left sleeve and, using No. 12 needles, k. the 7 sts. of left sleeve, pick up and k.13 sts. down left side of neck, k. the 11 (13) (15) sts. at centre front, pick up and k.13 sts. from right side of neck, k. the 7 sts. of right sleeve, pick up and k.7 sts. from shaped edge of back, k. the 19 (21) (23) sts. at centre and pick up and k.7 sts. from shaped edge of back — 84 (88) (92) sts.

Work 7 rows in single rib inserting contrast colours if required.

Cast off very loosely in rib.

To Make Up The Sweater

Press on wrong side, avoiding the ribbing, using a warm iron over a damp cloth. Join remaining raglan seam and neck band. Join sleeve and side seams.

The 'V' Neck Style

The Back and Sleeves

Work as given for Crew Neck Style.

The Front

With No. 12 needles cast on 68 (74) (80) sts. and work 15 rows in single rib.

Next (inc.) row: Rib 10, * inc. in next st., rib 7 (8) (9); repeat from * 5 times more, inc. in next st., rib 9 — 75 (81) (87) sts.

Change to No. 10 needles and, beginning with a k. row, st.st. 45 (51) (57) rows.

Now divide sts. for front neck.

Next row: P.37 (40) (43) and leave these sts. on a spare needle for right side, p. next st. and leave on safety-pin, p. to end and work on these 37 (40) (43) sts. for left side.

The left side: To shape the raglan armhole and slope front neck:

1st row: Cast off 2 (3) (4) sts., k. to last 3 sts., k.2 tog., k.1.

2nd row: All p.

3rd row: K.2, k.2 tog.b., k. to end.

4th row: All p.

5th row: K.2, k.2 tog.b., k. to last 3 sts., k.2 tog., k.1.

Repeat 2nd to 5th rows 7 (8) (9) times more – 10 (9) (8) sts.

Continue as follows:

1st row: All p.

2nd row: K.2, k.2 tog.b., k. to end.

Repeat these 2 rows 5 (4) (3) times more – 4 sts.

Next row: P.4.

Next row: K.2, k.2 tog.b.

Next row: P.3.

Next row: K.1, k.2 tog.b.

Next row: P.2.

Take these 2 sts. tog. and fasten off.

The right side: With right side of work facing, rejoin wool to sts. on spare needle and k. to end of row.

To shape the raglan armhole and slope front neck:

1st row: Cast off 2 (3) (4), p. to end.

2nd row: K.1, k.2 tog.b., k. to last 4 sts., k.2 tog. k.2.

3rd row: All p.

4th row: K. to last 4 sts., k.2 tog., k.2.

5th row: All p.

Repeat 2nd to 5th rows 7 (8) (9) times more, then work 2nd row again – 9 (8) (7) sts.

Continue as follows:

1st row: All p.

2nd row: K. to last 4 sts., k.2 tog., k.2.

Repeat these 2 rows 4 (3) (2) times more – 4 sts.

Next row: P.4.

Next row: K.2 tog., k.2.

Next row: P.3.

Next row: K.2 tog., k.1.

Next row: P.2.

Take these 2 sts. tog. and fasten off.

The Short Sleeves (both alike)

With No. 12 needles cast on 48 (50) (52) sts. and work 8 rows in single rib, increasing 1 st. at end of last row – 49 (51) (53) sts.

Change to No. 10 needles and, beginning with a k. row, st.st. 2 rows.

Inc. 1 st. at each end of next and following 4 (5) (6) right-side rows – 59 (63) (67) sts. St.st. 5 (5) (3) rows.

To shape the raglan sleeve top: Work as given for long sleeves .

The Neck Band

First join right raglan seams, then join left sleeve to front only. With right side of work facing, rejoin wool to top of left sleeve and, using No. 12 needles, k. these 7 sts., pick up and k.46 (48) (50) sts. down left side of neck, k. st. from safety-pin at centre, pick up and k.46 (48) (50) sts. from right side of neck, k. the 7 sts. of right sleeve, pick up and k.7 sts. from shaped edge of back, k. the 19 (21) (23) sts. at centre and pick up and k.7 sts. from other shaped edge of back – 140 (146) (152) sts.

1st row: * P.1, k.1 ; repeat from * to within 2 sts. of centre front st., p.2 tog., p.1, p.2 tog.b., ** k.1, p.1 ; repeat from ** to last st., k.1.

2nd row: Rib to within 2 sts. of centre st., k.2 tog.b., k.1, k.2 tog., rib to end.

Inserting contrast colours if required repeat these 2 rows 3 times more, then work 1st row again.

Cast off in rib.

To Make Up The Sweater

Work as given for Crew Neck Style.

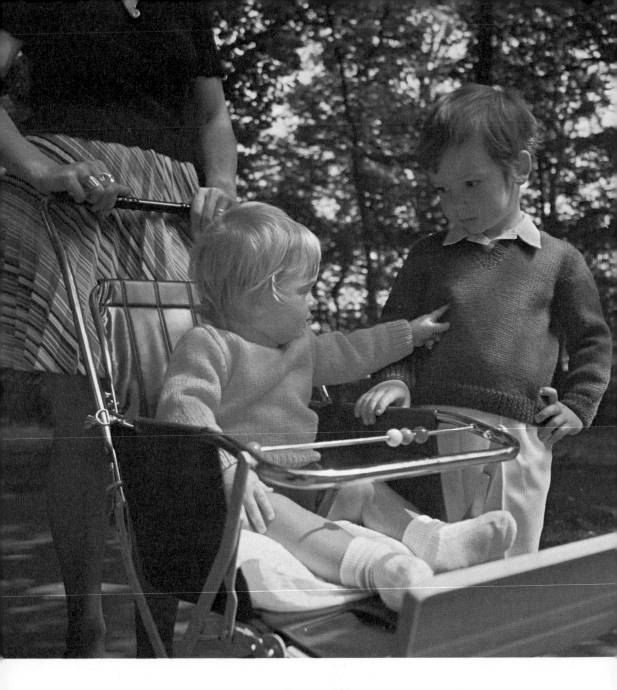

Crew and 'V' Neck
Sweaters

in Double Knitting

Materials

For either style: Five 25-gramme balls of Bairnswear Pleasure Double Knitting Wool for 1st size; six balls for 2nd size; seven balls for 3rd size.

For any one size: a pair each of No. 8 and No. 10 knitting needles; a set of four No. 10 double-pointed needles for V-neck style; 2 buttons for crew neck style.

Tension

Work at a tension of 11 stitches and 15 rows to 2 inches, over the stocking stitch, using No. 8 needles, to obtain the following measurements:

Measurements

	INCHES		
	1st size	2nd size	3rd size
All round at under-arms	23	24	25
Side seam	$7\frac{1}{4}$	8	$8\frac{3}{4}$
Length	12	13	14
Sleeve seam	7	8	9

Abbreviations

K., knit; p., purl; st., stitch; tog., together; k.2 tog.b., k.2 sts. tog. through back of loops; dec., decrease (by working 2 sts. tog.); inc., increase (by working twice into same st.); w.fwd., wool forward to make a st.; st.st., stocking st. (k. on right side and p. on wrong side); single rib is k.1 and p.1 alternately; garter st. is k. on every row.

● *The instructions are given for 1st size. Where they vary, work figures in first brackets for 2nd size; figures in second brackets for 3rd size.*

Crew Neck Style

The Back

With No. 10 needles cast on 64 (66) (70) sts. and work 10 rows in single rib.

Change to No. 8 needles and, beginning with a k. row, st.st. 44 (50) (56) rows.

To shape the armholes: Cast off 4 sts. at beginning of next 2 rows, then dec. 1 st. at each end of the next row and following 2 (2) (3) right-side rows — 50 (52) (54) sts. **

Work 10 (12) (12) rows, ending with a k. row.

Now divide sts. for back opening.

Next row: P.23 (24) (25) and leave these sts. on a spare needle for left side, p. to end and work on these 27 (28) (29) sts. for right side.

The right side:

1st row: All k.

2nd row: K.4, p. to end.

Repeat these 2 rows 4 times more.

Next (buttonhole) row: K. to last 4 sts., k.2 tog., w.fwd., k.2.

Keeping garter st. border as set, work 3 rows, ending at armhole edge.

To slope the shoulder: Cast off 7 (7) (8) sts. at beginning of next row and 7 (8) (8) sts. on following alternate row.

Work 1 row. Break off wool and leave remaining 13 sts. on a spare needle.

The left side: With right side of work facing; rejoin wool to sts. on spare needle, cast on 4 sts. for underlap, then k. to end of row.

1st row: P. to last 4 sts., k.4.

2nd row: All k.

Repeat these 2 rows 6 times more.

To slope the shoulder: Work as given for right side to end.

The Front

Work as given for back to **.

Work 14 (16) (16) rows, ending with a k. row.

Now divide sts. for front neck.

Next row: P.19 (20) (21) and leave these sts. on a spare needle for right side, cast off next 12 sts., p. to end and work on these 19 (20) (21) sts. for left side.

The left side: Dec. 1 st. at neck edge on next row and following 4 alternate rows – 14 (15) (16) sts.

Work 1 row back to armhole edge.

To slope the shoulder: Cast off 7 (7) (8) sts. at beginning of next row; work 1 row, then cast off remaining 7 (8) (8) sts.

The right side: With right side of work facing, rejoin wool to sts. left on spare needle and k. to end of row.

Now work as given for left side to end.

The Sleeves (both alike)

With No. 10 needles cast on 38 (38) (40) sts. and work 10 rows in single rib.

Change to No. 8 needles and, beginning with a k. row, st.st. 2 rows.

Inc. 1 st. at each end of the next row and every following 8th row until the 5th (6th) (6th) inc. row has been worked – 48 (50) (52) sts.

Work 7 (7) (15) rows.

To shape the sleeve top: Cast off 4 sts. at beginning of each of the next 2 rows, then dec. 1 st. at each end of the next row and following 6 (7) (8) alternate rows – 26 sts.

Work 1 row, then dec. 1 st. at each end of the next 5 rows – 16 sts.

Work 1 row.

Cast off.

The Neck Band

First join shoulder seams. With right side of work facing, rejoin wool to centre back and, using No. 10 needles, k. the 13 sts. from left side, pick up and k.13 sts. from left side of neck, 11 sts. from centre front, 13 sts. from right side of neck and finally k. the 13 sts. at back – 63 sts.

1st row: K.5, p.1, * k.1, p.1; repeat from * to last 5 sts., k.5.

2nd row: K.4, p.1, * k.1, p.1; repeat from * to last 4 sts., k.4.

3rd row: As 1st row.

4th (buttonhole) row: K.4, p.1, * k.1, p.1; repeat from * to last 4 sts., k.2 tog., w.fwd., k.2.

Work a further 3 rows in rib and garter st. as set.

Cast off.

To Make Up The Sweater

Press on wrong side, avoiding the ribbing, using a warm iron over a damp cloth. Set in sleeves, then join sleeve and side seams. Neaten lower edge of back opening. Sew on buttons.

The 'V' Neck Style

The Back

With No. 10 needles cast on 63 (65) (69) sts. and, beginning right-side rows with k.1 and wrong side rows with p.1, work 10 rows in single rib.

Change to No. 8 needles and, beginning with a k. row, st.st. 44 (50) (56) rows.

To shape the armholes: Cast off 4 sts. at beginning of next 2 rows, then dec. 1 st. at each end of the next row and following 2 (2) (3) right-side rows – 49 (51) (53) sts.

Work 25 (27) (27) rows.

To slope the shoulders: Cast off 7 (7) (8) sts. at beginning of next 2 rows and 7 (8) (8) sts. on following 2 rows.

Break off wool and leave remaining 21 sts. on a spare needle.

The Front

With No. 10 needles cast on 63 (65) (69) sts. and work 10 rows in single rib.

Change to No. 8 needles and, beginning with a k. row, st.st. 39 (45) (51) rows.

Now divide sts. for front neck.

Next row: P.31 (32) (34) sts. and leave these on a spare needle for right side, p. next st. and leave on safety-pin, p. to end and work on these 31 (32) (34) sts. for the left side.

The left side: Dec. 1 st. at neck edge on next row and following 3rd row – 29 (30) (32) sts.

To shape the armhole:

Next row: Cast off 4, work to end.

Now work 6 (6) (8) rows decreasing 1 st. at armhole edge on each right-side row and dec. 1 st. at neck edge on the 2nd and 5th (2nd and 5th) (2nd, 5th and 8th) of these rows. This completes armhole shaping – 20 (21) (21) sts.

Work 1 (1) (3) row(s), then dec. 1 st. at neck edge on the next row and every following 4th row until a further 6 (6) (5) dec. rows have been worked – 14 (15) (16) sts.

Work 3 (5) (7) rows.

To slope the shoulder: Cast off 7 (7) (8) sts. at beginning of next row; work 1 row, then cast off remaining 7 (8) (8) sts.

The right side: With right side of work facing, rejoin wool to sts. left on spare needle and k. to end of row.

Now work as given for the left side to end.

The Sleeves (both alike)

Work as given for Crew Neck Style.

The Neck Band

First join shoulder seams. With right side of work facing, using the set of double-pointed needles, rejoin wool to neck edge of left shoulder and pick up and k.36 (38) (40) sts. down left side of neck, k. st. from safety-pin, pick up and k.36 (38) (40) sts. from right side of neck and finally k. the 21 sts. at back – 94 (98) (102) sts.

Next round: * K.1, p.1; repeat from * to within 2 sts. of centre st., k.2 tog.b., k.1, k.2 tog., ** p.1, k.1; repeat from ** to last st., p.1.

Work a further 5 rounds decreasing each side of centre st. on every round.

Cast off still decreasing at centre.

To Make Up The Sweater

Press on wrong side, avoiding the ribbing, using a warm iron over a damp cloth. Set in sleeves, then join sleeve and side seams.

Crew and 'V' Neck Raglans

in Double Knitting

Materials

For either style: Six 25-gramme balls of Lee Target Motoravia Double Knitting Wool for 1st size; seven balls for 2nd and 3rd sizes. For any one size: a pair of No. 8 and No. 10 knitting needles; oddment of contrast colour if required.

Tension

Work at a tension of 11 stitches and 15 rows to 2 inches, over the stocking stitch, using No. 8 needles, to obtain the following measurements:

Abbreviations

K., knit; p., purl; st., stitch; tog., together; dec., decrease (by working 2 sts. tog.); inc., increase (by working twice into same st.); k. or p.2 tog.b., k. or p.2 sts. tog. through back of loops; st.st., stocking st. (k. on right side and p. on wrong side); single rib is k.1 and p.1 alternately.

● *The instructions are given for 1st size. Where they vary, work figures in first brackets for 2nd size; figures in second brackets for 3rd size.*

Measurements

	INCHES		
	1st size	2nd size	3rd size
All round at under-arms	23	24	25
Side seam	6¾	7½	8½
Length	12	13	14
Sleeve seam	7¼	8	8¾

Crew Neck Style

The Back

With No. 10 needles cast on 64 (66) (70) sts. and work 10 rows in single rib.

Change to No. 8 needles and, beginning with a k. row, st.st. 40 (46) (52) rows.

To shape the raglan armholes:
1st row: Cast off 4 sts., k. to end.
2nd row: Cast off 4 sts., p. to end.
3rd row: K.2 tog., k. to last 2 sts., k.2 tog.
4th row: All p.
5th row: All k.

6th row: All p.

Repeat 3rd to 6th rows twice more – 50 (52) (56) sts. **.

Repeat 3rd and 4th rows only 9 (10) (11) times, then work 3rd row again – 30 (30) (32) sts.

Now divide sts. for back neck.

Next row: P.8 and leave these sts. on spare needle for left side, p. next 14 (14) (16) sts. and leave on a st. holder for neck band, p. to end and work on these 8 sts. for right side.

The right side: Dec. 1 st. at each end of next and following 2 alternate rows.

P.2, then take 2 tog. and fasten off.

The left side: With right side of work facing, rejoin wool to 8 sts. and work as given for right side.

The Front

Work as back to **.

Repeat 3rd and 4th rows only 5 (6) (7) times, then work 3rd row again – 38 (38) (40) sts.

Now divide sts. for front neck.

Next row: P.14 and leave these sts. on a spare needle for right side, p. next 10 (10) (12) sts. and leave on st. holder for neck band, p. to end and work on these 14 sts. for left side.

The left side: Dec. 1 st. at each end of next and following 4 alternate rows – 4 sts.

Work 1 row, then dec. 1 st. at armhole edge only on next and following alternate row.

Take remaining 2 sts. tog. and fasten off.

The right side: With right side of work facing, rejoin wool to the 14 sts. and work as given for left side.

The Sleeves (both alike)

With No. 10 needles cast on 38 (38) (40) sts. and work 10 rows in single rib.

Change to No. 8 needles, and, beginning with a k. row, st.st. 2 rows.

Inc. 1 st. at each end of next row and every following 8th row until the 5th (6th) (6th) inc. row has been worked – 48 (50) (52) sts.

St.st. 9 (7) (13) rows.

To shape the raglan sleeve top: Work the first 6 rows of raglan armhole shaping given on back – 38 (40) (42) sts.

Repeat 3rd to 6th rows twice more – 34 (36) (38) sts.

Repeat 3rd and 4th rows only 13 (14) (15) times – 8 sts.

Break off wool and leave these sts. on a safety-pin.

The Neck Band

First join right raglan seams, then join left sleeve to front only. Rejoin wool to top of left sleeve and, using No. 10 needles, k. these 8 sts., pick up and k.14 sts. down left side of neck, k. the 10 (10) (12) sts. at centre front, pick up and k.14 sts. from right side of neck, k. the 8 sts. of right sleeve, pick up and k.7 sts. along shaped edge of back, k. the 14 (14) (16) sts. in centre, and pick up and k.7 sts. from other side of back – 82 (82) (86) sts.

Work 7 rows in single rib.

Cast off in rib.

To Make Up The Sweater

Press on wrong side, avoiding the ribbing, using a warm iron over a damp cloth. Join remaining raglan seam including neck band. Join sleeve and side seams.

The 'V' Neck Style

The Back

Work as Crew Neck style.

The Front

With No. 10 needles cast on 65 (67) (71) sts. and, beginning right-side rows with k.1 and wrong-side rows with p.1, work 10 rows in single rib.

Change to No. 8 needles and, beginning with a k. row, st.st. 39 (45) (51) rows.

Now divide sts. for 'V' neck.

Next row: P.32 (33) (35) and leave these sts. on a spare needle for right side, p. next st. and leave on safety-pin, p. to end and work on these 32 (33) (35) sts. for left side.

The left side: To shape armhole and slope neck:

1st row: Cast off 4, k. to last 3 sts., k.2 tog., k.1.

2nd row: All p.

3rd row: K.2 tog., k. to end.

4th row: All p.

5th row: K. to last 3 sts., k.2 tog., k.1.

6th row: All p.

Repeat 3rd to 6th rows twice more — 21 (22) (24) sts.

*** Now work 23 (23) (27) rows decreasing 1 st. at armhole edge on each right-side row and 1 st. at neck edge, as before, on the 3rd of these rows and each following 4th row — 3 (4) (3) sts.

P.1 row, then dec. 1 st. at armhole edge only on following 1 (2) (1) right-side row(s).

Take remaining 2 sts. tog. and fasten off.

The right side: With right side of work facing, rejoin wool to sts. on spare needle, k.1, k.2 tog.b., k. to end.

To shape the armhole and slope neck:

1st row: Cast off 4, p. to end.

2nd row: K. to last 2 sts., k.2 tog.

3rd row: All p.

4th row: K.1, k.2 tog.b., k. to end.

5th row: All p.

Repeat 2nd to 5th rows twice more — 21 (22) (24) sts.

Now work as given for left side from *** to end.

The Sleeves (both alike)

Work as Crew Neck style.

The Neck Band

First join right raglan seams, then join left sleeve to front only.

With right side of work facing, rejoin wool to sts. of left sleeve and, using No. 10 needles, k. these 8 sts., pick up and k.36 (38) (40) sts. down left side of neck, k. st. from centre, pick up and k.36 (38) (40) sts. from right side of neck, k.8 sts. of right sleeve, pick up and k.7 sts. from shaped edge of back, k.14 (14) (16) sts. across centre, and pick up and k. 7 sts. from other shaped edge — 117 (121) (127) sts.

1st row: *P.1, k.1; repeat from * to within 2 sts. of centre st., p.2 tog., p. centre st., p.2 tog.b., ** k.1, p.1; repeat from ** to end.

2nd row: Rib to within 2 sts. of centre st., k.2 tog.b., k.1, k.2 tog., rib to end.

Repeat these 2 rows twice more and the 1st row again, inserting contrast colour if required.

Cast off.

To Make Up The Sweater

Work as Crew Neck style.

Ribbed Jersey with Collar-cum-Hood

Materials

Seven 25-gramme balls of Bairnswear Pleasure 4-ply Wool for 1st size; eight balls for 2nd size. For either size: one ball in a contrast colour; a pair each of No. 9 and No. 10 knitting needles; a set of four double-pointed No. 9 needles.

Tension

Work at a tension of 14 stitches and 16 rows to 2 inches over the rib when slightly stretched, using No. 9 needles, to obtain the following measurements:

Measurements

	INCHES	
	1st size	2nd size
All round at underarms— unstretched	22	24
Side seam	$8\frac{3}{4}$	$9\frac{1}{4}$
Length	$14\frac{1}{2}$	$15\frac{1}{2}$
Sleeve seam with cuff turned back	9	9

Abbreviations

K., knit; p., purl; st., stitch; tog., together; dec., decrease (by working 2 sts. tog.); inc., increase (by working twice into same st.); up 1 (pick up the thread which lies between the needles and k. into back of it, thus making a st.); double rib is k.2 and p.2 alternately; m., main colour; c., contrast colour.

● *The instructions are given for 1st size. Where they vary, work figures in brackets for 2nd size.*

The Back

With No. 9 needles and m., cast on 78 (86) sts.
1st row: K.2, * p.2, k.2; repeat from * to end.
2nd row: P.2, * k.2, p.2; repeat from * to end.
Mark right side of work with a coloured thread for easier identification.
Repeat these 2 rows 34 (36) times more.

To shape the armholes: Cast off 4 sts. at beginning of next 2 rows, then dec. 1 st. at each end of next and following 3 (5) right-side rows – 62 (66) sts. **

Work 27 rows straight, ending with a wrong-side row.

To slope for saddle shoulders: Cast off 8 (9) sts. at beginning of next 2 rows and 9 (10) sts. on following 2 rows.

On remaining 28 sts., work 10 rows straight.

Break off wool and leave sts. on a spare needle.

The Front

Work as given for back to **.

On these 62 (66) sts., work 16 rows straight, ending with a right-side row.

Now divide sts. for front neck.

Next row: Rib 22 (24) and leave these sts. on a spare needle for right side, rib next 18 sts. and leave these on a stitch-holder, rib to end and work on these 22 (24) sts. for left side.

The left side: Dec. 1 st. at neck edge on next and following 4 alternate rows — 17 (19) sts.

Work 1 row back to armhole edge.

To slope the shoulder: Cast off 8 (9) sts. at beginning of next row; work 1 row, then cast off remaining 9 (10) sts.

The right side: With right side of work facing, rejoin wool to sts. on spare needle and rib to end of row.

Now work as given for left side to end.

The Sleeves (both alike)

With No. 10 needles and m., cast on 42 (46) sts. and work 10 rows in rib as back.

Change to No. 9 needles and rib 2 rows.

Inc. 1 st. at each end of next and every following 6th row until the 12th inc. row has been worked — 66 (70) sts.

Work 1 row to end with a wrong-side row. Join on c.

With c., k.1 row and rib 3 rows.

With m., k.1 row and rib 1 row.

With c., k.1 row and rib 3 rows.

Break off c.

With m., k.1 row and rib 1 row.

To shape the sleeve top: Cast off 4 sts. at beginning of next 2 rows, then dec. 1 st. at each end of next and following 3 (5) right-side rows — 50 sts.

Work 1 row, then cast off 2 sts. at beginning of each of next 14 rows — 22 sts.

Break off m., join on c.

With c., k.1 row and rib 17 (19) rows for saddle shoulder extension.

Cast off.

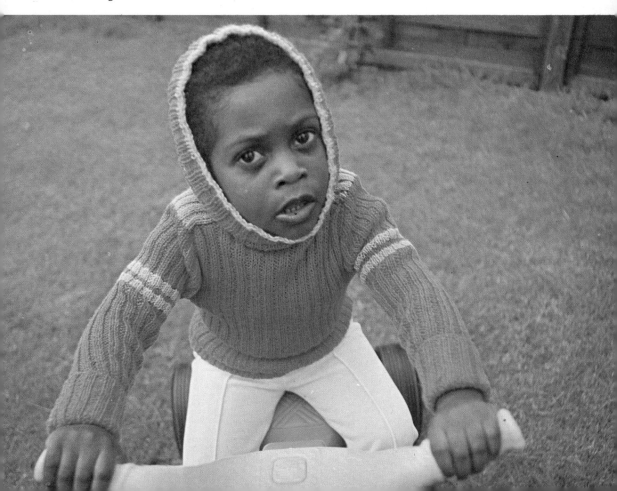

The Collar-cum-Hood

First set in sleeves sewing the straight row-ends of saddle shoulder extensions to the sts. cast-off for shoulders on back and front, then sew the 10 straight row-ends at top of back halfway across the cast-off edge on saddle shoulder extensions, leaving remainder of this edge free to form part of the neck edge.

With right side of work facing, rejoin m. to sts. at back and, using the set of double-pointed No. 9 needles, rib these 28 sts., pick up and k.9 sts. from sleeve top, 8 sts. from left side of neck, rib the 18 sts. at centre front, pick up and k.8 sts. from right side of neck and finally, pick up and k.9 sts. from sleeve top – 80 sts.

Work 62 rounds in double rib.

Next (inc.) round: K.1, * p.2, k.1, up 1, k.1 ; repeat from * to last 3 sts., p.2, k.1, up 1 (for your guidance, on this round, you work the up 1 between each of the 2 k. sts.) – 100 sts.

Work 34 rounds in k.3, p.2 rib as now set. Break off m., join on c. and work 4 rounds. Cast off very loosely in rib.

To Make Up The Jersey

Press very lightly on wrong side, taking care not to lose the natural stretch of the fabric. Join sleeve and side seams. Roll collar over several times for polo neck.

White Cricket Sweater

(see illustration p. 108)

**Add dad's club colours to the neck band and
you'll have a winner**

Materials

Seven ounces of Lister Lavenda
Double Crêpe Wool in white for the
1st size; eight ounces for the 2nd size.
For either size: oddments in 2
contrasting colours; a pair each of
No. 8 and No. 10 knitting needles;
a cable needle.

Tension

Work at a tension of 11 stitches and 15
rows to 2 inches, over the stocking stitch,
using No. 8 needles, to obtain the following
measurements:

Measurements

	INCHES	
	1st size	2nd size
All round at underarms	23	24
Side seam	$8\frac{1}{4}$	$8\frac{3}{4}$
Length	13	$13\frac{3}{4}$
Sleeve seam	$8\frac{1}{2}$	$9\frac{1}{4}$

Abbreviations

K., knit; p., purl; st., stitch; tog., together;
dec., decrease (by working 2 sts. tog.); inc.,
increase (by working twice into same st.);
sl., slip; c.6f., cable 6 front (sl. next 3 sts.
onto cable needle and leave at front of work,
k.3, then k.3 from cable needle); c.6b.,
cable 6 back (sl. next 3 sts. onto cable needle
and leave at back of work, k.3, then k.3 from
cable needle); st.st., stocking st. (k. on
right side and p. on wrong side); single rib
is k.1 and p.1 alternately; k. or p.2 tog.b.,
k. or p.2 sts. tog. through back of loops.

● *The instructions are given for 1st size.
Where they vary, work figures in brackets
for 2nd size.*

The Back

With No. 10 needles cast on 77 (81) sts.
and, beginning right-side rows with k.1 and
wrong-side rows with p.1, work 10 rows in
single rib.

Change to No. 8 needles.

1st foundation row: K.8 (9), p.2, k.6, p.2,
k.11 (12), p.2, k.6, p.1, k.1, p.1, k.6, p.2,
k.11 (12), p.2, k.6, p.2, k.8 (9).

2nd foundation row: P.8 (9), k.2, p.6, k.2,
p.11 (12), k.2, p.6, k.1, p.1, k.1, p.6, k.2,
p.11 (12), k.2, p.6, k.2, p.8 (9).

Repeat these 2 rows once more.

Now work in pattern as follows:

1st row: K.8 (9), p.2, c.6b., p.2, k.11 (12),
p.2, c.6b., p.1, k.1, p.1, c.6f., p.2., k.11
(12), p.2, c.6f., p.2, k.8 (9).

2nd row: P.8 (9), k.2, p.6, k.2, p.11 (12),
k.2, p.6, k.1, p.1, k.1, p.6, k.2, p,11 (12),
k.2, p.6, k.2, p.8 (9).

3rd row: K.8 (9), p.2, k.6, p.2, k.11 (12),
p.2, k.6, p.1, k.1, p.1, k.6, p.2, k.11 (12),
p.2, k.6, p.2, k.8 (9).

4th row: As 2nd row.

5th to 8th rows: Repeat 3rd and 4th rows
twice **.

Repeat these 8 rows 5 times (5 times and
first 4 rows again).

White cricket sweater

To shape the armholes: Cast off 4 sts. at beginning of next 2 rows, then dec. 1 st. at each end of next and following 3 (4) right-side rows – 61 (63) sts.

Work 25 rows.

To slope the shoulders: Cast off 10 sts. at beginning of next 4 rows.

Break off wool and leave the remaining 21 (23) sts. on a spare needle.

The Front

Work as given for back to **.

Repeat these 8 rows 3 times more, then work the first 3 (7) rows again.

Now divide sts. for front neck.

Next row: Pattern 38 (40) and leave these sts. on spare needle for right half, p. next st. and leave on safety-pin, pattern to end and work on these 38 (40) sts. for left half.

The left half:

1st row: Pattern to last 11 sts., k.2 tog., pattern to end.

2nd, 3rd and 4th rows: Work in pattern.

Repeat these 4 rows twice more – 35 (37) sts.

To shape the armhole:

1st row: Cast off 4, pattern to last 11 sts., k.2 tog., pattern to end.

2nd row: Work in pattern.

3rd row: K.2 tog., pattern to end.

4th row: Work in pattern.

*** Work 5 (7) rows decreasing 1 st. at armhole edge on each right-side row and 1 st. at neck edge – inside cable panel as before – on the 1st and 5th of these rows – 24 (25) sts. This completes armhole shaping.

Work 3 (1) row(s) straight, then dec. 1 st. at neck edge, as before, on the next row and every following 4th row until a further 4 (5) dec. rows have been worked – 20 sts.

Work 9 (7) rows straight, ending at armhole edge; work 10 (8) rows here on right half.

To slope the shoulder: Cast off 10 sts. at beginning of next row; work 1 row, then cast off remaining 10 sts.

The right half: With right side of work facing, rejoin wool to sts. left on spare needle.

1st row: Pattern 9, k.2 tog.b., pattern to end.

2nd, 3rd and 4th rows: Work in pattern.

Repeat last 4 rows twice more, then work

the 1st row again – 34 (36) sts.

To shape the armhole:

1st row: Cast off 4, pattern to end.
2nd row: Pattern to last 2 sts., k.2 tog.
3rd row: Work in pattern.

Now work as given for left half from ***
to end, noting extra row to be worked before
sloping shoulder.

The Left Sleeve

With No. 10 needles cast on 38 sts. and
work 11 rows in single rib.
Next (inc.) row: Rib 6, * inc. in next st.,
rib 7; repeat from * 3 times – 42 sts.
Change to No. 8 needles.
1st foundation row: K.16, p.2, k.6, p.2,
k.16.
2nd foundation row: P.16, k.2, p.6, k.2,
p.16.
Repeat these 2 rows once more.
Now work in pattern as follows:
1st row: K.16, p.2, c.6b., p.2, k.16.
2nd row: P.16, k.2, p.6, k.2, p.16.

These 2 rows set position of the sts. for
cable panel. Keeping continuity of the panel
by working c.6b. on every 8th row from
previous cable row, inc. 1 st. at each end of
the next row and every following 8th row
until the 6th (7th) inc. row has been
worked – 54 (56) sts.
Work 5 (3) rows.
To shape the sleeve top: Cast off 4 sts.
at beginning of next 2 rows, then dec. 1 st.
at each end of next and following 5 (6)
right-side rows – 34 sts.
Work 1 row, then dec. 1 st. at each end
of the next 6 rows.
Cast off remaining 22 sts.

The Right Sleeve

Work as given for left sleeve but work c.6f.
instead of c.6b. on the cable row.

The Neck Band

First join right shoulder seam. With right
side of work facing, rejoin wool to neck edge
of left half and, using No. 10 needles, pick
up and k.46 (48) sts. down left side of neck,
k. st. on safety-pin, pick up and k.46 (48)
sts. from right side of neck and k. the 21 (23)
sts. across back – 114 (120) sts.

1st row: K.1, * p.1, k.1; repeat from * to
within 2 sts. of centre st., p.2 tog., p.1,
p.2 tog.b., ** k.1, p.1; repeat from ** to
end.
2nd row: Rib to within 2 sts. of centre st.,
k.2 tog.b., k.1, k.2 tog., rib to end.
3rd row: As 1st row.

With 1st contrast colour, still decreasing at
each side of centre st., k.1 row and rib 1 row.
With main colour, repeat last 2 rows.
With 2nd contrast, repeat last 2 rows.
With main colour, repeat last 2 rows.
Cast off.

To Make Up The Sweater

Press on wrong side, using a warm iron
over a damp cloth. Join left shoulder seam,
continuing seam across neck band.
Set in sleeves; join sleeve and side seams.

Chunky sweater (pattern p. 110).

Chunky Sweater

(see illustration p. 109)

**This roll-neck sweater has saddle shoulders
for that grown-up look**

Materials

Eight 25-gramme balls of Wendy
Double Knit Nylonised for 1st size;
ten balls for 2nd size. For either size:
a pair each of No. 8 and No. 10
knitting needles; a set of four double-
pointed No. 9 needles; a cable needle.

Tension

Work at a tension of 11 stitches and 15
rows to 2 inches, over the stocking stitch,
using No. 8 needles, to obtain the following
measurements:

Measurements

	INCHES	
	1st size	2nd size
All round at underarms	$23\frac{1}{2}$	25
Side seam	$7\frac{3}{4}$	$8\frac{3}{4}$
Length	$12\frac{3}{4}$	14
Sleeve seam	8	9

Abbreviations

K., knit; p., purl; st., stitch; tog., together;
dec., decrease (by working 2 sts. tog.); inc.,
increase (by working twice into same st.);
tw.2 rt., twist 2 right (k. into front of 2nd
st. on left-hand needle then p. into front of
1st st. and slip both sts. off needle tog.);
tw.2 lt., twist 2 left (slip next st. onto cable
needle and leave at front of work, p.1, then
k. st. from cable needle); c.6f., cable 6 front
(slip next 3 sts. onto cable needle and leave
at front of work, k.3, then k.3 from cable
needle); st.st., stocking st. (k. on right side
and p. on wrong side); double rib is k.2 and
p.2 alternately.

●*The instructions are given for 1st size.
Where they vary, work figures in brackets
for 2nd size.*

The Back

With No. 10 needles cast on 74 (78) sts.
1st row: K.2, * p.2, k.2; repeat from * to
end.
2nd row: P.2, * k.2, p.2; repeat from * to
end.
Repeat these 2 rows 4 times more.
Change to No. 8 needles and work in
pattern as follows:
1st row: K.10 (12), * p.4, tw.2 rt., k.6,
tw.2 lt., p.4 *, k.18, work from * to * once,
k.10 (12).
2nd row: P.10 (12), * k.4, p.1, k.1, p.6, k.1,
p.1, k.4 *, p.18, work from * to * once,
p. 10 (12).

3rd row: K.10 (12), * p.3, tw.2 rt., p.1, k.6,
p.1, tw.2 lt., p.3, * k.18, work from * to *
once, k.10 (12).
4th row: P.10 (12), * k.3, p.1, k.2, p.6, k.2,
p.1, k.3, * p.18, work from * to * once,
p.10 (12).
5th row: K.10 (12), * p.2, tw.2 rt., p.2,
c.6f., p.2, tw.2 lt., p.2, * k.18, work from
* to * once, k.10 (12).
6th row: P.10 (12), * k.2, p.1, k.3, p.6, k.3,
p.1, k.2, * p.18, work from * to * once,
p.10 (12).
7th row: K.10 (12), * p.1, tw.2 rt., p.3, k.6,
p.3, tw.2 lt., p.1, * k.18, work from * to *
once, k.10 (12).

8th row: P.10 (12), * k.1, p.1, k.4, p.6, k.4, p.1, k.1, * p.18, work from * to * once, p.10 (12).

9th row: K.10 (12), * p.1, tw.2 lt., p.3, k.6, p.3, tw.2 rt., p.1, * k.18, work from * to * once, k.10 (12).

10th row: As 6th row.

11th row: K.10 (12), * p.2, tw.2 lt., p.2, c.6f., p.2, tw.2 rt., p.2, * k.18, work from * to * once, k.10 (12).

12th row: As 4th row.

13th row: K.10 (12), * p.3, tw.2 lt., p.1, k.6, p.1, tw.2 rt., p.3, * k.18, work from * to * once, k.10 (12).

14th row: As 2nd row.

15th row: K.10 (12), * p.4, tw.2 lt., k.6, tw.2 rt., p.4, * k.18, work from * to * once, k.10 (12).

16th row: P.10 (12), * k.5, p.8, k.5, * p.18, work from * to * once, p. 10 (12).

These 16 rows form the pattern; repeat them twice more (twice more and first 8 rows again).

To shape the armholes: Keeping continuity of the pattern panels cast off 3 (4) sts. at beginning of each of next 2 rows, then dec. 1 st. at each end of the next row and following 4 right-side rows **.

On these 58 (60) sts., work 15 (17) rows straight.

To slope for saddle shoulders: Cast off 6 sts. at beginning of each of the next 6 rows.

On the remaining 22 (24) sts., work 8 rows straight.

Cast off.

The Front

Work as given for back to **.

On 58 (60) sts., work 10 (12) rows straight, ending with a right-side row.

Now divide sts. for front neck.

Next row: Pattern 21 and leave these sts. on a spare needle for right side, pattern next 16 (18) sts. and leave these on a stitch-holder, pattern to end and work on these 21 sts. for the left side.

The left side: Dec. 1 st. at neck edge on next 3 rows; work 1 row back to armhole edge.

To slope for saddle shoulder: Cast off 6 sts. at beginning of next row and following alternate row; work 1 row, then cast off the remaining 6 sts.

The right side: With right side of work facing, rejoin yarn to the 21 sts. left on spare needle and pattern to end of row.

Now work as given for the left side to end.

The Sleeves (both alike)

With No. 10 needles cast on 38 sts. and work 10 rows in double rib as given for back increasing 1 st. at each end of the last row – 40 sts.

Change to No. 8 needles.

1st row: K.11, p.4, tw.2 rt., k.6, tw.2 lt., p.4, k.11.

2nd row: P.11, k.4, p.1, k.1, p.6, k.1, p.1, k.4, p.11.

These 2 rows set position of the sts. for the pattern panel in centre.

Continuing in pattern as set out between * and * on the pattern rows given for back and taking the extra sts. into the st.st. at each side as they occur, inc. 1 st. at each end of the next row and every following 8th row until the 5th (7th) inc. row has been worked – 50 (54) sts.

Work 15 (7) rows straight.

To shape the sleeve top: Cast off 3 (4) sts. at beginning of next 2 rows, then dec. 1 st. at each end of the next row and following 2 (3) right-side rows – 38 sts.

Work 1 row, then dec. 1 st. at each end of the next 10 rows.

On the remaining 18 sts., work 20 rows for the saddle shoulder extension.

Cast off.

The Collar

First set in sleeves sewing the row ends of saddle shoulder extensions to the sts. cast off for shoulders on back and front and sewing the 8 row ends at top of back halfway across the sts. cast off at top of saddle shoulder extension on sleeves.

With right side of work facing, rejoin yarn to top of left sleeve and, using the set of No. 9 double-pointed needles, pick up and k.9 sts. from remaining half of saddle shoulder extension, 8 sts. down left side of neck, k. the 16 (18) sts. at centre front, pick up and k.8 sts. from right side of neck, 9 sts. from right sleeve top and, finally, k. the 22 (24) sts. at back – 72 (76) sts.

Work 30 rounds in double rib.
Cast off loosely in rib.

Press on wrong side, avoiding the ribbing, using a warm iron over a damp cloth. Join side and sleeve seams. Fold collar to right side.

Tank Tops
Striped and Squared

Contributed by Eugenie Hammond

Materials

The Striped Version: For either size: Two ¾-ounce balls of Lee Target Super Crimp Bri-Nylon Double Knitting in main colour and two balls in a contrast colour; a pair each of No. 8 and No. 10 knitting needles.

The Squared Version: For either size: Four balls in main colour and one ball in contrast colour; a pair each of No. 8 and No. 10 needles.

Abbreviations

K., knit; p., purl; st., stitch; tog., together; dec., decrease (by working 2 sts. tog.); st.st., stocking st. (k. on right side and p. on wrong side); single rib is k.1 and p.1 alternately; m., main colour; c., contrast colour.

● *The instructions are given for 1st size. Where they vary, work figures in brackets for 2nd size.*

Tension

Work at a tension of 6 stitches and 9 rows to 1 inch, over the stocking stitch, using No. 8 needles, to obtain the following measurements:

Measurements

INCHES

	1st size	2nd size
All round at underarms	22	24
Side seam, including armhole band	8¼	8½
Length	11½	12¼

The Striped Version

The Back

With No. 10 needles and m., cast on 66 (72) sts. and work 10 (12) rows in single rib.

Change to No. 8 needles and k.1 row and p.1 row.

Join on c. and k.1 row and p.1 row.

Continuing in stripe sequence of 2 rows m. and 2 rows c., st.st. 12 rows.

** With m., work 4 rows, with c., work 4 rows; repeat from ** 3 times more.

With m., work 6 rows, with c., work 6 rows ***.

113

Continuing in stripe sequence of 6 rows m. and 6 rows c. continue as follows:

To shape the armholes: Cast off 4 sts. at beginning of next 2 rows, then dec. 1 st. at each end of next and following 4 (5) right-side rows – 48 (52) sts.

P.1 row.

To shape the back neck:

Next row: K.17 (18) turn, and leaving remaining 31 (34) sts. on a spare needle work on these sts. for 1st side.

First side: Dec. 1 st. at neck edge on next 7 rows – 10 (11) sts.

Work 12 (14) rows straight, ending at armhole edge – work 13 (15) rows here on second side.

To slope the shoulder: Cast off 5 sts. at beginning of next row. Work 1 row.

Cast off remaining 5 (6) sts.

Second side: With right side of work facing, slip centre 14 (16) sts. onto stitch-holder for neck band, rejoin yarn to next st. and k. to end of row.

Now work as given for first side to end.

The Front

Work as back to ***.

Continuing in stripe sequence of 6 rows m. and 6 rows c., continue as follows:

To shape the armholes: Cast off 4 sts. at beginning of next 2 rows – 58 (64) sts.

To shape the neck and continue shaping armhole:

Next row: K.2 tog., k.20 (22) turn and, leaving remaining 36 (40) sts. on a spare needle work on these 21 (23) sts. for first side.

First side: Work 7 rows decreasing 1 st. at neck edge on each row and 1 st. at armhole edge on each right-side row – 11 (13) sts.

Dec. 1 st. at armhole edge only on next 1 (2) right-side row(s) – 10 (11) sts.

Work 21 (23) rows straight ending at armhole edge – work 22 (24) rows here on second side.

To slope the shoulder: Cast off 5 sts. at beginning of next row. Work 1 row.

Cast off remaining 5 (6) sts.

Second side: With right side of work facing, slip centre 14 (16) sts. onto a stitch-holder, rejoin yarn to next st., k. to last 2 sts., k.2 tog.

Now work as given for first side noting the extra row to be worked before sloping shoulder.

The Neck Band

First join right shoulder seam. With right side of work facing, rejoin m. to neck edge of left front shoulder and, using No. 10 needle, pick up and k.26 (30) sts. down left side of neck, k. the 14 (16) sts. at centre front, pick up and k.26 (30) sts. from right side of neck, 18 (20) sts. from right side of back, k. the 14 (16) sts. at centre and finally, pick up and k.18 (20) sts. from left side of back – 116 (132) sts.

Work 5 rows in single rib.

Cast off.

The Armhole Bands (both alike)

First join left shoulder seam. With right side of work facing, rejoin m. at underarm and, using No. 10 needle, pick up and k.60 (64) sts. along entire armhole edge.

Work 5 rows in single rib.

Cast off.

To Make Up The Tank Top

Press on wrong side, avoiding the ribbing, using a COOL iron over a DRY cloth. Join side seams.

The Squared Version

The Back

Work as given for Striped Version, using m. throughout.

The Front

With No. 10 needles and m., cast on 66 (72) sts. and work 10 (12) rows in single rib.

Change to No. 8 needles and k.1 row and p.1 row.

Continuing in st.st. and twisting the yarns at back of work at each colour change to avoid a gap in the knitting, work as follows:

1st row: K.11 (14) m., join on c. and with c., k.14, join on another ball of m. and k.41 (44) m.

2nd row: P.41 (44) m., 14 c., 11 (14) m.

Repeat these 2 rows 7 times more. Cut c. and one ball of m.

Next row: K.28 (31) m., join on c., k.10 c., join on another ball of m. and k.28 (31) m.

Next row: P.28 (31) m., 10 c., 28 (31) m.

Repeat these 2 rows 12 times more. Cut c. and one ball of m.

Next row: K.41 (44) m., join on c., k.14 c., join on another ball of m. and k. 11 (14) m.

Next row: P.11 (14) m., 14 c., 41 (44) m.

Repeat these 2 rows 7 times more. Cut c. and one ball of m.

Continuing with m. only, shape armholes and neck as given for Striped Version.

The Neck Band

Work as Striped Version.

The Armhole Bands

Work as Striped Version.

To Make Up The Tank Top

Work as Striped Version.

Three First-Size Cardigans

(see illustration p. 28)

Materials

Four 25-gramme balls of Patons Quickerknit Baby Wool for each style; a pair each of No. 8 and No. 10 knitting needles; 4 buttons.

Tension and Size

Worked at a tension of 6 stitches and 8 rows to 1 inch, over the stocking stitch and pattern when pressed, using No. 8 needles, the cardigans will be suitable for baby aged birth to 6 months.

Abbreviations

K., knit; p., purl; st., stitch; tog., together; dec., decrease (by working 2 sts. tog.); inc., increase (by working twice into same st.); 3 from 3 (k.3 sts. tog. but do not slip sts. from left-hand needle, bring wool to front between the needles to make a st. then k. through the same 3 sts. and let original sts. drop off left-hand needle in the usual way); k.2 tog.b., k.2 sts. tog. through back of loops; 3 in 1 (k.1, p.1 and k.1 all into next st.); w.o.n., wool over needle to make a st.; st.st., stocking st. (k. on right side and p. on wrong side); single rib is k.1 and p.1 alternately.

The Yellow Cardigan

The Back

With No. 10 needles cast on 62 sts. and work 14 rows in single rib.

Change to No. 8 needles.

1st row: P.2, * k.3, p.2; repeat from * to end.

2nd row: K.2, * p.3, k.2; repeat from * to end.

3rd row: P.2, * 3 from 3, p.2; repeat from * to end.

4th row: As 2nd row.

These 4 rows form the pattern; repeat them 6 times more **.

To shape the square armholes: Cast off 5 sts. at beginning of next 2 rows – 52 sts.

Work 3rd and 4th pattern rows, then work the 4 pattern rows 6 times more and first 2 rows again.

To slope the shoulders: Cast off 8 sts. at beginning of next 4 rows.

Cast off remaining 20 sts.

The Left Front

With No. 10 needles cast on 32 sts. and work as given for back to **.

To shape the square armhole and slope front edge:

Next row: Cast off 5, pattern to last 2 sts., dec.

Work 2 rows straight, then dec. 1 st. at front edge on next and every following 3rd row until a further 9 dec. rows have been worked – 17 sts.

Work 2 rows straight.

To slope the shoulder:
Next row: Cast off 8, pattern to last 2 sts., doc.
Work 1 row, then cast off remaining 8 sts.

The Right Front

With No. 10 needles cast on 32 sts. and work as given for back to **.
Work 1 row more to finish at side edge.
To shape the square armhole, slope front and shoulder: Work as given for left front.

The Sleeves (both alike)

With No. 10 needles cast on 37 sts. and beginning right-side rows with k.1 and wrong-side rows with p.1, work 14 rows in single rib.
Change to No. 8 needles and work the 4 pattern rows given for back once.
Keeping continuity of pattern and, taking the extra sts. into the pattern as they occur, inc. 1 st. at each end of next and every following 3rd row until the 9th inc. row has been worked – 55 sts.
Work 4 rows straight.
Mark each end of work with a coloured thread to denote end of sleeve seam, then work a further 7 rows straight.
Cast off.

The Front Band

With No. 10 needles cast on 9 sts.
1st row: K.1, * p.1, k.1; repeat from * to end.
2nd row: K.2, * p.1, k.1; repeat from * ending last repeat with k.2.
Repeat these 2 rows once more.
Next (buttonhole) row: K.1, p.1, k.1, p.1, w.o.n., k.2 tog., k.1, p.1, k.1.
Rib 13 rows.
Repeat last 14 rows twice more, then work buttonhole row again.
Continue in rib until band is long enough, when slightly stretched, to fit all round front edge.
Cast off when correct length is assured.

To Make Up The Cardigan

Pin out and press firmly using a warm iron over a damp cloth.
Join shoulder seams. Set in sleeves sewing row-ends above the markers to the sts. cast off on back and fronts. Sew front band in place with last buttonhole level with first front shaping. Sew on buttons.

The Green Cardigan

The Back

With No. 10 needles cast on 62 sts. and work 14 rows in single rib.
Change to No. 8 needles.
1st row: All p.
2nd row: K.1, * p.3 tog., 3 in 1; repeat from * to last st., k.1.
3rd row: All p.
4th row: K.1, * 3 in 1, p.3 tog., repeat from * to last st., k.1.
5th row: As 1st row.
6th row: As 2nd row.
This completes border.
Beginning with a k. row, st.st. 24 rows **

To shape the raglan armholes:
1st row: Cast off 4, k. to end.
2nd row: Cast off, 4, p. to end.
3rd row: K.2, k.2 tog.b., k. to last 4 sts., k.2 tog., k.2.
4th row: All p.
Repeat 3rd and 4th rows 16 times more – 20 sts.
Cast off.

The Left Front

With No. 10 needles cast on 30 sts. and work as given for back to **

117

To shape the raglan armhole and slope front edge:
1st row: Cast off 4, k. to last 2 sts., dec.
2nd row: All p.
3rd row: K.2, k.2 tog.b., k. to end.
4th row: All p.
5th row: K.2, k.2 tog.b., k. to last 2 sts., dec.
Repeat 2nd to 5th rows 5 times more – 7 sts.
Work 1 row, then dec. 1 st. at armhole edge only on next and following 3 right-side rows – 3 sts.
Next row: P.3.
Next row: K.1, k.2 tog.b.
Next row: P.2.
Take remaining 2 sts. tog. and fasten off.

The Right Front

With No. 10 needles cast on 30 sts. and work as given for back to **.
Work 1 more row to finish at side edge.
To shape the raglan armhole and slope front edge:
1st row: Cast off 4, p. to last 2 sts., dec.
2nd row: K. to last 4 sts., k.2 tog., k.2.
3rd row: All p.
4th row: K. to last 4 sts., k.2 tog., k.2.
5th row: P. to last 2 sts., dec.
Repeat 2nd to 5th rows 5 times more – 7 sts.
Dec. 1 st. at armhole edge on next and

following 3 right-side rows – 3 sts.
Next row: P.3.
Next row: K.2 tog., k.1.
Next row: P.2.
Take remaining 2 sts. tog. and fasten off.

The Sleeves (both alike)

With No. 10 needles cast on 38 sts. and work 14 rows in single rib.
Change to No. 8 needles and, beginning with a k. row, st.st. 2 rows.
Inc. 1 st. at each end of next and every following 6th row until the 5th inc. row has been worked – 48 sts.
Work 3 rows straight.
To shape the raglan sleeve top: Work exactly as given for raglan armhole shaping on back when 6 sts. will remain.
Cast off.

The Front Band

Work as given for yellow cardigan.

To Make Up The Cardigan

Press as given for yellow cardigan. Join raglan seams, then join sleeve and side seams. Sew front band in place. Sew on buttons.

The White Cardigan

The Back

With No. 10 needles cast on 62 sts. and work 14 rows in single rib.
Change to No. 8 needles and, beginning with a k. row, st.st. 10 rows **.
To shape for sleeves: Inc. 1 st. at each end of next and following 5 right-side rows – 74 sts.
P.1 row then cast on 14 sts. at beginning of next 2 rows – 102 sts.
St.st. 30 rows.
To shape the top of sleeves and shoulders: Cast off 10 sts. at beginning of next 6 rows and 11 sts. on following 2 rows.
Cast off remaining 20 sts.

The Left Front

With No. 10 needles cast on 32 sts. and work as given for back to **.
To shape for sleeve: Inc. 1 st. at beginning of next and following 5 right-side rows – 38 sts.
P.1 row.
*** Cast on 14 sts. at beginning of next row – 52 sts.
St.st. 7 rows.
To slope the front edge: Dec. 1 st. at front edge on next and following 10 alternate rows – 41 sts.
St.st. 3 rows, ending at sleeve edge.
To shape the top of sleeve and

shoulder: Cast off 10 sts. at beginning of next and following 2 alternate rows – 11 sts.

Work 1 row.

Cast off.

The Right Front

With No. 10 needles cast on 32 sts. and work as given for back to **.

To shape for sleeve: Inc. 1 st. at end of next and following 5 right-side rows – 38 sts.

Work 2 rows, ending at side edge.

Now work as given for left front from *** to end.

The Front Band

Work as given for yellow cardigan.

To Make Up The Cardigan

Pin out and press. Join upper sleeve seams.

The cuffs (both alike): With right side of work facing, rejoin wool to sleeve edge and, using No. 10 needles, pick up and k.38 sts. along sleeve edge.

Work 14 rows in single rib.

Cast off loosely in rib.

Join underarm and side seams. Sew band in place. Sew on buttons.

Zipped Lumber Jacket

**Suitable for boys and girls, worked in a
broken rib stitch which gives a chunky look
to the fabric**

Materials

Eight 25-gramme balls of Lister
Lavenda Double Knitting Wool and a
10-inch open-end zip for 1st size;
ten balls and a 12-inch zip for 2nd
size. For either size: a pair each of
No. 8 and No. 9 knitting needles.

Tension

Work at a tension of 12 stitches and 17
rows to 2 inches, over the broken rib pattern
when lightly pressed, using No. 8 needles,
to obtain the following measurements:

Measurements

	INCHES	
	1st size	2nd size
All round at underarms	23	24¼
Side seam	8½	9½
Length	13	14½
Sleeve seam	8	9

Abbreviations

K., knit; p., purl; st., stitch; tog., together;
inc., increase (by working twice into same
st.); single rib is k.1 and p.1 alternately.

● *The instructions are given for 1st size.
Where they vary, work figures in brackets
for 2nd size.*

The Main Part (worked in one piece to armholes)

With No. 9 needles cast on 139 (147) sts.
1st row: K.2, * p.1, k.1; repeat from * to
last 3 sts., p.1, k.2.
2nd row: K.3, * p.1, k.1; repeat from * to
last 2 sts., k.2 more.
Repeat these 2 rows 6 times more.
Change to No. 8 needles.
1st row: K.2, p. to last 2 sts., k.2.
2nd row: K.3, * p.1, k.1; repeat from * to
last 2 sts., k.2 more.
These 2 rows form the broken rib pattern;
repeat them 28 (32) times more.
Now divide sts. for back and fronts.
Next row: K.2, p.31 (33) for right front,
cast off 4 for armhole – 1 st. left on right-
hand needle – p. next 64 (68) sts., cast off
4, p. to last 2 sts., k.2 and work on these
33 (35) sts. for left front.
**The left front: To shape the raglan
armhole:**
1st row: Work in pattern.
2nd row: P.1, p.2 tog., p. to last 2 sts., k.2.

**Zipped lumber jacket; embroidered
cardigan (pattern p. 126).**

Repeat these 2 rows 14 (16) times more — 18 sts. — ending at front edge.

To shape the neck:

1st row: Cast off 7, pattern to end.

2nd row: P.1, p.2 tog., p. to last 2 sts., p.2 tog.

3rd row: P.2 tog., pattern to end.

Repeat 2nd and 3rd rows twice more.

Take remaining 2 sts. tog. and fasten off.

The back: With wrong side of work facing, rejoin wool to the 65 (69) sts.

1st row: Work in pattern.

2nd row: P.1, p.2 tog., p. to last 3 sts., p.2 tog., p.1.

Repeat these 2 rows 17 (19) times more — 29 sts.

Work 5 rows straight — These rows are sewn across top of sleeve.

Cast off.

The right front: With wrong side of work facing, rejoin wool to remaining 33 (35) sts.

1st row: Work in pattern.

2nd row: K.2, p. to last 3 sts., p. 2 tog., p. 1.

Repeat these 2 rows 13 (15) times more, then work 1st row again — 19 sts. — ending at front edge.

To shape the neck:

1st row: Cast off 7, p. to last 3 sts., p.2 tog., p.1.

2nd row: Work in pattern.

3rd row: P.2 tog., p. to last 3 sts., p.2 tog., p.1.

4th row: Work in pattern to last 2 sts., k.2 tog.

Repeat 3rd and 4th rows twice more.

Take remaining 2 sts. tog. and fasten off.

The Sleeves (both alike)

With No. 9 needles cast on 39 (41) sts. and beginning right-side rows with k.1 and wrong-side rows with p.1, work 12 rows in single rib.

Change to No. 8 needles.

1st row: All p.

2nd row: P.1, * k.1, p.1 ; repeat from * to end.

Repeat these 2 rows once more.

Keeping continuity of pattern inc. 1 st. at each end of next and every following 8th row until the 7th (8th) inc. row has been worked — 53 (57) sts.

Work 3 rows straight.

To shape the raglan sleeve top:

1st row: Cast off 2, p. to end.

2nd row: Cast off 2, pattern to end.

3rd row: P.1, p.2 tog., p. to last 3 sts., p.2 tog., p.1.

4th row: Work in pattern.

Repeat 3rd and 4th rows 17 (19) times more — 13 sts.

Cast off.

The Collar

With No. 8 needles cast on 89 sts.

1st row: K.1, * p.1, k.1 ; repeat from * to end.

2nd row: P.1, * k.1, p.1 ; repeat from * to end.

Repeat these 2 rows 7 times more.

Change to No. 9 needles and work a further 4 rows.

To shape the neck edge: Cast off 16 sts. at beginning of next 2 rows and 18 sts. on following 2 rows.

Cast off remaining 21 sts. loosely in rib.

To Make Up The Lumber Jacket

Press lightly on wrong side, using a warm iron over a damp cloth. Join raglan seams sewing the straight row-ends at top of back across the first 6 sts. cast-off at top of sleeves leaving remainder of sleeve edge free to form part of neck edge. Join sleeve seams. Sew the cast-off edge of collar evenly to neck edge. Insert zip from neck edge to lower edge leaving remainder of lower edge free.

Cardigan in Tricel

(see illustration p. 124)

Materials

Six 20-gramme balls of Lee Target Duo 4-ply Crêpe Tricel with Nylon for 1st size; six balls for 2nd size; seven balls for 3rd size. For any one size: a pair of No. 11 and No. 9 knitting needles; 7 buttons.

Tension

Work at a tension of 7 stitches and 9 rows to 1 inch, over the stocking stitch, using No. 9 needles, to obtain the following measurements:

Measurements

INCHES

	1st size	2nd size	3rd size
All round at under-arms	23	25	26
Side seam	6¼	7	8
Length	11½	12½	13¾
Sleeve seam	8¼	8¾	9¼

Abbreviations

K., knit; p., purl; st., stitch; tog., together; dec., decrease (by working 2 sts. tog.); inc., increase (by working twice into same st.); k.2 tog.b., k.2 sts. tog. through back of loops; y.fwd., yarn forward to make a st.; sl., slip; p.s.s.o., pass slipped st. over; s.k.p.o., sl.1, k.1, pass slipped st. over; st.st., stocking st. (k. on right side and p. on wrong side); single rib is k.1 and p.1 alternately.

● *The instructions are given for 1st size. Where they vary, work figures in first brackets for 2nd size; work figures in second brackets for 3rd size.*

The Back

With No. 11 needles cast on 72 (78) (84) sts. and work 13 rows in single rib.

Next (inc.) row: Rib 9, * inc. in next st., rib 8 (9) (10); repeat from * 5 times more, inc. in next st., rib 8 – 79 (85) (91) sts.

Change to No. 9 needles and, beginning with a k. row, st.st. 44 (52) (60) rows.

To shape the raglan armholes:

1st row: Cast off 3 (4) (5) sts., k. to end.

2nd row: Cast off 3 (4) (5) sts., p. to end.

3rd row: K.2, k.2 tog.b., k. to last 4 sts., k.2 tog., k.2.

4th row: All p.

Repeat 3rd and 4th rows 23 (24) (25) times more.

Cast off remaining 25 (27) (29) sts.

The Left Front

With No. 11 needles cast on 34 (36) (38) sts. and work 13 rows in single rib.

Next (inc.) row: Rib 7 (5) (7), * inc. in next st., rib 8 (5) (5); repeat from * once (3 times) (3 times) more, inc. in next st., rib 8 (6) (6) – 37 (41) (43) sts.

Change to No. 9 needles and work in pattern as follows:

123

1st row: K.8 (10) (11), p.1, k.1, * k.2 tog., y.fwd., k.1, y.fwd., s.k.p.o., k.1; repeat from * twice more, p.1, k.8 (10) (11).

2nd, 4th and 6th rows: All p.

3rd row: K.8 (10) (11), p.1, k.2 tog., y.fwd., k.3, y.fwd., sl.1, k.2 tog., p.s.s.o.; repeat from * once more, y.fwd., k.3, y.fwd., s.k.p.o., p.1, k.8 (10) (11).

5th row: K.8 (10) (11), p.1, k.1, * y.fwd., s.k.p.o., k.1, k.2 tog., y.fwd., k.1; repeat from * twice more, p.1, k.8 (10) (11).

7th row: K.8 (10) (11), p.1, k.2, * y.fwd., sl.1, k.2 tog., p.s.s.o., y.fwd., k.3; repeat from * once more, y.fwd., sl.1, k.2 tog., p.s.s.o., y.fwd., k.2, p.1, k.8 (10) (11).

8th row: All p.

These 8 rows form the pattern; repeat them 4 (5) (6) times more, then work the first 4 rows again **.

To shape the raglan armhole:

1st row: Cast off 3 (4) (5) sts., pattern to end.

2nd row: All p.

3rd row: K.2, k.2 tog.b., pattern to end.

4th row: All p.

This completes front pattern panel. Continue as follows:

1st row: K.2, k.2 tog.b., k. to end.

2nd row: All p.

Repeat 1st and 2nd rows 16 (17) (18) times more, then work 1st row again – 15 (17) (17) sts., ending at front edge.

To shape the neck: Cast off 4 (6) (6) sts. at beginning of next row, then dec. 1 st. at armhole edge, as before, and 1 st. at neck edge on next and following 2 right-side rows – 5 sts.

Next row: P.5.

Next row: K.2, k.2 tog.b., k.1.

Next row: P.4.

Next row: K.2, k.2 tog.b.

Next row: P.3.

Take these 3 sts. tog. and fasten off.

The Right Front

Work as left front to **.

Work 1 row more to end at side edge.

To shape the raglan armhole:

1st row: Cast off 3 (4) (5) sts., p. to end.

2nd row: Pattern to last 4 sts., k.2 tog., k.2.

3rd row: All p.

This completes front pattern panel. Continue as follows:

1st row: K. to last 4 sts., k.2 tog., k.2.

2nd row: All p.

Repeat 1st and 2nd rows 16 (17) (18) times more – 16 (18) (18) sts. – ending at front edge.

To shape the neck:

1st row: Cast off 4 (6) (6) sts., k. to last 4 sts., k.2 tog., k.2.

2nd row: All p.

Dec. 1 st. at neck edge and 1 st. at armhole edge, as before, on next and following 2 right-side rows – 5 sts.

Next row: P.5.

Next row: K.1, k.2 tog., k.2.

Next row: P.4.

Next row: K.2 tog., k.2.

Next row: P.3.

Take these 3 sts. tog. and fasten off.

The Sleeves (both alike)

With No. 11 needles cast on 40 (44) (48) sts. and work 13 rows in single rib.

Next (inc.) row: Rib 10 (11) (12), * inc. in next st., rib 9 (10) (11); repeat from * twice more – 43 (47) (51) sts.

Change to No. 9 needles and, beginning with a k. row, st.st. 6 rows.

Inc. 1 st. at each end of next and every following 6th row until the 9th inc. row has been worked – 61 (65) (69) sts.

St.st. 11 (15) (21) rows straight.

To shape the raglan sleeve top: Work exactly as given for raglan armholes on back when 7 sts. will remain.

Cast off.

The Button Band

With No. 11 needles cast on 9 sts.

1st row: K.1, * p.1, k.1; repeat from * to end.

2nd row: K.2, p.1, k.1, p.1, k.1, p.1, k.2.

Repeat these 2 rows 53 (59) (65) times more.

Leave sts. on safety-pin.

The Buttonhole Band

With No. 11 needles cast on 9 sts. and work 4 rows in rib as given for button band.

1st (buttonhole) row: Rib 3, cast off 3, rib to end.

2nd (buttonhole) row: Rib 3, turn, cast on 3, turn, rib to end.

Rib 16 (18) (20) rows.

Repeat last 18 (20) (22) rows 4 times more, then work the 2 buttonhole rows again.

Rib 12 (14) (16) rows.

Leave sts. on safety-pin.

The Neck Band

First join raglan seams. Slip the 9 sts. of right front band onto No. 11 needle, then with point to inner edge of right front, pick up and k.14 (15) (16) sts. along right front neck edge, 5 sts. from sleeve top, 23 (25) (27) sts. across back, 5 sts. from sleeve top, 14 (15) (16) sts. from left front neck edge and finally rib across the 9 sts. of left front band – 79 (83) (87) sts.

Work 3 rows in single rib.

Work a buttonhole over next 2 rows.

Rib 2 rows.

Cast off in rib.

To Make Up The Cardigan

Press on wrong side using a cool iron over a dry cloth. Join sleeve and side seams. Sew front bands in place. Sew on buttons.

Opposite – Gold cardigan in Tricel (pattern p. 123); pink cardigan in 4-ply (pattern p. 132); white 'V' neck cardigan (pattern p. 134).

White Embroidered Cardigan

(see illustration p. 121)

The girls will love this cardigan with the flower embroidery but, for the boys, try pillar box red and leave it plain

Materials

Eight 25-gramme balls of Robin Vogue Double Knitting for 1st size; nine balls for 2nd size. For either size; a pair each of No. 8 and No. 10 knitting needles; a cable needle; 6 buttons; oddments of contrasting colours for embroidery.

Tension

Work at a tension of 11 stitches and 15 rows to 2 inches, over the stocking stitch, using No. 8 needles, to obtain the following measurements:

Measurements

INCHES

	1st size	2nd size
All round at underarms	24½	26
Side seam	7¾	8¾
Length	13	14½
Sleeve seam	8	9

Abbreviations

K., knit; p., purl; st., stitch; tog., together; dec., decrease (by working 2 sts. tog.) : inc., increase (by working twice into same st.); cr.2b., cross 2 back (slip next st. onto cable needle and leave at back of work, k.1 then p. st. from cable needle); cr.2f., cross 2 front (slip next st. onto cable needle and leave at front of work, p.1 then k. st. from cable needle); MB., make a bobble (k.1, p.1 and k.1 all into next st., turn, k. these 3 sts., turn, p.3, turn, k.3, turn and p.3 tog.); st.st., stocking st. (k. on right side and p. on wrong side); single rib is k.1 and p.1 alternately; double rib is k.2 and p.2 alternately.

● *The instructions are given for 1st size. Where they vary, work figures in brackets for 2nd size.*

The Back

With No. 10 needles cast on 74 (78) sts.
1st row: K.2, * p.2, k.2; repeat from * to end.
2nd row: P.2, * k.2, p.2; repeat from * to end.
Repeat these 2 rows 4 times more.
Change to No. 8 needles and work in st.st. with pattern panels as follows:

1st row: K.9 (10), * p.6, k.1, MB., k.1, p.6 *, k.26 (28), work from * to * once, k.9, (10).
2nd row: P.9 (10), * k.6, p.1, k.1, p.1, k.6 *, p.26 (28), work from * to * once, p.9 (10).
3rd row: K.9 (10), * p.5, cr.2b., p.1, cr.2f., p.5 *, k.26 (28), work from * to * once, k.9 (10).

4th row: P.9 (10), * k.5, p.1, k.3, p.1, k.5 *, p.26 (28), work from * to * once, p.9 (10).

5th row: K.9 (10), * p.4, cr.2b., p.3, cr.2f., p.4 *, k.26 (28), work from * to * once, k.9 (10).

6th row: P.9 (10), * k.4, p.1, k.5, p.1, k.4 *, p.26 (28), work from * to * once, p.9 (10).

7th row: K.9 (10), * p.3, cr.2b., p.5, cr.2f., p.3 *, k.26 (28), work from * to * once, k.9 (10).

8th row: P.9 (10), * k.3, p.1, k.7, p.1, k.3 *, p.26 (28), work from * to * once, p.9 (10).

9th row: K.9 (10), * p.1, MB., p.1, k.1, p.7, k.1, p.1, MB., p.1, * k.26 (28), work from * to * once, k.9 (10).

10th row: P.9 (10), * k.3, p.1, k.7, p.1, k.3 *, p.26 (28), work from * to * once, p.9 (10).

11th row: K.9 (10), * p.3, cr.2f., p.5, cr.2b., p.3 *, k.26 (28), work from * to * once, k.9 (10).

12th row: P.9 (10), * k.4, p.1, k.5, p.1, k.4 *, p.26 (28), work from * to * once, p.9 (10).

13th row: K.9 (10), * p.4, cr.2f., p.3, cr.2b., p.4 *, k.26 (28), work from * to * once, k.9 (10).

14th row: P.9 (10), * k.5, p.1, k.3, p.1, k.5 *, p.26 (28), work from * to * once, p. 9 (10).

15th row: K.9 (10), * p.5, cr.2f., p.1, cr.2b., p.5 *, k.26 (28), work from * to * once, k.9 (10).

16th row: P.9 (10), * k.6, p.1, k.1, p.1, k.6 *, p.26 (28), work from * to * once, p.9 (10).

These 16 rows form the pattern; repeat them twice more, then work the first 2 (8) rows again.

To shape the armholes: Keeping continuity of the pattern panels cast off 4 sts. at beginning of next 2 rows, then dec. 1 st. at each end of next and following 3 (4) right-side rows – 58 (60) sts.

Work 15 (17) rows straight.

To slope the saddle shoulders: Cast off 6 sts. at beginning of next 6 rows – 22 (24) sts.

Work 8 rows straight.

Cast off.

The Left Front

With No. 10 needles cast on 34 sts. and work 10 rows in double rib as given for back, increasing 1 st. at each end of last row on the 2nd size only – 34 (36) sts.

Change to No. 8 needles and work in pattern as follows:

1st row: K.9 (10), p.6, k.1, MB., k.1, p.6, k.10 (11).

2nd row: P.10 (11), k.6, p.1, k.1, p.1, k.6, p.9 (10).

These 2 rows set position of the sts. for the pattern panel.

Continuing in pattern as set out between * and * on the 16 pattern rows of back, work a further 48 (54) rows.

To shape the armhole: Keeping continuity of pattern cast off 4 sts. at beginning of next row; work 1 row, then dec. 1 st. at armhole edge on next and following 3 (4) right-side rows – 26 (27) sts.

Work 10 (12) rows straight, ending at front edge.

To shape the neck: Cast off 5 (6) sts. at beginning of next row, then dec. 1 st. at neck edge on next 3 rows – 18 sts.

Work 1 row back to armhole edge.

To slope the saddle shoulder: Cast off 6 sts. at beginning of next and following alternate row; work 1 row, then cast off remaining 6 sts.

The Right Front

With No. 10 needles cast on 34 sts. and work 10 rows in double rib as given for back, increasing 1 st. at each end of last row on the 2nd size only – 34 (36) sts.

Change to No. 8 needles and work in pattern as follows:

1st row: K.10 (11), p.6, k.1, MB., k.1, p.6, k.9 (10).

2nd row: P.9 (10), k.6, p.1, k.1, p.1, k.6, p.10 (11).

These 2 rows set position of sts. for pattern panel.

Continuing in pattern as set out between * and * on pattern rows of back, work a further 49 (55) rows, ending at side edge.

To shape the armhole: Cast off 4 sts. at beginning of next row, then dec. 1 st. at armhole edge on next and following 3 (4) right-side rows – 26 (27) sts.

Work 11 (13) rows straight, ending at front edge.

To shape the neck: Cast off 5 (6) sts. at beginning of next row, then dec. 1 st. at neck edge on next 3 rows – 18 sts.

Work 1 row back to armhole edge.

To slope the shoulder: Cast off 6 sts. at beginning of next and following alternate row; work 1 row, then cast off remaining 6 sts.

The Sleeves (both alike)

With No. 10 needles cast on 38 sts. and work 10 rows in rib as given for back, increasing 1 st. at end of last row – 39 sts.

Change to No. 8 needles and work in pattern as follows:

1st row: K.12, p.6, k.1, MB., k.1, p.6, k.12.

2nd row: P.12, k.6, p.1, k.1, p.1, k.6, p.12.

These 2 rows set position of sts. for pattern panel.

Continuing in pattern and taking the extra sts. into the st.st. as they occur, inc. 1 st. at each end of next and every following 8th row until the 5th (6th) inc. row has been worked – 49 (51) sts.

Work 15 (13) rows straight.

To shape the sleeve top: Cast off 4 sts. at beginning of next 2 rows, then dec. 1 st. at each end of next and following 3 (4) right-side rows – 33 sts.

Work 1 row, then dec. 1 st. at each end of next 8 rows – 17 sts.

Work 20 rows straight in pattern for saddle shoulder extension.

Cast off.

The Button Band

With No. 10 needles cast on 9 sts.

1st row: K.1, * p.1, k.1 ; repeat from * to end.

2nd row: K.2, * p.1, k.1 ; repeat from * ending last repeat with k.2.

Repeat these 2 rows 40 (45) times more.

Break off wool and leave sts. on spare needle.

The Buttonhole Band

With No. 10 needles cast on 9 sts. and work 6 rows in rib as given for button band.

1st (buttonhole) row: Rib 3, cast off 3, rib to end.

2nd (buttonhole) row: Rib 3, turn, cast on 3, turn, rib to end.

Rib 14 (16) rows.

Repeat last 16 (18) rows 3 times more, then work the 2 buttonhole rows again.

Rib 11 (13) rows.

Do not break off wool.

The Neck Band

First set in sleeves, sewing the row ends of the saddle shoulder extensions to the sts. cast off for shoulders on back and fronts then sew the straight row ends at top of back halfway across the cast-off edge of sleeve extensions leaving remainder of this edge free to form part of the neck edge.

With the needle holding the 9 sts. of right-front band, pick up and k.12 (13) sts. from right front neck edge, 6 sts. from sleeve top, 21 (23) sts. across back, 6 sts. from sleeve top, 12 (13) sts. from left front neck edge and finally rib across the 9 sts. of left-front band.

On these 75 (79) sts. work 3 rows in single rib.

Make a buttonhole over next 2 rows, then rib 2 rows.

Cast off.

To Make Up The Cardigan

Press on wrong side using a warm iron over a damp cloth. Join sleeve and side seams. Sew front bands in place. Work flower embroidery as shewn in photograph. Sew on buttons.

Hooded Jacket

**Worked in double moss stitch. Just right
for an afternoon outing**

Materials

Seven 25-gramme balls of Patons
Quickerknit Baby Wool for 1st size;
eight balls for 2nd size. For either size:
a pair of No. 9 and No. 11 knitting
needles; 6 buttons.

Tension

Work at a tension of 7 stitches and 9 rows
to 1 inch, over the pattern, using No. 9
needles, to obtain the following measurements:

Measurements

	INCHES	
	1st size	2nd size
All round at underarms	23	25
Side seam	6½	7
Length	11	12
Sleeve seam	7½	8½

Abbreviations

K., knit; p., purl; st., stitch; tog., together;
dec., decrease (by working 2 sts. tog.); inc.,
increase (by working twice into same st.);
single rib is k.1 and p.1 alternately.

● *The instructions are given for 1st size.
Where they vary, work figures in brackets
for 2nd size.*

The Back

With No. 11 needles cast on 79 (87) sts. and, beginning right-side rows with k.1 and wrong-side rows with p.1, work 16 rows in single rib.

Change to No. 9 needles.

1st row: P.1, * k.1, p.1; repeat from * to end.

2nd row: K.1, * p.1, k.1; repeat from * to end.

3rd row: K.1, * p.1, k.1; repeat from * to end.

4th row: P.1, * k.1, p.1; repeat from * to end.

These 4 rows form the double moss st. pattern; repeat them 10 (11) times more, then work first 2 rows again.

To shape the armholes: Cast off 3 (4) sts. at beginning of next 2 rows, then dec. 1 st. at each end of next and following 4 (5) alternate rows — 63 (67) sts.

Work 29 (31) rows straight.

To slope the shoulders: Cast off 10 (11) sts. at beginning of next 4 rows.

Cast off remaining 23 sts.

The Left Front

With No. 11 needles cast on 37 (41) sts. and work 16 rows in single rib as given for back.

Change to No. 9 needles and work the 4 pattern rows 11 (12) times and first 2 rows again.

To shape the armhole: Cast off 3 (4) sts. at beginning of next row, work 1 row, then dec. 1 st. at armhole edge on next and following 4 (5) alternate rows — 29 (31) sts.

Work 18 (20) rows straight, ending at front edge.

To shape the neck: Cast off 4 sts. at beginning of next row, then dec. 1 st. at neck edge on following 5 alternate rows — 20 (22) sts.

To slope the shoulder: Cast off 10 (11) sts. at beginning of next row, work 1 row, then cast off remaining 10 (11) sts.

The Right Front

With No. 11 needles cast on 37 (41) sts. and work 16 rows in single rib as given for back.

Change to No. 9 needles and work the 4 pattern rows 11 (12) times and first 3 rows again.

To shape the armhole: Cast off 3 (4) sts. at beginning of next row, then dec. 1 st. at armhole edge on next and following 4 (5) alternate rows — 29 (31) sts.

Work 19 (21) rows straight, ending at front edge.

To shape the neck and shoulder: Work as given for left front.

The Sleeves (both alike)

With No. 11 needles cast on 43 (45) sts. and work 16 rows in single rib as given for back.

Change to No. 9 needles and work the 4 pattern rows once.

Inc. 1 st. at each end of next and every following 6th row until the 9th (10th) inc. row has been worked — 61 (65) sts.

Work 3 (5) rows straight.

To shape the sleeve top: Cast off 3 (4) sts. at beginning of next 2 rows, then dec. 1 st. at each end of next and following 5 (7) alternate rows — 43 (41) sts.

Work 1 row, then dec. 1 st. at each end of next 8 (6) rows.

Cast off remaining 27 (29) sts.

The Button Band

With No. 11 needles cast on 9 sts. and work 88 (98) rows in single rib as given for back.

Cast off.

The Buttonhole Band

With No. 11 needles cast on 9 sts. and work 4 rows in rib as given for back.

1st (buttonhole) row: Rib 3, cast off 2, rib to end.

2nd (buttonhole) row: Rib 4, turn, cast on 2, turn, rib to end.

Rib 14 (16) rows.

Repeat last 16 (18) rows 4 times more, then work the 2 buttonhole rows again.

Rib 2 rows.

Cast off.

The Hood

With No. 11 needles cast on 113 sts. and work 12 rows in rib as given for back.

Change to No. 9 needles and work the 4 pattern rows given for back 8 times.

Cast off 10 sts. at beginning of next 6 rows and 11 sts. on following 2 rows.

On centre 31 sts. work 52 rows straight for back section.

Cast off.

To Make Up The Jacket

Press lightly using a warm iron over a damp cloth. Join shoulder seams, set in sleeves, then join sleeve and side seams. Sew front bands in place. Join cast-off edges of hood to the row-ends of back section. Turn back ribbed edge and catch in place. Beginning and ending at inner edge of front bands, sew hood in place all round neck edge. Sew on buttons.

Cardigan

(see illustration p. 124)

in 4-ply

Materials

For either size: Six 25-gramme balls of Bairnswear Pleasure 4-ply Wool; a pair each of No. 10 and No. 12 knitting needles; 7 buttons.

Tension

Work at a tension of 7 stitches and 9 rows to 1 inch, over the stocking stitch, using No. 10 needles, to obtain the following measurements:

Measurements

INCHES

	1st size	2nd size
All round at underarms	22½	24¾
Side seam	7¼	8
Length	13	14
Sleeve seam	8	9

Abbreviations

K., knit; p., purl; st., stitch; tog., together; dec., decrease (by working 2 sts. tog.); inc., increase (by working twice into same st.); k.2 tog.b., k.2 tog. through back of loops; w.fwd., wool forward to make a st.; sl., slip; p.s.s.o., pass slipped st. over; single rib is k.1 and p.1 alternately; st.st., stocking st. (k. on right side and p. on wrong side).

● *The instructions are given for 1st size. Where they vary, work figures in brackets for 2nd size.*

The Back

With No. 12 needles cast on 72 (80) sts. and work 13 rows in single rib.

Next (inc.) row: Rib 9 (10), * inc. in next st., rib 8 (9); repeat from * to end — 79 (87) sts.

Change to No. 10 needles and, beginning with a k. row, st.st. 44 (50) rows.

To shape the raglan armholes:

1st row: Cast off 3 (4) sts., k. to end.

2nd row: Cast off 3 (4) sts., p. to end.

3rd row: K.2, k.2 tog.b., k. to last 4 sts., k.2 tog., k.2.

4th row: All p.

Repeat 3rd and 4th rows 24 (25) times more — 23 (27) sts.

Break off wool and leave sts. on spare needle.

The Left Front

With No. 12 needles cast on 34 (38) sts. and work 13 rows in single rib.

Next (inc.) row: Rib 7 (8), * inc. in next st., rib 8 (9); repeat from * to end — 37 (41) sts. **.

Change to No. 10 needles and work in pattern as follows:

1st row: K.20 (24), p.1, k.1, * w.fwd., sl.1, k.2 tog., p.s.s.o., w.fwd., k.1; repeat from * twice more, p.1, k.2.

2nd row: P.2, k.1, p.13, k.1, p.20 (24).

Repeat these 2 rows 21 (24) times more.

To shape the raglan armholes:

1st row: Cast off 3 (4) sts., pattern to end.

2nd row: Work in pattern.

3rd row: K.2, k.2 tog.b., pattern to end.

4th row: Work in pattern.

Repeat 3rd and 4th rows 17 (18) times more, then work 3rd row again – 15 (17) sts., ending at front edge.

To shape the neck.

Next row: Cast off 4 (6) sts., pattern to end.

Now dec. 1 st. at armhole edge, as before, and dec. 1 st. at neck edge on next and following 2 alternate rows – 5 sts.

Work 1 row, then dec. 1 st. at armhole edge only on next and following alternate row – 3 sts.

Next row: P.3.

Next row: K.1, k.2 tog.b.

Take remaining 2 sts. tog. and fasten off.

The Right Front

Work as left front to **.

Change to No. 10 needles.

1st row: K.2, p.1, * k.1, w.fwd., sl.1, k.2 tog., p.s.s.o., w.fwd. ; repeat from * twice, k.1, p.1, k.20 (24).

2nd row: P.20 (24), k.1, p.13, k.1, p.2.

Repeat these 2 rows 21 (24) times more, then work 1st row again.

To shape the raglan armhole:

1st row: Cast off 3 (4) sts., pattern to end.

2nd row: Pattern to last 4 sts., k.2 tog., k.2.

3rd row: Work in pattern.

Repeat 2nd and 3rd rows 17 (18) times more – 16 (18) sts.

To shape the neck:

Next row: Cast off 4 (6) sts. pattern to last 4 sts., k.2 tog., k.2.

Work 1 row, then dec. 1 st. at armhole edge, as before, and 1 st. at neck edge on next and following 2 alternate rows – 5 sts.

Work 1 row, then dec. 1 st. at armhole edge only on next and following alternate row.

Next row: P.3.

Next row: K.2 tog., k.1.

Take remaining 2 sts. tog. and fasten off.

The Sleeves (both alike)

With No. 12 needles cast on 40 (42) sts. and work 13 rows in single rib.

Next (inc.) row: Rib 1 (2), * inc. in next st., rib 8 ; repeat from * 3 times more, inc. in next st., rib 2 (3) – 45 (47) sts.

Change to No. 10 needles and, beginning with a k. row, st.st. 4 rows.

Inc. 1 st. at each end of next and every

following 6th row until the 9th (10th) inc. row has been worked – 63 (67) sts.

Work 5 (9) rows straight.

To shape the raglan sleeve top: Work exactly as given for raglan armhole shaping on back when 7 sts. will remain.

Break off wool and leave sts. on safety-pin.

The Button Band

With No. 12 needles cast on 7 sts.

1st row: K.1, * p.1, k.1 ; repeat from * to end.

2nd row: K.2, p.1, k.1, p.1, k.2.

Repeat these 2 rows 43 (48) times more. Break off wool and leave sts. on safety-pin.

The Buttonhole Band

With No. 12 needles cast on 7 sts. and work 6 (4) rows in rib as given for button band.

Next (buttonhole) row: K.1, p.1, k.1, w.fwd., k.2 tog., p.1, k.1.

Rib (13) (15) rows.

Repeat last 14 (16) rows 4 times more, then work buttonhole row again.

Rib 11 (13) rows. Break off wool and leave sts. on safety-pin.

The Neck Band

First join raglan seams. Slip the sts. of right front band onto No. 12 needle with point to inner edge, rejoin yarn to neck edge and, with this needle, pick up and k.16 (17) sts. along right front neck edge, k. the 7 sts. of right sleeve, 23 (27) sts. across back, 7 sts. of left sleeve and pick up and k.16 (17) sts. from left front neck edge then rib across the sts. of left front band – 83 (89) sts.

Work 3 rows in single rib.

Work a buttonhole on next row, then rib a further 3 rows.

Cast off in rib.

To Make Up The Cardigan

Press on wrong side, avoiding the ribbing, using a warm iron over a damp cloth. Join sleeve and side seams. Sew front bands in place. Sew on buttons.

White 'V' Neck Cardigan

(see illustration p. 124)

Materials

Six 25-gramme balls of Lee Target Motoravia Double Knitting Wool for 1st size; seven balls for 2nd and 3rd sizes. For any one size: a pair each of No. 8 and No. 10 knitting needles; 5 buttons; oddments of contrast colours if required.

Tension

Work at a tension of 11 stitches and 15 rows to 2 inches, over the stocking stitch, using No. 8 needles, to obtain the following measurements:

Abbreviations

K., knit; p., purl; st., stitch; tog., together; dec., decrease (by working 2 sts. tog.); inc., increase (by working twice into same st.); w.fwd., wool forward to make a st.; st.st., stocking st. (k. on right side and p. on wrong side); single rib is k.1 and p.1 alternately.

● *The instructions are given for 1st size. Where they vary, work figures in first brackets for 2nd size; figures in second brackets for 3rd size.*

Measurements

	INCHES		
	1st size	2nd size	3rd size
All round at under- arms	23	24	25
Side seam	7	$7\frac{3}{4}$	$8\frac{3}{4}$
Length	12	13	$14\frac{1}{4}$
Sleeve seam	7	$7\frac{3}{4}$	$8\frac{3}{4}$

The Back

With No. 10 needles cast on 64 (66) (70) sts. and work 16 rows in single rib, inserting contrast colours as required.

Change to No. 8 needles and, beginning with a k. row, st.st. 40 (46) (52) rows.

To shape the raglan armholes: Cast off 4 sts. at beginning of next 2 rows, then dec. 1 st. at each end of next and following 17 (18) (19) right-side rows – 20 (20) (22) sts.

P.1 row.

Cast off.

The Left Front

With No. 10 needles cast on 29 (31) (33) sts. and, beginning right-side rows with k.1 and wrong-side rows with p.1, work 16 rows in single rib inserting contrast colours if required, and increasing 1 st. in centre of last row on the 1st size only – 30 (31) (33) sts.

Change to No. 8 needles.

Beginning with a k. row, st.st. 40 (46) (52) rows **.

To shape the raglan armhole and slope front edge:

1st row: Cast off 4, k. to last 2 sts., dec.

Work 8 rows decreasing 1 st. at armhole edge on each right-side row and 1 st. at front edge on the 4th and 8th of these rows – 19 (20) (22) sts.

*** Now work 18 (18) (24) rows decreasing 1 st. at armhole edge on each right-side row and 1 st. at front edge on the 6th of these rows and each following 6th row – 7 (8) (6) sts.

Work 1 row, then dec. 1 st. at armhole edge only on next and following 4 (5) (3) right-side rows.

P.2, then take these 2 sts. tog. and fasten off.

The Right Front

Work as given for left front to **

To shape the raglan armhole and slope front edge:

1st row: K.2 tog., k. to end.

2nd row: Cast off 4, p. to end.

Now work 7 rows decreasing 1 st. at armhole edge on each right-side row and 1 st. at front edge on the 3rd and 7th of these rows – 19 (20) (22) sts.

Now work as given for left front from *** to end.

The Sleeves (both alike)

With No. 10 needles cast on 38 (38) (40) sts. and work 16 rows in single rib as given for back.

Change to No. 8 needles and, beginning with a k. row, st.st. 2 rows.

Inc. 1 st. at each end of next and every following 8th row until the 5th (6th) (6th) inc. row has been worked – 48 (50) (52) sts.

St.st. 5 (3) (9) rows straight.

To shape the raglan sleeve top: Cast off 4 sts. at beginning of next 2 rows, then dec. 1 st. at each end of next and following 4th row – 36 (38) (40) sts.

Work 1 row, then dec. 1 st. at each end of next and following 14 (15) (16) right-side rows – 6 sts.

Work 1 row, then cast off.

The Front Band

First join raglan seams. With No. 10 needles cast on 7 sts.

1st row: K.1, * p.1, k.1; repeat from * to end.

2nd row: K.2, p.1, k.1, p.1, k.2.

Repeat these 2 rows once.

Next (buttonhole) row: K.1, p.1, k.1, w.fwd., k.2 tog., p.1, k.1.

Mark positions for a further 4 buttonholes on front, evenly spaced to first front shaping then continue in rib, making buttonholes to correspond with marked positions, until band is long enough, when slightly stretched, to fit all round front edge. Cast off when correct length is assured.

To Make Up The Cardigan

Press on wrong side, avoiding the ribbing, using a warm iron over a damp cloth. Join sleeve and side seams. Sew front band in place. Sew on buttons.

White Dress

3-ply

**Designed to match the Matinee Set on
page 76**

Materials

Four 25-gramme balls of Patons
Beehive Baby Wool 3-ply; a pair of
No. 11 knitting needles; 3 buttons;
3 yards narrow ribbon.

Tension

Worked at a tension of 17 stitches and 22
rows to 2 inches, over the stocking stitch,
the dress will fit baby aged birth to 3 months.

Abbreviations

K., knit; p., purl; st., stitch; tog., together;
dec., decrease (by working 2 sts. tog.); inc.,
increase (by working twice into same st.);
sl., slip; p.s.s.o., pass slipped st. over;
w.fwd., wool forward to make a st.; w.r.n.,
wool round needle to make a st.; st.st.,
stocking stitch (k. on the right side and p.
on the wrong side).

The Back

With No. 11 needles cast on 123 sts. and
k.2 rows.

Now work in pattern as follows:

1st row: K.2, * w.fwd., k.3, sl.1, k.2 tog.,
p.s.s.o., k.3, w.fwd., k.1; repeat from *
ending last repeat with k.2.

2nd row: All p.

3rd row: K.3, * w.fwd., k.2, sl.1, k.2 tog.,
p.s.s.o., k.2, w.fwd., k.3; repeat from * to
end.

4th row: All p.

5th row: K.1, k.2 tog., * w.fwd., k.1, w.fwd.,
k.1, sl.1, k.2 tog., p.s.s.o., k.1, w.fwd., k.1,
w.fwd., sl.1, k.2 tog., p.s.s.o.; repeat from *
to last 10 sts., w.fwd., k.1, w.fwd., k.1,
sl.1, k.2 tog., p.s.s.o., k.1, w.fwd., k.1,
w.fwd., k.2 tog., k.1.

6th row: All p.

Repeat these 6 rows 13 times more.

Next (dec.) row: K.2 tog., k.2 tog., * k.1,
k.2 tog.; repeat from * to last 2 sts., k.2
tog. — 81 sts.

Now work as follows:

1st row (wrong side): All k.

2nd row: All k.

3rd row: P.2, * w.r.n., p.2 tog.; repeat from
* to last st., p.1.

4th row: All k.

5th row (wrong side): All k.

6th to 10th rows: Beginning with a k. row,
st.st. 5 rows.

Work these 10 rows once more, then work
the first 5 rows again **

K.1 row and p.1 row.

To shape the raglan armholes: Cast
off 4 sts. at beginning of next 2 rows, then
dec. 1 st. at each end of next row and
following 19 right-side rows – 33 sts.

P.1 row.

Cast off.

The Front

Work as back to **.

K.1 row.

Now divide sts. for front opening.

Next row: P.43 and leave these sts. on a spare needle for right side, p. to end and work on these 38 sts. for left side.

The left side: To shape raglan arm hole:

1st row: Cast off 4, k. to end, turn and cast on 5 sts. for underlap – 39 sts.

2nd row: K.5, p. to end.

3rd row: K.2 tog., k. to end.

Repeat 2nd and 3rd rows 13 times more – 25 sts. – ending at front edge.

To shape the neck:

1st row: K.5 and leave these sts. on a safety-pin, cast off 2, p. to end.

2nd row: K.2 tog., k. to last 2 sts., k.2 tog.

3rd row: P.2 tog., p. to end.

Repeat 2nd and 3rd rows 3 times more – 6 sts.

Next row: K.2 tog., k.2, k.2 tog.

Next row: P.4.

Next row: K.2 tog., k.2 tog.

P.2 tog. and fasten off.

The right side: With right side of work facing, rejoin wool to sts. on spare needle and k. to end of row.

To shape the raglan armhole:

1st row: Cast off 4, p. to last 5 sts., k.5.

2nd row: K. to last 2 sts., k.2 tog.

3rd row: P. to last 5 sts., k.5.

Repeat 2nd and 3rd rows once.

Next (buttonhole) row: K.2, w.fwd., k.2 tog., k. to last 2 sts., k.2 tog.

Work 3rd row, then repeat 2nd and 3rd rows 6 times.

Work buttonhole row; work 3rd row, then repeat 2nd and 3rd rows 4 times more – 25 sts. – ending at front edge.

To shape the neck:

1st row: K.5 and leave these sts. on a safety-pin, cast off 2, k. to last 2 sts., k.2 tog.

2nd row: P. to last 2 sts., p.2 tog.

3rd row: K.2 tog., k. to last 2 sts., k.2 tog.

Repeat 2nd and 3rd rows 3 times more – 5 sts.

Next row: P.5.

Next row: K.2 tog., k.1, k.2 tog.

Next row: P.3.

Next row: K.1, k.2 tog.

P.2 tog. and fasten off.

The Sleeves (both alike)

With No. 11 needles cast on 51 sts. and k.3 rows.

Next row: P.2, * w.r.n., p.2 tog.; repeat from * to last st., p.1.

Next row: All k.

Next row (wrong side): All k.

Beginning with a k. row, st.st. 4 rows.

Inc. 1 st. at each end of next row and following 4th row – 55 sts.

St.st. 3 rows.

To shape the raglan sleeve top: Work exactly as given for raglan armhole shaping on back when 7 sts. will remain.

Cast off.

The Neck Band

First join raglan seams. With right side of work facing sl. the 5 sts. of buttonhole band onto No. 11 needle with point to inner edge, rejoin wool and pick up and k.14 sts. along shaped edge, 5 sts. from sleeve top, 31 sts. across back, 5 sts. from sleeve top, 14 sts. along shaped edge and finally, k. the 5 sts. of button band – 79 sts.

K.2 rows.

Next row: K.5, p.1, * w.r.n., p.2 tog.; repeat from * to last 5 sts., k.5.

Next (buttonhole) row: K.2, w.fwd., k.2 tog., k. to end.

K.2 rows.

Cast off.

To Make Up The Dress

Press st.st. parts only using a warm iron over a damp cloth. Join sleeve and side seams. Neaten lower edge of front opening. Sew on buttons. Thread with ribbon.

Yellow First-Size Dress

(see illustration p. 140)

Materials

Five 20-gramme balls of Lister 2 Spun 4-ply Crêpe Tricel with Nylon; a pair each of No. 10 and No. 12 knitting needles; a 4-inch zip; ribbon and motifs for trimming.

Tension and Size

Worked at a tension of 15 stitches and 19 rows to 2 inches, over the stocking stitch, using No. 10 needles, the dress will fit baby aged birth to six months.

Abbreviations

K., knit; p., purl; st., stitch; tog., together; dec., decrease (by working 2 sts. tog.); inc., increase (by working twice into same st.); sl., slip; p.s.s.o., pass slipped st. over; y.fwd., yarn forward to make a st.; s.k.p.o., sl.1, k.1, pass slipped st. over; up 1 (pick up the thread which lies between the needles and k. into back of it, thus making a st.); st.st., stocking st. (k. on right side and p. on wrong side); single rib is k.1 and p.1 alternately.

SPECIAL NOTE: If baby is above average size, use one size larger needle.

The Back

With No. 10 needles cast on 101 sts. and k.2 rows.

Now work in pattern as follows:

1st row: K.2, y.fwd., k.5, sl.1, k.2 tog., p.s.s.o., * k.5, y.fwd., k.1, y.fwd., k.5, sl.1, k.2 tog., p.s.s.o.; repeat from * to last 7 sts., k.5, y.fwd., k.2.

2nd row: All p.

These 2 rows form the pattern; repeat them 32 times more.

Next (dec.) row: * K.1, k.2 tog.; repeat from * to last 2 sts., k.2 – 68 sts.

Beginning with a p. row, st.st. 5 rows.

To shape the raglan armholes:

1st row: Cast off 4, k. to end.

2nd row: Cast off 4, p. to end.

3rd row: K.1, s.k.p.o., k. to last 3 sts., k.2 tog., k.1.

4th row: All p. **.

Repeat 3rd and 4th rows once more, then work 3rd row again – 54 sts.

Now divide sts. for back opening.

Next row: P.27 and leave these sts. on a spare needle for left side, p. to end and work on these 27 sts. for right side.

The right side: Dec. 1 st. at armhole edge, as before, on next and following 16 right-side rows – 10 sts.

P.1 row ***.

Break off yarn and leave sts. on a spare needle.

The left side: With right side of work facing, rejoin yarn to 27 sts. on spare needle and work as given for right side to ***.

K.1 row.

Break off yarn and leave sts. on a spare needle.

The Front

Work as back to **.

Repeat 3rd and 4th rows 11 times more, then work 3rd row again – 34 sts.

Now divide sts. for front neck.

Next row: P.12 and leave these sts. on a spare needle for right side, p. next 10 sts. and leave these on a stitch-holder for neck band, p. to end and work on these 12 sts. for left side.

The left side: Work 5 rows decreasing 1 st. at armhole edge, as before, and 1 st. at neck edge on each right-side row – 6 sts.

P.1 row.

Now dec. 1 st. at armhole edge only on next and following 3 right-side rows.

P.2, then take these 2 sts. tog. and fasten off.

The right side: With right side of work facing, rejoin yarn to the 12 sts. left on spare needle and work as given for left side to end.

The Sleeves (both alike)

With No. 12 needles cast on 32 sts. and k. 7 rows.

Change to No. 10 needles.

Next (increase) row: K.2, * up.1, k.3; repeat from * 9 times – 42 sts.

Beginning with a p. row, st.st. 5 rows.

Inc. 1 st. at each end of next and every following 6th row until the 6th inc. row has been worked – 54 sts.

St.st. 11 rows.

To shape the raglan sleeve top: Work the first 4 rows of raglan shaping given for back, then repeat 3rd and 4th rows 19 times more – 6 sts.

Break off yarn and leave sts. on a safety-pin.

The Neck Band

First join raglan seams. With right side of work facing, slip the 10 sts. of left side of back onto No. 12 needle with point to sleeve edge, rejoin yarn and k. the 6 sts. of left sleeve, pick up and k.13 sts. down left side of neck, k.10 sts. at centre front, pick up and k.13 sts. from right side of neck, k.6 sts. of right sleeve and finally k. the 10 sts. at right side of back – 68 sts.

Work 5 rows in single rib.

Cast off loosely in rib.

To Make Up The Dress

Press on wrong side using a cool iron over a dry cloth.

Join sleeve and side seams. Insert zip. Trim front with ribbon and motifs. Trim neck with motifs.

First- and second-size dresses.

Blue Second-Size Dress

Materials

Seven 20 gramme balls of Lee Target Duo 4 ply Crêpe Tricel with Nylon; a pair each of No. 10 and No. 12 knitting needles; a 4-inch zip; daisy motif trimming.

Tension and Size

Worked at a tension of 15 stitches and 19 rows to 2 inches over the stocking stitch, using No. 10 needles, the dress will fit baby aged six to twelve months.

Abbreviations

K., knit; p., purl; st., stitch; tog., together; dec., decrease (by working 2 sts. tog.); inc., increase (by working twice into same st.); sl., slip; p.s.s.o., pass slipped st. over; y.fwd., yarn forward to make a st.; s.k.p.o., sl.1, k.1, pass slipped st. over; up 1 (pick up the thread which lies between the needles and k. into back of it, thus making a st.); single rib is k.1 and p.1 alternately; st.st. stocking st. (k. on right side and p. on wrong side).

● *Instructions in brackets must be worked the number of times stated after 2nd bracket.*

SPECIAL NOTE: If baby is above average size, use one size larger needle.

The Back

With No. 10 needles cast on 107 sts. and k.2 rows.

1st row: K.2, * s.k.p.o., k.1, y.fwd., k.1, y.fwd., k.1, k.2 tog., k.1; repeat from * to last st., k.1 more.

2nd and every alternate row: All p.

3rd row: As 1st row.

5th row: K.2, * y.fwd., s.k.p.o., k.3, k.2 tog., y.fwd., k.1; repeat from * to last st., k.1 more.

7th row: K.3, * y.fwd., s.k.p.o., k.1, k.2 tog., y.fwd., k.3; repeat from * to end.

9th row: K.4, * y.fwd., sl.1, k.2 tog., p.s.s.o., y.fwd., k.5; repeat from * ending last repeat with k.4.

10th row: All p.

These 10 rows form the pattern; repeat them 8 times more, then work first 6 rows again.

Next (dec.) row: K.3, (k.2 tog., k.2) 5 times, (k.2 tog., k.1) 20 times, (k.2 tog., k.2) 6 times – 76 sts.

Beginning with a p. row, st.st. 11 rows.

To shape the raglan armholes:

1st row: Cast off 5, k. to end.

2nd row: Cast off 5, p. to end.

3rd row: K.1, s.k.p.o., k. to last 3 sts., k.2 tog., k.1.

4th row: All p. **.

Repeat 3rd and 4th rows 3 times more, then work 3rd row again – 56 sts.

Now divide sts. for back opening.

Next row: P.28 and leave these sts. on a spare needle for left side, p. to end and work on these 28 sts. for right side.

The right side: Dec. 1 st. at armhole edge, as before, on next and following 16 right-side rows – 11 sts.

P.1 row ***.

Break off yarn and leave sts. on a spare needle.

The left side: With right side of work facing, rejoin yarn to the 28 sts. on spare needle and work as given for right side to ***.

K.1 row.

Break off yarn and leave sts. on a spare needle.

The Front

Work as back to **.

Repeat 3rd and 4th rows 13 times more, then work 3rd row again — 36 sts.

Now divide sts. for front neck.

Next row: P.12 and leave these sts. on a spare needle for right side, p. next 12 sts. and leave on stitch-holder for neck band, p. to end and work on these 12 sts. for left side.

The left side: Work 5 rows decreasing 1 st. at armhole edge, as before, and 1 st. at neck edge on each right-side row — 6 sts.

P.1 row, then dec. 1 st. at armhole edge only on next and following 3 right-side rows.

P.2, then take these 2 sts. tog. and fasten off.

The right side: With right side of work facing, rejoin yarn to 12 sts. on spare needle and work as given for left side to end.

The Sleeves (both alike)

With No. 12 needles cast on 36 sts. and k.7 rows.

Change to No. 10 needles.

Next (inc.) row: K.2, * up 1, k.3; repeat from * 10 times more, up 1, k.1 — 48 sts.

Beginning with a k. row, st.st. 4 rows.

Inc. 1 st. at each end of next and every following 8th row until the 6th inc. row has been worked — 60 sts.

St.st. 7 rows.

To shape the raglan sleeve top: Work the first 4 rows of raglan armhole shaping given for back, then repeat 3rd and 4th rows 21 times more — 6 sts.

Break off yarn and leave sts. on a safety pin.

The Neck Band

First join raglan seams. With right side of work facing, slip the 11 sts. of left side of back onto No. 12 needle with point to sleeve edge, rejoin yarn and k. the 6 sts. of left sleeve, then pick up and k.13 sts. down left side of neck, k.12 sts. at centre, pick up and k.13 sts. from right side of neck, k.6 sts. of right sleeve and k. the 11 sts. at right side of back — 72 sts.

Work 5 rows in single rib.

Cast off loosely in rib.

To Make Up The Dress

Press on wrong side, using a cool iron over a dry cloth. Join sleeve and side seams. Insert zip. Trim neck and front with daisy motifs.

Shift Dress

(see illustration p. 144)

**Worked in one piece, only the back seam
and shoulders to join**

Materials

Six 20-gramme balls of Emu Tricel
Nylon Double Knitting for 1st size;
eight balls for 2nd size. For either size:
a pair of long No. 9 knitting needles;
a 4-inch zip.

Tension

Work at a tension of 6 stitches and 8 rows
to 1 inch, over the stocking stitch, using
No. 9 needles, to obtain the following
measurements:

Measurements

	INCHES	
	1st size	2nd size
All round at underarms	22	24
Side seam	11	13
Length	14¼	16¾

Abbreviations

K., knit; p., purl; st., stitch; tog., together;
dec., decrease (by working 2 sts. tog.); inc.,
increase (by working twice into same st.);
k.2 tog.b., k.2 sts. tog. through back of
loops; y.fwd., yarn forward; sl., slip; 3 in 1
(k.1, y.fwd., k.1 all into same st.); 5 in 1
(k.1, y.fwd., k.1, y.fwd., k.1 all into same st.);
k.3 or 5 dbl., k.3 or 5 sts. double (k. 3 or
5 sts. taking yarn twice round needle for each
st.); sl.3 or 5 tog. (sl.3 or 5 sts. p.wise onto
right-hand needle dropping extra loops to
make 3 or 5 long sts., place them back onto
left-hand needle, then p. these 3 or 5 loops
together); st.st., stocking st. (k. on right side
and p. on wrong side).

● *The instructions are given for 1st size.
Where they vary, work figures in brackets
for 2nd size.*

The Main Part (worked in one piece to armholes)

With No. 9 needles cast on 195 (207) sts.
and k.8 rows.

Now work border pattern as follows:

1st row: K.1, 3 in 1, * k.5 dbl., 5 in 1;
repeat from * to last 7 sts., k.5 dbl., 3 in 1,
k.1.

2nd row: K.4, * sl.5 tog., k.5; repeat from *
ending last repeat with k.4.

3rd row: All k.

4th row: All k.

5th row: K.1, k.3 dbl., * 5 in 1, k.5 dbl.;
repeat from * to last 5 sts., 5 in 1, k.3 dbl.,
k.1.

6th row: K.1, sl.3 tog., * k.5, sl.5 tog.;
repeat from * to last 9 sts., k.5, sl.3 tog.,
k.1.

7th row: All k.

8th row: All k. increasing 1 st. in centre of
this row – 196 (208) sts.

This completes border pattern.

Now shape as follows:

1st (shaping) row: K.22 (23), k.2 tog.,
k.23 (25), k.2 tog., k.2 tog.b., k.30 (32),
k.2 tog.b., k.30 (32), k.2 tog., k.30 (32),
k.2 tog., k.2 tog.b., k.23 (25), k.2 tog.b.,
k.22 (23) – 188 (200) sts.

Beginning with a p. row, st.st. 7 (9) rows.

2nd (shaping) row: K.21 (22), k.2 tog., k.22 (24), k.2 tog., k.2 tog.b., k.29 (31), k.2 tog.b., k.28 (30), k.2 tog., k.29 (31), k.2 tog., k.2 tog.b., k.22 (24), k.2 tog.b., k.21 (22) – 180 (192) sts.
St.st. 7 (9) rows.

3rd (shaping) row: K.20 (21), k.2 tog., k.21 (23), k.2 tog., k.2 tog.b., k.28 (30), k.2 tog.b., k.26 (28), k.2 tog., k.28 (30), k.2 tog., k.2 tog.b., k.21 (23), k.2 tog.b., k.20 (21) – 172 (184) sts.
St.st. 7 (9) rows.

4th (shaping) row: K.19 (20), k.2 tog., k.20 (22), k.2 tog., k.2 tog.b., k.27 (29), k.2 tog.b., k.24 (26), k.2 tog., k.27 (29), k.2 tog., k.2 tog.b., k.20 (22), k.2 tog.b., k.19 (20) – 164 (176) sts.
St.st. 7 (9) rows.

5th (shaping) row; K.18 (19), k.2 tog., k.19 (21), k.2 tog., k.2 tog.b., k.26 (28), k.2 tog.b., k.22 (24), k.2 tog., k.26 (28), k.2 tog., k.2 tog.b., k.19 (21), k.2 tog.b., k.18 (19) – 156 (168) sts.
St.st. 7 (9) rows.

6th (shaping) row: K.17 (18), k.2 tog., k.18 (20), k.2 tog., k.2 tog.b., k.25 (27), k.2 tog.b., k.20 (22), k.2 tog., k.25 (27), k.2 tog., k.2 tog.b., k.18 (20), k.2 tog.b., k.17 (18) – 148 (160) sts.
St.st. 7 (9) rows.

7th (shaping) row: K.16 (17), k.2 tog., k.17 (19), k.2 tog., k.2 tog.b., k.24 (26), k.2 tog.b., k.18 (20), k.2 tog., k.24 (26), k.2 tog., k.2 tog.b., k.17 (19), k.2 tog.b., k.16 (17) – 140 (152) sts.
St.st. 7 (9) rows.

8th (shaping) row: K.15 (16), k.2 tog., k.16 (18), k.2 tog., k.2 tog.b., k.23 (25), k.2 tog.b., k.16 (18), k.2 tog., k.23 (25), k.2 tog., k.2 tog.b., k.16 (18), k.2 tog.b., k.15 (16) – 132 (144) sts.
St.st. 12 (14) rows.
Now divide sts. for back and front.

Next row: P.30 (33), cast off next 6 sts. for armhole – 1 st. left on right-hand needle – p. next 59 (65) sts. cast off 6, p. to end and work on these 30 (33) sts. for left back.

Shift dress; tangerine dress (pattern p. 148); Aran style dress (pattern p. 151); flared dress (pattern p. 154).

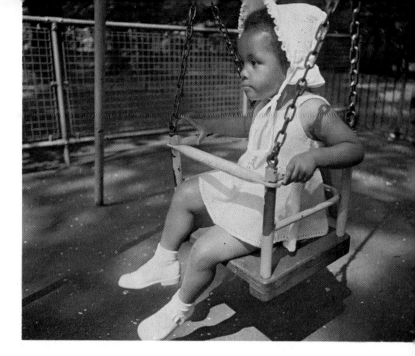

Sun dress (pattern p. 146).

The left back: To shape the armhole: Dec. 1 st. at armhole edge on next row and following 4 (5) alternate rows – 25 (27) sts.

St.st. 16 (18) rows.

To slope the shoulder: Cast off 6 (7) sts. at beginning of next row and 7 sts. on following alternate row; work 1 row, then cast off remaining 12 (13) sts.

The front: With right side of work facing, rejoin yarn to the 60 (66) sts.

To shape the armholes: Dec. 1 st. at each end of next row and following 4 alternate rows – 50 (56) sts.

Next row (wrong side): All k. increasing 1 st. in centre of the row – 51 (57) sts.

Work the 8 pattern rows of border.

K.1 row decreasing 1 st. in centre of row for the 1st size and dec. 1 st. at each end as well as 1 st. in centre for the 2nd size – 50 (54) sts.

Now divide sts. for front neck.

Next row: P.16 (17), cast off next 18 (20) sts., p. to end and work on these 16 (17) sts. for left side.

The left side: Dec. 1 st. at neck edge on the next 3 rows – 13 (14) sts.

Work 1 (5) row(s).

To slope the shoulder: Cast off 6 (7) sts. at beginning of next row; work 1 row, then cast off the remaining 7 sts.

The right side: With right side of work facing, rejoin yarn to remaining 16 (17) sts. and k. to end of row.

Now work as given for left side to end.

The right back: With right side of work facing, rejoin yarn to remaining 30 (33) sts. and k. to end of row.

Now work as given for left back to end.

The Armhole Bands (both alike)

With right side of work facing, rejoin yarn to shoulder and pick up and k.58 (64) sts. along armhole edge.

K.5 rows.

Cast off.

The Neck Band

First join shoulder seams. With right side of work facing, rejoin yarn to centre back and pick up and k.12 (13) sts. across back, 8 (11) sts. down left side of neck, 18 (20) sts. across centre front, 8 (11) sts. from right side of neck and finally 12 (13) sts. across back – 58 (68) sts.

K.5 rows.

Cast off.

To Make Up The Dress

Press on wrong side using a cool iron over a dry cloth. Join centre back seam to within 4 inches of neck edge. Insert zip.

145

Sun Dress

(see illustration p. 145)

**This full-skirted sun dress has a separate
collar which buttons to cover the shoulders**

Contributed by Eugenie Hammond

Materials

Six 20-gramme balls of Lister 2 Spun
4-ply Crêpe Tricel with Nylon for 1st
size; seven balls for 2nd size. For either
size: a pair of No. 9 knitting needles;
a 24-inch No. 9 circular knitting needle;
3 small buttons; 2 medium buttons.

Tension

Work at a tension of 7 stitches and 9 rows
to 1 inch, over the stocking stitch, using No.
9 needles, to obtain the following measurements:

Measurements

INCHES

	1st size	2nd size
All round at underarms	23	24
Length	15	16

Abbreviations

K., knit; p., purl; st., stitch; tog., together;
y.fwd., yarn forward to make a st.; k.2 tog.b.,
k.2 sts. tog. through back of loops; y.o.n.,
yarn over needle to make a st.; sl., slip;
p.s.s.o., pass slipped st. over; st.st., stocking
st. (k. on right side and p. on wrong side);
single rib is k.1 and p.1 alternately.

● *The instructions are given for 1st size.
Where they vary, work figures in brackets
for 2nd size.*

The Bodice

With No. 9 needles cast on 165 (173) sts.
loosely.
1st row: * K.1, p.1; repeat from * 25 (26)
times more, k.61 (65) ,** p.1, k.1; repeat
from ** 25 (26) times more.
2nd row: * P.1, k.1; repeat from * 25 (26)
times more, p.61 (65), ** k.1, p.1; repeat
from ** 25 (26) times more.
Repeat these 2 rows 2 (4) times more.
Next (buttonhole) row: Work to last 3
sts., y.o.n., p.2 tog., k.1.
Work 9 rows straight.

Repeat last 10 rows once more, then work
buttonhole row again.
Work 3 rows straight.
Cast off 48 (50) sts. at beginning of next
2 rows – 69 (73) sts.
This completes back.
Continue on remaining sts. for front.
1st row: K.1, p.1, k.1, p.1, k.2 tog., k. to last
6 sts., k.2 tog.b., p.1, k.1, p.1, k.1.
2nd row: P.1, k.1, p.1, k.1, p. to last 4 sts.,
k.1, p.1, k.1, p.1.
Repeat these 2 rows 4 (5) times more –
59 (61) sts.

To shape the neck:

1st row: Rib 4, k.2 tog., k.9, k.2 tog.b., * p.1, k.1 ; repeat from * 11 (12) times more, p.1, k.2 tog., k.9, k.2 tog.b., rib 4.

2nd row: Rib 4, p.11, rib 25 (27), p.11, rib 4.

3rd row: Rib 4, k.2 tog., k.7, k.2 tog.b., rib 25 (27), k.2 tog., k.7, k.2 tog.b., rib 4.

4th row: Rib 4, p.9, rib 25 (27), p.9, rib 4.
Now divide sts. for front neck.

Next row: Rib 4, k.2 tog., k.5, k.2 tog.b., rib 4, cast off next 17 (19) sts. – 1 st. left on right-hand needle – rib next 3 sts., k.2 tog., k.5, k.2 tog.b., rib 4.

1st side:

1st row: Rib 4, p.7, rib 4.

2nd row: Rib 4, k.2 tog., k.3, k.2 tog.b., rib 4.

3rd row: Rib 4, p.5, rib 4.

4th row: Rib 4, k.2 tog., k.1, k.2 tog.b., rib 4.

5th row: Rib 4, p.3, rib 4.

6th row: Rib 4, sl.1, k.2 tog., p.s.s.o., rib 4 – 9 sts.
Work 40 rows in single rib.
Cast off.

2nd side: With wrong side of work facing, rejoin yarn to remaining 15 sts. and work as given for 1st side to end.

The Skirt

With right side of work facing overlap 5 sts. of buttonhole border at lower edge, rejoin yarn to centre and, using the No. 9 circular knitting needle, working through both thicknesses of overlap, pick up and k.160 (168) sts. all round lower edge. Mark 1st st. to denote beginning of round, then k.1 round.

Shaping round: K.1, y.fwd., * k.19 (20) – work 2 sts. more here on each repeat – y.fwd., k.1, y.fwd.; repeat from * 6 times more, k.19 (20) – work 2 sts. more here on each repeat – y.fwd. – 176 (184) sts.
K.3 rounds.
Repeat last 4 rounds 15 (16) times more, working 2 sts. more in each section where indicated on each repeat of the shaping round, then work shaping round again – 432 (456) sts.
K.1 round.

Next round: * K.2 tog., y.fwd.; repeat from * to end of round.
K.1 round and p.1 round.
Cast off.

The Collar

With No. 9 needles cast on 59 (63) sts. and, beginning right side rows with k.1 and wrong-side rows with p.1, work 4 rows in single rib.
Now work in st.st. with ribbed borders as follows:

1st row: Rib 4, k. to last 4 sts., rib 4.

2nd row: Rib 4, p, to last 4 sts., rib 4.
Repeat these 2 rows 10 (11) times more.
Continue as follows:

1st row: Rib 4, k.13, * p.1, k.1; repeat from * 11 (13) times more, p.1, k.13, rib 4.

2nd row: Rib 4, p.13, * k.1, p.1; repeat from * 11 (13) times more, k.1, p.13, rib 4.
Repeat these 2 rows once more.
Now divide sts. for back neck.

Next row: Rib 4, k.2 tog., k.9, k.2 tog.b., rib 4, cast off next 17 (21) sts. – 1 st. left on right-hand needle – rib next 3 sts., k.2 tog., k.9, k.2 tog.b., rib 4.

1st side:

1st row: Rib 4, p.11, rib 4.

2nd row: Rib 4, k.2 tog., k.7, k.2 tog.b., rib 4.

3rd row: Rib 4, p.9, rib 4.

4th row: Rib 4, k.2 tog., k.5, k.2 tog.b., rib 4.

5th row: Rib 4, p.7, rib 4.

6th row: Rib 4, k.2 tog., k.3, k.2 tog.b., rib 4.

7th row: Rib 4, p.5, rib 4.

8th row: Rib 4, k.2 tog., k.1, k.2 tog.b., rib 4.

9th row: Rib 4, p.3, rib 4.

10th row: Rib 4, sl.1, k.2 tog., p.s.s.o., rib 4 – 9 sts.

11th row: Rib 4, cast off 1 st., rib to end.

12th row: K.1, p.1, k.2 tog., y.fwd., k.2 tog.b., p.1, k.1.

13th row: Rib 7.

14th row: K.1, p.1, sl.1, k.2 tog., p.s.s.o., p.1, k.1.

15th row: Rib 5.

16th row: K.1, sl.1, k.2 tog., p.s.s.o., k.1.
Take remaining 3 sts. tog. and fasten off.

2nd side: With wrong side of work facing, rejoin yarn to remaining 19 sts. and work as given for 1st side to end.

To Make Up The Dress

Press on wrong side using a cool iron over a dry cloth. Sew straps to back and sew on small buttons. Sew medium button to each side of front and attach collar.

Tangerine Dress with White Stitching

(see illustration p. 144)

The front panel is outlined with embroidered chain stitch and hems are edged with an attractive picot

Materials

Five 25-gramme balls of Bairnswear Crêpe Wool, knits as 4-ply for 1st size; six balls for 2nd size; seven balls for 3rd size. For any one size: a pair each of No. 10 and No. 12 knitting needles; 3 buttons; oddment of contrast colour.

Tension

Work at a tension of 15 stitches and 20 rows to 2 inches, over the stocking stitch, using No. 10 needles, to obtain the following measurements:

Abbreviations

K., knit; p., purl; st., stitch; tog., together; dec., decrease (by working 2 sts. tog.); inc., increase (by working twice into same st.); w.fwd., wool forward to make a st.; s.k.p.o., slip 1, k.1, pass slipped st. over; sl., slip; p.s.s.o., pass slipped st. over; st.st., stocking st. (k. on right side and p. on wrong side); garter st. is k. on every row.

● *The instructions are given for 1st size. Where they vary, work figures in first brackets for 2nd size; figures in second brackets for 3rd size.*

Measurements

	INCHES		
	1st size	2nd size	3rd size
All round at under-arms	22	$23\frac{1}{2}$	25
Side seam	$10\frac{3}{4}$	$11\frac{3}{4}$	$12\frac{3}{4}$
Length	$15\frac{1}{2}$	$16\frac{3}{4}$	18
Sleeve seam	$2\frac{1}{4}$	$2\frac{1}{2}$	$2\frac{3}{4}$

The Back

With No. 10 needles cast on 121 (129) (137) sts. and, beginning with a k. row, st.st. 6 rows.

Next (picot) row: K.1, * w.fwd., k.2 tog.; repeat from * to end.

Next row: All p. **

Continuing in st.st. work 12 rows then dec. 1 st. at each end of the next row and every following 5th row until the 19th (20th) (21st) dec. row has been worked — 83 (89) (95) sts.

Work 3 (8) (13) rows.

To shape the armholes: Cast off 3 sts. at beginning of next 2 rows, then dec. 1 st. at each end of the next row and following 7 (8) (9) right-side rows — 61 (65) (69) sts.

Now divide sts. for back opening.

Next row: P.28 (30) (32) and leave these sts. on a spare needle for left side, p. to end and work on these 33 (35) (37) sts. for the right side.

The right side:

1st row: All k.

2nd row: K.4, p. to end.

Repeat these 2 rows once more.

Next (buttonhole) row: K. to last 3 sts., w.fwd., k.2 tog., k.1.

Work 7 rows.

Work last 8 rows once more.

Repeat buttonhole row, then work 1 row, ending at armhole edge.

To slope the shoulder: Cast off 5 (6) (7) sts. at beginning of next row; 6 (6) (7) sts. on following alternate row and 6 (7) (7) sts. on next alternate row.

Work 1 row.

Cast off remaining 16 sts.

The left side: With right side of work facing, rejoin wool to the sts. left on spare needle, cast on 5 sts. k. to end of row.

1st row: P. to last 4 sts., k.4.

2nd row: All k.

Repeat these 2 rows 10 times more.

To slope the shoulder: Work as given for right side.

The Front

Work as given for back to **

Now work in st.st. with centre panel as follows:

1st row: K.51 (55) (59), p.1, k.2, k.2 tog., w.fwd., k.1, w.fwd., s.k.p.o., k.3, k.2 tog., w.fwd., k.1, w.fwd., s.k.p.o., k.2, p.1, k.51 (55) (59).

2nd and every alternate row: P. 51 (55) (59), k.1, p.17, k.1, p.51 (55) (59).

3rd row: K.51 (55) (59), p.1, k.1, * k.2 tog., w.fwd., k.3, w.fwd., s.k.p.o., k.1; repeat from * once, p.1, k.51 (55) (59).

5th row: K.51 (55) (59), p.1, k.2 tog., w.fwd., k.5, w.fwd., sl.1, k.2 tog., p.s.s.o., w.fwd., k.5, w.fwd., s.k.p.o., p.1, k.51 (55) (59).

7th row: K.51 (55) (59), p.1, k.1, * w.fwd., s.k.p.o., k.3, k.2 tog., w.fwd., k.1; repeat from * once, p.1, k.51 (55) (59).

9th row: K.51 (55) (59), p.1, k.2, w.fwd., s.k.p.o., k.1, k.2 tog., w.fwd., k.3, w.fwd., s.k.p.o., k.1, k.2 tog., w.fwd., k.2, p.1, k.51 (55) (59).

11th row: K.51 (55) (59), p.1, k.3, w.fwd., sl.1, k.2 tog., p.s.s.o., w.fwd., k.5, w.fwd., sl.1, k.2 tog., p.s.s.o., w.fwd., k.3, p.1, k.51 (55) (59).

12th row: As 2nd row.

These 12 rows form the pattern; keeping continuity of the pattern dec. 1 st. at each end of the next row and every following 5th row until the 19th (20th) (21st) dec. row has been worked — 83 (89) (95) sts.

Work 3 (8) (13) rows straight.

To shape the armholes: Cast off 3 sts. at beginning of next 2 rows, then dec. 1 st. at each end of the next row and following 7 (8) (9) right-side rows — 61 (65) (69) sts.

Work 14 rows, ending with a right-side row.

Now divide sts. for front neck.

Next row: P.21 (23) (25) and leave these sts. on a spare needle for right side, cast off the next 19 sts., p. to end and work on these 21 (23) (25) sts. for the left side.

The left side: Dec. 1 st. at neck edge on the next row and following 3 alternate rows.

On 17 (19) (21) sts., work 1 row back to armhole edge.

To slope the shoulder: Cast off 5 (6) (7) sts. at beginning of next row and 6 (6) (7) sts. on the following alternate row.

Work 1 row, then cast off remaining 6 (7) (7) sts.

The right side: With right side of work facing, rejoin wool to sts. left on spare needle and k. to end of row.

Now work as given for the left side to end.

The Sleeves (both alike)

With No. 12 needles cast on 46 (48) (50) sts. and work as given for back to **.

Change to No. 10 needles and st.st. 2 rows.

Inc. 1 st. at each end of the next row and following 2 right-side rows – 52 (54) (56) sts.

Work 3 rows, then inc. 1 st. at each end of next row and the 2 following 4th rows – 58 (60) (62) sts.

Work 1 (3) (5) row(s).

To shape the sleeve top: Cast off 3 sts. at beginning of next 2 rows, then dec. 1 st. at each end of next row and following 9 (10) (11) right-side rows – 32 sts.

P.1 row.

Cast off.

The Neck Band

First join shoulder seams. With *wrong* side of work facing, rejoin wool to inner edge of garter st. border at centre back and, using No. 12 needles, pick up and k.13 sts. across back, 13 sts. from neck edge, 19 sts. from centre front, 13 sts. from neck and 13 sts. across back to garter st. border – 71 sts.

Beginning with a p. row, st.st. 3 rows.

Work picot row as given for back.

Beginning with a p. row, st.st. 5 rows.

Cast off very loosely.

To Make Up The Dress

Press on wrong side, using a warm iron over a damp cloth. Using a contrast colour and bodkin, work a row of chain stitch along the 'p' st. ridge at each side of centre panel. Set in sleeves, then join sleeve and side seams. Fold neck band to right side at picot row and slip st. in place on right side. Fold hems at picot rows and sew in place. Neaten lower edge of back opening. Sew on buttons.

Aran Style Dress

(see illustration p. 144)

Don't be put off by the stitch detail in this design. There are only 4 rows to the pattern

Materials

For either size : Eleven 25 gramme balls of Lister Lavenda Double Knitting Wool; a pair each of No. 8 and No. 10 knitting needles; a cable needle.

Tension

Work at a tension of 12 stitches and 15 rows to 2 inches, over the double moss stitch, using No. 8 needles, to obtain the following measurements :

Measurements

	INCHES	
	1st size	2nd size
All round at underarms	$23\frac{1}{2}$	25
Side seam	11	12
Length	$16\frac{1}{4}$	$17\frac{1}{2}$
Sleeve seam	8	9

Abbreviations

K., knit; p., purl; st., stitch; tog., together; dec., decrease (by working 2 sts. tog.); inc., increase (by working twice into same st.); sl., slip; 3 in 1 (k. into next st. but do not sl. st. off needle, bring wool to front between the needles to make a st., then k. into same st. again); tw.2 rt., twist 2 right (k. into front of 2nd st. on left-hand needle then k. into front of 1st st. and sl. both sts. off needle tog.); tw.2 lt., twist 2 left (sl. next st. onto cable needle and leave at front of work, k.1, then k. st. from cable needle); c.3b., cable 3 back (sl. next 2 sts. onto cable needle and leave at back of work, k.1, then k.2 from cable needle); c.3f., cable 3 front (sl. next st. onto cable needle and leave at front of work, k.2, then k. st. from cable needle); k. or p.1b., k. or p.1 st. through back of loop; single rib is k.1 and p.1 alternately; d.m.st., double moss st. (k.1 and p.1 alternately on 2 rows and on subsequent 2 rows the sts. are reversed).

● *The instructions are given for 1st size. Where they vary, work figures in brackets for 2nd size.*

The Back

With No. 8 needles cast on 105 (109) sts.
1st foundation row: * K.1, p.1; repeat from * 7 (8) times, k.1, p.2, k.2, p.2, k.6, p.2, k.2, p.1, k.1b., p.12, k.1b., p.1, k.3, p.1, k.3, p.1, k.1b., p.12, k.1b., p.1, k.2, p.2, k.6, p.2, k.2, p.2, ** k.1, p.1; repeat from ** 7 (8) times, k.1.

2nd foundation row: * P.1, k.1; repeat from * 7 (8) times, p.1, k.2, p.2, k.2, p.6, k.2, p.2, k.1, p.1b., ** 3 in 1, p.3 tog.; repeat from ** twice, p.1b., k.1, p.3, k.1, p.3, k.1, p.1b., *** p.3 tog., 3 in 1; repeat from *** twice, p.1b., k.1, p.2, k.2, p.6, k.2, p.2, k.2, **** p.1, k.1; repeat from **** 7 (8) times, p.1.

Now work in pattern as follows:

1st row: * P.1, k.1; repeat from * 7 (8) times, p.3, tw.2 rt., p.2, c.3b., c.3f., p.2, tw.2 lt., p.1, k.1b., p.12, k.1b., p.1, c.3b., p.1, c.3f., p.1, k.1b., p.12, k.1b., p.1, tw.2 rt., p.2, c.3b., c.3f., p.2, tw.2 lt., p.3, ** k.1, p.1; repeat from ** 7 (8) times.

2nd row: * K.1, p.1; repeat from * 7 (8) times, k.3, p.2, k.2, p.6, k.2, p.2, k.1, p.1b., ** p.3 tog., 3 in 1; repeat from ** twice, p.1b., k.1, p.3, k.1, p.3, k.1, p.1b., *** 3 in 1, p.3 tog.; repeat from *** twice, p.1b., k.1, p.2, k.2, p.6, k.2, p.2, k.3, **** p.1, k.1; repeat from **** 7 (8) times.

3rd row: * K.1, p.1; repeat from * 7 (8) times, k.1, p.2, tw.2 rt., p.2, c.3b., c.3f., p.2, tw.2 lt., p.1, k.1b., p.12, k.1b., p.1, c.3b., p.1, c.3f., p.1, k.1b., p.12, k.1b., p.1, tw.2 rt., p.2, c.3b., c.3f., p.2, tw.2 lt., p.2, ** k.1, p.1; repeat from ** 7 (8) times, k.1.

4th row: * P.1, k.1; repeat from * 7 (8) times, p.1, k.2, p.2, k.2, p.6, k.2, p.2, k.1, p.1b., ** 3 in 1, p.3 tog.; repeat from ** twice, p.1b., k.1, p.3, k.1, p.3, k.1, p.1b., *** p.3 tog., 3 in 1; repeat from *** twice, p.1b., k.1, p.2, k.2, p.6, k.2, p.2, k.2, **** p.1, k.1; repeat from **** 7 (8) times, p.1.

These 4 rows form the pattern; keeping continuity of the pattern work 2 rows, then dec. 1 st. at each end of next and every following 8th row until the 8th dec. row has been worked – 89 (93) sts.

Work 17 (25) rows straight.

To shape the armholes: Cast off 4 sts. at beginning of next 2 rows, then dec. 1 st. at each end of next 5 rows – 71 (75) sts.

Work 1 row, then dec. 1 st. at each end of next row – 69 (73) sts.

This completes armhole shaping.

Work 25 (27) rows, ending with a wrong-side row.

To slope the shoulders: Cast off 7 sts. at beginning of next 4 rows and 7 (8) sts. on following 2 rows.

Break off wool and leave remaining 27 (29) sts. on a spare needle for collar.

The Front

Work as back until armhole shaping has been completed – 69 (73) sts.

Work 12 (14) rows straight, ending with a right-side row.

Now divide sts. for front neck.

Next row: Pattern 29 (31) and leave these sts. on spare needle for right side, pattern next 11 sts. and leave these on a stitch-holder for collar, pattern to end and work on these 29 (31) sts. for left side.

Note: When shaping neck be careful to count the sts. over the 'Blackberry St. Panel' and work the 3 in 1 only when you have enough sts. to work a compensating p.3 tog.

The left side: To shape the neck: Dec. 1 st. at neck edge on next 8 (9) rows – 21 (22) sts.

Work 4 (3) rows, ending at armhole edge.

To slope the shoulder: Cast off 7 sts. at beginning of next and following alternate row; work 1 row, then cast off remaining 7 (8) sts.

The right side: With right side of work facing, rejoin wool to the 29 (31) sts. on spare needle and pattern to end of row.

Now work as given for left side to end.

The Sleeves (both alike)

With No. 10 needles cast on 39 sts. and, beginning right-side rows with k.1 and wrong-side rows with p.1, work 13 rows in single rib.

Next (inc.) row: Rib 7, * inc. in next st., rib 7; repeat from * to end – 43 sts.

Change to No. 8 needles.

1st row: * P.1, k.1; repeat from * 4 times, p.2, k.2, p.2, k.1b., p.1, k.3, p.1, k.3, p.1, k.1b., p.2, k.2, p.2, ** k.1, p.1; repeat from ** 4 times.

2nd row: * K.1, p.1; repeat from * 4 times, k.2, p.2, k.2, p.1b., k.1, p.3, k.1, p.3, k.1, p.1b., k.2, p.2, k.2, ** p.1, k.1; repeat from ** 4 times.

3rd row: * K.1, p.1; repeat from * 3 times, k.1, p.3, tw.2 rt., p.2, k.1b., p.1, c.3b., p.1, c.3f., p.1, k.1b., p.2, tw.2 lt., p.3, ** k.1, p.1; repeat from ** 3 times, k.1.

4th row: * P.1, k.1; repeat from * 3 times, p.1, k.3, p.2, k.2, p.1b., k.1, p.3, k.1, p.3, k.1, p.1b., k.2, p.2, k.3, ** p.1, k.1; repeat from ** 3 times, p.1.

These 4 rows set the d.m.st. pattern for the sleeves.

Keeping continuity of the pattern – that is work the twist and cable on each right-side row – work 2 rows, then inc. 1 st. at each end of next and every following 6th row until the 5th (6th) inc. row has been worked – 53 (55) sts.

Work 16 rows straight, ending with a wrong-side row.

To shape the sleeve top: Cast off 4 sts. at beginning of next 2 rows, then dec. 1 st. at each end of next and following 3 right-side rows – 37 (39) sts.

Work 1 row, then cast off 2 sts. at beginning of next 8 rows.

Cast off remaining 21 (23) sts.

The Collar

First join right shoulder seam. With right side of work facing, rejoin wool to neck edge at left shoulder and, using No. 10 needles, pick up and k.20 sts. down left side of neck, k. the 11 sts. at centre front, pick up and k.20 sts. from right side of neck and k. the 27 (29) sts. at back.

On these 78 (80) sts. work 9 rows in single rib.

Change to No. 8 needles and rib a further 14 rows.

Cast off very loosely in rib.

To Make Up The Dress

Press lightly on wrong side, avoiding the ribbing, using a warm iron over a damp cloth. Join left shoulder seam, continuing seam across collar. Set in sleeves ; join sleeve and side seams. Fold collar to right side.

Flared Dress

(see illustration p. 144)

**All little girls love to twist and twirl. This
dress is a must for them**

Materials

Eight 20 gramme balls of Lee Target
Duo 4-ply Crêpe Tricel with Nylon for
1st size; nine balls for 2nd size. For
either size; a pair each of No. 9 and
No. 10 knitting needles; a 24-inch
No. 9 circular needle; 9 motifs; 6
buttons.

Tension

Work at a tension of 7 stitches and 9 rows
to 1 inch, over the stocking stitch, using
No. 9 needles, to obtain the following
measurements:

Measurements

INCHES

	1st size	2nd size
All round at underarms	23	24
Side seam	$12\frac{1}{2}$	$13\frac{1}{2}$
Length	$16\frac{3}{4}$	18

Abbreviations

K., knit; p., purl; st., stitch; tog., together;
dec., decrease (by working 2 sts. tog.);
y.r.n., yarn round needle to make a st.;
y.fwd., yarn forward to make a st.; st.st.,
stocking st. (k. on right side and p. on wrong
side); garter st. is k. on every row.

● *The instructions are given for 1st size.
Where they vary, work figures in brackets
for 2nd size.*

The Bodice

With No. 9 needles cast on 164 (172) sts.
loosely.
1st row: All k.
2nd row: K.4, p. to last 4 sts., k.4.
Repeat these 2 rows 3 (6) times more.
Next (buttonhole) row: K. to last 3 sts.,
y.fwd., k.2 tog., k.1.
Keeping garter st. borders as set, st.st. 11
rows.
Work the buttonhole row, then work a
further 9 (7) rows.
Now divide sts. for front and backs.

Next row: K.38 (39), cast off 8 (10) sts. –
1 st. left on right-hand needle not included in next item, k.71 (73) sts., cast off
8 (10), k. to end and work on these 38 (39)
sts. for the right back.
The right back:
1st row: K.4, p. to end.
Keeping the garter st. border at centre back
edge work 15 rows decreasing 1 st. at
armhole edge on each right-side row and
making a buttonhole, as before, on the 1st
and 13th (3rd and 15th) of these rows. This
completes armhole shaping – 30 (31) sts.
Work 17 (19) rows making a buttonhole

on the 10th (12th) of these rows, ending at armhole edge.

To slope the shoulder: Cast off 8 sts. at beginning of next row and 9 sts. on following alternate row; work 1 row; cast off remaining 13 (14) sts.

The front: With wrong side of work facing, rejoin yarn to centre 72 (74) sts. and p. 1 row.

Dec. 1 st. at each end of next and following 7 right-side rows — 56 (58) sts.

Work 7 (9) rows, ending with a p. row.

Now divide sts. for front neck.

Next row: K. 20, turn and p. to end for 1st side.

Dec. 1 st. at neck edge on next and following 2 alternate rows — 17 sts.

Work 3 rows, ending at armhole edge.

To slope the shoulder: Cast off 8 sts. at beginning of next row; work 1 row, then cast off remaining 9 sts.

With right side facing, rejoin yarn to dividing row, cast off next 16 (18) sts., k. to end.

Now work as given for 1st side to end.

The left back: With wrong side of work facing, rejoin yarn to the 38 (39) sts., p. to last 4 sts., k.4.

Keeping garter st. border, dec. 1 st. at armhole edge on next and following 7 right-side rows — 30 (31) sts.

Work 18 (20) rows, ending at armhole edge.

To slope the shoulder: Cast off 8 sts. at beginning of next row and 9 sts. on following alternate row; work 1 row, then cast off remaining 13 (14) sts.

The Skirt

With right side of work facing, overlap the garter st. borders at lower edge, rejoin yarn to centre and, using the No. 9 circular needle, pick up and k. 2 sts. through both thicknesses of border, then pick up and k.150 (158) sts. evenly all round lower edge and 2 sts. through both thicknesses of borders — 154 (162) sts.

Mark 1st st. to denote beginning of round.

1st round: All p.

2nd round: * Y.r.n., p.2 tog.; repeat from * to end.

3rd round: All k.

4th round: All p.

K.6 rounds decreasing 1 st. at end of last round on the 1st size only — 153 (162) sts.

Now shape skirt as follows:

Next (shaping) round: K.8 (9), y.fwd., k.1, y.fwd., * k.16 (17), y.fwd., k.1, y.fwd.; repeat from * 7 times more, k.8 — 171 (180) sts.

K.3 rounds.

Next (shaping) round: K.9 (10), y.fwd., k.1, y.fwd., * k.18 (19), y.fwd., k.1, y.fwd.; repeat from * 7 times more, k.9 — 189 (198) sts.

K.3 rounds.

Repeat last 4 rounds 15 (16) times more working 1 st. more at each end and 2 sts. more between the shapings on each repeat — 459 (486) sts.

Next round: All p.

Next round: All k. increasing 1 st. at end of this round on the 1st size only — 460 (486) sts.

Next round: * Y.r.n., p.2 tog.; repeat from * to end.

Next round: All k.

Next round: All p.

Cast off k.wise.

The Armhole Bands (both alike)

With right side of work facing, rejoin yarn to shoulder edge and, using No. 10 needles, pick up and k.63 (65) sts. all round armhole edge.

K.3 rows.

Cast off.

The Neck Band

First join shoulder seams. With right side of work facing, rejoin yarn to centre back and, using No. 10 needles, pick up and k.12 (13) sts. across back, 34 (38) sts. all round front neck and 12 (13) sts. across back — 58 (64) sts.

K.3 rows.

Work a buttonhole on next row.

K.3 rows.

Cast off.

To Make Up The Dress

Press on wrong side using a cool iron over a dry cloth. Sew on buttons. Make a length of twisted cord for waist. Trim with motifs.

Yellow Beret

Materials

Two 25-gramme balls of Wendy Double Knit Nylonised for 1st size; three balls for 2nd size. For either size: a set of four double-pointed No. 9 knitting needles.

Tension and Size

Worked at a tension of 1 repeat of the pattern to $2\frac{1}{4}$ inches in width across widest part the hat will be suitable for the 1 to 3-year-olds.

Abbreviations

K., knit; p., purl; st., stitch; tog., together; sl., slip; p.s.s.o., pass the slipped st. over; k.2 tog.b., k.2 tog. through back of loops; up 1 (pick up the thread which lies between the needles and k. into back of it thus making a st.); single rib is k.1 and p.1 alternately.

● *The instructions are given for 1st size. Where they vary, work figures in brackets for 2nd size.*

Left to right – Pill box hat (pattern p. 162); bobble cap and scarf (pattern p. 218); pink helmet (pattern p. 159); two-colour hat (pattern p. 160); yellow beret (pattern above); red balaclava (pattern p. 158).

To Make

Cast on 84 (96) sts. evenly between three needles and work 12 rounds in single rib.
Next (inc.) round: * K.5, up 1, p.7, up 1; repeat from * to end – 98 (112) sts.
Now work in pattern as follows:
1st round: * K.5, p.9; repeat from * to end.
2nd round: * K.1, up 1, k.3, up 1, k.1, p.9; repeat from * to end.
3rd round: * K.7, p.9; repeat from * to end.
4th round: * K.1, up 1, k.5, up 1, k.1, p.9; repeat from * to end.
5th round: * K.9, p.9; repeat from * to end.
6th round: * K.1, up 1, k.7, up 1, k.1, p.9; repeat from * to end.
7th round: * K.11, p.9; repeat from * to end.
8th round: * K.1, up 1, k.9, up 1, k.1, p.9; repeat from * to end.
9th round: * K.13, p.9: repeat from * to end.
10th round: * K.1, up 1, k.11, up 1, k.1, p.9; repeat from * to end – 168 (192) sts.
11th to 18th rounds: * K.15, p.9; repeat from * to end.
To shape the crown:
1st round: * K.1, k.2 tog.b., k.9, k.2 tog., k.1, p.9; repeat from * to end.
2nd round: * K.13, p.9; repeat from * to end.
3rd round: * K.1, k.2 tog.b., k.7, k.2 tog., k.1, p.9; repeat from * to end.
4th round: * K.11, p.9; repeat from * to end.
5th round: * K.1, k.2 tog.b., k.5, k.2 tog., k.1, p.9; repeat from * to end.
6th round: * K.9, p.9; repeat from * to end.
7th round: * K.1, k.2 tog.b., k.3, k.2 tog., k.1, p.9; repeat from * to end.
8th round: * K.7, p.9; repeat from * to end.
9th round: * K.1, k.2 tog.b., k.1, k.2 tog., k.1, p.9; repeat from * to end.
10th round: * K.5, p.9; repeat from * to end.
11th round: * K.1, sl.1, k.2 tog., p.s.s.o., k.1, p.9; repeat from * to end.
12th round: * K.3, p.9; repeat from * to end.
13th round: * Sl.1, k.2 tog., p.s.s.o., p.9; repeat from * to end.
14th round: * K.1, p.9; repeat from * to end.
15th round: * K.1, p.2 tog., p.5, p.2 tog.; repeat from * to end.
16th round: * K.1, p.7; repeat from * to end.
17th round: * K.1, p.2 tog., p.3, p.2 tog.; repeat from * to end.
18th round: * K.1, p.5; repeat from * to end.
19th round: * K.1, p.2 tog., p.1, p.2 tog.; repeat from * to end.
20th round: * K.1, p.3; repeat from * to end.
21st round: * K.1, sl.1, k.2 tog., p.s.s.o.; repeat from * to end.
Break off wool; run end through remaining 14 (16) sts., draw up and fasten off securely.
Press with a warm iron over a damp cloth.

Red Balaclava

(see illustration p. 156)

Materials

For either size: Three 25-gramme balls of Lee Target Motoravia Double Knitting Wool; a pair each of No. 9 and No. 10 knitting needles.

Abbreviations

K., knit; p., purl; st., stitch; single rib is k.1 and p.1 alternately.

Tension and Size

Worked at a tension of 12 stitches and 16 rows to 2 inches, slightly stretched, over the double rib, using No. 9 needles, the balaclava will fit the 1 to 3-year olds.

To Make

With No. 10 needles cast on 114 (122) sts. and work 6 rows in single rib.

Next row: Rib 12 and leave these sts. on safety-pin, rib until 12 sts. remain, turn and leave these 12 sts. on safety-pin.

Change to No. 9 needles and on 90 (98) sts. work in double rib as follows:

1st row: P.2, * k.2, p.2; repeat from * to end.

2nd row: K.2, * p.2, k.2; repeat from * to end.

Repeat these 2 rows 15 (16) times more.

To shape for back section: Cast off 32 (36) sts. at beginning of next 2 rows — 26 sts.

Work 34 (38) rows straight.

Break off wool and leave sts. on spare needle.

Slip the 12 sts. at right-hand side onto No. 10 needle with point to inner edge, rejoin wool and using this needle, pick up and k.26 (28) sts. along row ends of main part, k. across the 26 sts. on spare needle, pick up and k.26 (28) sts. along other side of main part, then rib the 12 sts. on safety-pin at left-hand side — 102 (106) sts.

Work 13 rows in single rib.

Change to No. 9 needles and rib a further 14 rows.

Cast off very loosely in rib.

To Make Up The Balaclava

Join the two back seams, then join front seam.

Pink Helmet

(see illustration p. 156)

Materials

Two $\frac{3}{4}$-ounce balls of Lee Target Super Crimp Bri-Nylon Double Knitting; a pair each of No. 6 and No. 8 knitting needles.

Tension and Size

Worked at a tension of 11 stitches and 14 rows to 2 inches, over the pattern, using No. 6 needles, the helmet will fit the one to three-year-olds.

Abbreviations

K., knit; p., purl; st., stitch; tog., together; up 1 (pick up the thread which lies between the needles and k. into back of it thus making a st.); 3 in 1 (k. into front of next st. but do not slip st. off needle, bring yarn to front between the needles to make a st., then k. into same st. again and slip st. off needle).

The Main Part

With No. 6 needles cast on 90 sts. and k.1 row.

Now work in pattern as follows:

1st row: K.1, * p.3 tog., 3 in 1; repeat from * to last st., k.1.

2nd row: All p.

3rd row: K.1, * 3 in 1, p.3 tog.; repeat from * to last st., k.1.

4th row: All p.

Repeat these 4 rows 4 times more, then work first 2 rows again.

Next (dec.) row: K.44, k.2 tog., k.44 – 89 sts.

To shape the crown:

1st (shaping) row: * K.9, k.2 tog.; repeat from * to last st., k.1.

K.3 rows.

2nd (shaping) row: * K.8, k.2 tog.; repeat from * to last st., k.1.

K.3 rows.

Repeat last 4 rows 5 times more working 1 st. less between the decreases on each repeat, then work shaping row again – 25 sts.

Next row: All k.

Next row: K.1, * k.2 tog., k.1; repeat from * to end – 17 sts.

Next row: K.1, * k.2 tog., repeat from * to end – 9 sts.

Break off yarn; run end through remaining sts., draw up and fasten off securely, then join row ends to form back seam.

The Ear Flaps (make 2)

With No. 8 needles cast on 5 sts. and k.38 rows.

1st (shaping) row: K.2, up 1, k.1, up 1, k.2. K.3 rows.

2nd (shaping) row: K.2, up 1, k. to last 2 sts., up 1, k.2. K.3 rows.

Repeat last 4 rows 8 times more – 25 sts. Cast off.

To Make Up The Helmet

Do not press. Sew ear flaps in place.

Two-Colour Hat

(see illustration p. 156)

Materials

Two 25-gramme balls of Lee Target Motoravia Double Knitting Wool in main colour and one ball in contrast colour; a pair each of No. 8 and No.10 knitting needles.

Tension and Size

Worked at a tension of 4 repeats of the bobble pattern to 2 inches in width, using No. 8 needles, the hat will fit the 2–3-year-olds.

Abbreviations

K., knit; p., purl; st., stitch; tog., together; up 1 (pick up the thread which lies between the needles and k. into back of it thus making a st.); 5 in 1 (k. into front of next st. but do not slip st. off needle,* bring wool to front between the needles to make a st. and k. into same st. again; repeat from * once more thus working 5 sts. in 1 st.); m., main colour; c., contrast colour.

The Main Part

With No. 8 needles and c., cast on 63 sts. *very* loosely.

1st row: With c., all k.
2nd row: With c., k.1, * 5 in 1, k.1; repeat from * to end.
3rd row: With c., all p.
4th row: With c., k.1, * p.5 tog., k.1; repeat from * to end.
  Join on m.
5th row: With m., all k.
6th row: With m., k.2, * 5 in 1, k.1; repeat from * to last st., k.1 more.
7th row: With m., all p.
8th row: With m., k.2, * p.5 tog., k.1; repeat from * to last st., k.1 more.
  Repeat these 8 rows once more, then work first 4 rows again.
  Break off c. and continue with m. only.
Next (inc.) row: K.1, * up 1, k.2; repeat from * to end – 93 sts.
Next row (wrong side): All k.

K.1 row and p.1 row.
Next (dec.) row: K.17, * k.2 tog., k.17; repeat from * 3 times – 89 sts.
Next row (wrong side): All k.
  To shape the crown:
1st row: * K.9, k.2 tog.; repeat from * to last st., k.1.
2nd row: All p.
3rd row: * K.8, k.2 tog.; repeat from * to last st., k.1.
4th row (wrong side): All k.
  Repeat these 4 rows twice more working 1 st. less between the decreases on each repeat – 41 sts.
Next row: * K.3, k.2 tog.; repeat from * to last st., k.1.
Next row: All p.
Next row: * K.2, k.2 tog.; repeat from * to last st., k.1.
Next row: All p.
Next row: * K.1, k.2 tog.; repeat from * to last st., k.1.

Next row: All p.

Next row: * K.2 tog.; repeat from * to loot ot., k.1.

Break off yarn; run end through remaining 9 sts., draw up and fasten off securely, then join row ends to form back seam.

The Ear Flaps (make 2)

With No. 10 needles and m., cast on 4 sts and k.46 rows.

1st (shaping) row: K.2, up 1, k.2.
K.3 rows.

2nd (shaping) row: K.2, up 1, k.1, up 1, k.2.
K.3 rows.

3rd (shaping) row: K.2, up 1, k. to last 2 sts., up 1, k.2.
K.3 rows.

Repeat last 4 rows 7 times more, then work 3rd shaping row again – 25 sts.
K.1 row.
Cast off.

To Make Up The Hat

Press lightly on wrong side using a warm iron over a damp cloth. Sew ear flaps in place.

Pill Box Hat

(See illustration p. 156)

Materials

Three 25-gramme balls of Lee Target Motoravia Double Knitting Wool; a pair each of No. 9 and No. 10 knitting needles; canvas and lining for crown section.

Tension and Size

Worked at a tension of 6 stitches and 8 rows to 1 inch, over the stocking stitch, using No. 9 needles the hat will fit the 2-3-year-olds.

Abbreviations

K., knit; p., purl; st., stitch; tog., together; up 1 (pick up the thread which lies between the needles and k. into back of it thus making a st.); st.st., stocking st. (k. on right side and p. on wrong side).

The Main Part

With No. 9 needles cast on 95 sts. and k.7 rows.

Now work in pattern as follows:

1st (loop st.) row: K.1, * insert needle into next st., wind wool clockwise over needle and first finger of left hand then over needle only and draw these 2 loops through onto right-hand needle letting original st. drop off needle in the usual way, slip the 2 loops back onto left-hand needle and k. them tog. through back of loops; repeat from * to last st., k.1.

2nd row: All k.

3rd row: All p.

4th row: All k.

Repeat these 4 rows 3 times more, then work first 2 rows again.

Cast off.

The Crown

With No. 9 needles cast on 100 sts. and k.2 rows.

Next row: All p.

To shape the crown:

1st row: K.1, * k.2 tog., k.9; repeat from * to end.

2nd row: All p.

3rd row: K.1, * k.2 tog., k.8; repeat from * to end – 82 sts.

4th row: All p.

Repeat 3rd and 4th rows 6 times more working 1 st. less between the decreases on each repeat, then work the shaping row again – 19 sts.

Next row: P.1, * p.2 tog.; repeat from * to end – 10 sts.

Break off wool; run end through remaining sts., draw up and fasten off securely, then join row ends.

The Ear Flaps (make 2)

With No. 10 needles cast on 4 sts. and k.46 rows.

1st (shaping) row: K.2, up 1, k.2.

K.3 rows.

2nd (shaping) row: K.2, up 1, k.1, up 1, k.2.

K.3 rows.

3rd (shaping) row: K.2, up 1, k. to last 2 sts., up 1, k.2.

K.3 rows.

Repeat last 4 rows 7 times more, then work 3rd shaping row again — 25 sts.

K.1 row.

Cast off.

To Make Up The Hat

Join row ends of main part to form a circle. Press crown flat. Cut circle of canvas and lining to fit crown and sew in place, then join crown to main part. Sew ear flaps in position.

Angel Top and Tights

Two-colour top with ribbed tights. The lacy pattern is repeated at ankle on tights to make a matching set

Materials

Eight 25 gramme balls of Wendy 4-ply Nylonised in main colour and four balls in a contrast colour; a pair of No. 10 knitting needles; a set of four double-pointed No. 10 needles; 2 buttons; a waist length of elastic.

Tension and Size

Worked at a tension of 15 stitches — 3 repeats of the pattern — to 2 inches in width and 3 repeats of the pattern to 2 inches in depth, the set will fit baby aged six to twelve months.

Abbreviations

K., knit; p., purl; st., stitch; tog., together; dec., decrease (by working 2 sts. tog.); inc., increase (by working twice into same st.); sl., slip; p.s.s.o., pass slipped st. over; y.fwd., yarn forward to make a st.; k. or p. 2 tog.b., k. or p. 2 sts. tog. through back of loops; up 1 (pick up the thread which lies between the needles and k. into back of it thus making a st.); st.st., stocking st. (k. on right side and p. on wrong side); garter st. is k. on every row; single rib is k.1 and p.1 alternately; m., main colour; c., contrast colour.

● *If baby is above average size the set can be made on size 9 needles giving a slightly looser texture to the fabric.*

The Angel Top

The Back and Front (both alike)

With No. 10 needles and m., cast on 104 sts. and k.3 rows.

Join on c. and work in pattern as follows:

1st row (right side): With c., k.2, * k.1 winding yarn 3 times round needle; repeat from * to last 2 sts., k.2.

2nd row: With c., k.2, * sl. next 5 sts. onto right-hand needle dropping extra loops to make 5 long sts., sl. these back onto left-hand needle and, working through front of all 5 loops together, work k.1, p.1, k.1, p.1, k.1 and let original sts. drop off needle; repeat from * to last 2 sts., k.2.

3rd row: With m., all k.

4th row: With m., all k.

These 4 rows form the pattern; repeat them 9 times more, then work 1st and 2nd rows again. Break off c. and continue with m. only.

To shape the armholes:

1st row: Cast off 4, k. to end.

2nd row: Cast off 4, k. to end.

3rd row: K.2 tog., k. to last 2 sts., k.2 tog.

4th row: All p.

Repeat 3rd and 4th rows 3 times more – 88 sts.

Next (dec.) row (right side): * P.2 tog.; repeat from * to end – 44 sts.

Break off yarn and leave sts. on spare needle until required for yoke.

The Sleeves (both alike)

With No. 10 needles and m., cast on 36 sts. and work 10 rows in single rib.

Next (inc.) row: K.1, * up 1, k.2; repeat from * to last st., up 1, k.1 – 54 sts.

P.1 row, then k.2 rows.

Join on c. and work the 4 pattern rows 7 times, then work first 2 rows again.

Break off c. and continue with m. only.

To shape the sleeve top:

1st row: Cast off 4, k. to end.

2nd row: Cast off 4, k. to end.

3rd row: K.2 tog., k. to last 2 sts., k.2 tog.

4th row: All p.

Repeat 3rd and 4th rows 3 times more – 38 sts.

Next (dec.) row (right side): P.1, * p.2 tog., p.1; repeat from * to last 4 sts., p.2 tog., p.2 – 26 sts.

Break off yarn and leave sts. on spare needle until required for yoke.

The Yoke

Sl. first 24 sts. of back onto a spare needle, join m. to next st. then, using the set of four double-pointed No. 10 needles, cast on 4 sts. for underlap, k. these 4 sts. and k. across remaining 20 sts. of back, k. across 26 sts. of one sleeve, k. 44 sts. of front, k.26 sts. of other sleeve and finally, k. the 24 sts. left on spare needle, turn – 144 sts. with opening at centre back.

Working backwards and forwards in rows continue as follows:

1st row: K.4, p. to last 4 sts., k.4.

2nd row: All k.

Repeat these 2 rows twice more, then work 1st row again.

1st (shaping) row (right side): K.12, * sl.1, k.2 tog., p.s.s.o., k.9; repeat from * 3 times, sl.1, k.2 tog., p.s.s.o., k.18, ** sl.1, k.2 tog., p.s.s.o., k.9; repeat from ** 3 times, sl.1, k.2 tog., p.s.s.o., k.12 – 124 sts. Keeping 4 sts. at each end in garter st., st.st. 5 rows.

2nd (shaping and buttonhole) row: K.11, * sl.1, k.2 tog., p.s.s.o., k.7; repeat from * 3 times, sl.1, k.2 tog., p.s.s.o., k.16, ** sl.1, k.2 tog., p.s.s.o., k.7; repeat from ** 3 times, sl.1, k.2 tog., p.s.s.o., k.8, y.fwd., k.2 tog., k.1 – 104 sts. Work 5 rows.

3rd (shaping) row: K.10, * sl.1, k.2 tog., p.s.s.o., k.5; repeat from * 3 times, sl.1, k.2 tog., p.s.s.o., k.14, ** sl.1, k.2 tog., p.s.s.o., k.5; repeat from ** 3 times, sl.1, k.2 tog., p.s.s.o., k.10 – 84 sts.

You can now continue knitting on two needles only.

Next row: K.4, p.37, p.2 tog., p.37, k.4 – 83 sts.

Next row: K.4, * p.1, k.1 ; repeat from * to last 5 sts., p.1, k.4.

Keeping garter st. borders work a further 3 rows in single rib.

Next (buttonhole) row: Work to last 4 sts., k.1, y.fwd., k.2 tog., k.1.

Work a further 3 rows.

Cast off.

To Make Up The Angel Top

Press on wrong side, avoiding the ribbing, using a warm iron over a damp cloth. Join underarm, side and sleeve seams. Neaten lower edge of back opening. Sew on buttons.

The Tights

The Left Leg

With No. 10 needles and m., cast on 39 sts. and k.1 row.

To shape the foot:

1st row: K.5, up 1, k.1, up 1, k.19, up 1, k.1, up 1, k.13.

2nd and 4th rows: All p.

3rd row: K.6, up 1, k.1, up 1, k.21, up 1, k.1, up 1, k.14.

5th row: K.7, up 1, k.1, up 1, k.23, up 1, k.1, up 1, k.15.

6th row: All p.

On these 51 sts., k.1 row and p.1 row.

Next row: All p. on right side to form ridge.

Beginning with a p. row, st.st. 7 rows.

To shape the instep:

1st row: K.32, k.2 tog.b., k.1, k.2 tog., k.14.

2nd row: P.13, p.2 tog., p.1, p.2 tog.b., p.31.

3rd row: K.30, k.2 tog.b., k.1, k.2 tog., k.12.

4th row: P.11, p.2 tog., p.1, p.2 tog.b., p.29.

5th row: K.28, k.2 tog.b., k.1, k.2 tog., k.10.

6th row: P.9, p.2 tog., p.1, p.2 tog.b., p.27.

7th row: K.26, k.2 tog.b., k.1, k.2 tog., k.8.

On these 37 sts., p.1 row then k.2 rows.

Join on c. and work the 4 pattern rows given for top once but begin and end 1st and 2nd rows with k.1 instead of k.2.

*** Break off c. and continue with m. only.

Beginning right-side rows with k.1 and wrong-side rows with p.1, work 4 rows in single rib.

Continuing in single rib, inc. 1 st. at each end of next and every following 4th row until the 6th inc. row has been worked — 49 sts. — work 1 row, then inc. 1 st. at each end of next and following 28 alternate rows.

On these 107 sts., work 2 rows, ending with a right-side row — work 3 rows here

ending with a wrong-side row when working right leg.

To shape the crotch:

1st row: Cast off 2, rib to last 2 sts., dec.

2nd row: Work without shaping.

3rd row: Cast off 2, rib to end.

Work 3 rows straight, then dec. 1 st. at each end of next and following 6th row — 98 sts.

Work 9 rows straight, then dec. 1 st. at each end of next and every following 10th row until a further 4 dec. rows have been worked — 90 sts.

To shape for extra length on back:

1st and 2nd (turning) rows: Rib 45 for 1st row, turn and rib to end for 2nd row.

3rd and 4th rows: Rib 35, turn and rib to end.

5th and 6th rows: Rib 25, turn and rib to end.

7th and 8th rows: Rib 15, turn and rib to end.

Next row: Rib across all sts. picking up a thread at each point where work was turned and taking this together with next st. to avoid a gap in the knitting.

Rib 4 rows.

Next (slot) row: Rib 2, * y.fwd., rib 2 tog., rib 4 ; repeat from * ending last repeat with rib 2.

Rib 3 rows.

Cast off loosely in rib.

The Right Leg

With No. 10 needles and m., cast on 39 sts. and k.1 row.

To shape the foot:

1st row: K.13, up 1, k.1, up 1, k.19, up 1, k.1, up 1, k.5.

2nd and 4th rows: All p.

3rd row: K.14, up 1, k.1, up 1, k.21, up 1, k.1, up 1, k.6.

5th row: K.15, up 1, k.1, up 1, k.23, up 1, k.1, up 1, k.7.

6th row: All p.

On these 51 sts., k.1 row and p.1 row.

Next row: All p. on right side to form ridge. Beginning with a p. row, st.st. 7 rows.

To shape the instep:

1st row: K.14, k.2 tog.b., k.1, k.2 tog., k.32.

2nd row: P.31, p.2 tog., p.1, p.2 tog.b., p.13.

3rd row: K.12, k.2 tog.b., k.1, k.2 tog., k.30.

4th row: P.29, p.2 tog., p.1, p.2 tog.b., p.11.

5th row: K.10, k.2 tog.b., k.1, k.2 tog., k.28.

6th row: P.27, p.2 tog., p.1, p.2 tog.b., p.9.

7th row: K.8, k.2 tog. b., k.1, k.2 tog., k.26.

On these 37 sts., p.1 row and k.2 rows.

Join on c. and work the 4 pattern rows given for top once but begin and end 1st and 2nd rows with k.1 instead of k.2.

Now work as given for left leg from *** to end noting the extra row to be worked before shaping the crotch.

To Make Up The Tights

Press lightly. Join inner leg and underfoot seams, then join front and back seams. Thread elastic through holes at waist.

Navy Dungarees

Dungaree Style Crawlers worn with the first size striped sweater. Instructions on page 171

Contributed by Eugenie Hammond

Materials

Three 50 gramme balls of Patons Purple Heather 4-ply; a pair each of No. 10 and No. 12 knitting needles; 3 buttons; motif.

Tension and Size

Worked at a tension of 7 stitches and 9 rows to 1 inch, over the stocking stitch, using No. 10 needles, the dungarees will fit baby aged six to twelve months.

Abbreviations

K., knit; p., purl; st., stitch; tog., together; dec., decrease (by working 2 sts. tog.); inc., increase (by working twice into same st.); k. or p. 2 tog.b., k. or p. 2 sts. tog. through back of loops; up 1 (pick up the thread which lies between the needles and k. into back of it, thus making a st.); st.st., stocking st. (k. on right side and p. on wrong side); single rib is k.1 and p.1 alternately.

The Left Leg

With No. 10 needles cast on 39 sts. and k.1 row.

To shape the foot:

1st row: K.5, up 1, k.1, up 1, k.19, up 1, k.1, up 1, k.13.

2nd and 4th rows: All p.

3rd row: K.6, up 1, k.1, up 1, k.21, up 1, k.1, up 1, k.14.

5th row: K.7, up 1, k.1, up 1, k.23, up 1, k.1, up 1, k.15.

6th row: All p.

On these 51 sts., k.1 row and p.1 row.

Next row (right side): All p.

Next row: All k.

Next row: All p. The last 3 rows form a ridge.

Beginning with a p. row, st.st. 5 rows.

To shape the instep:

1st row: K.32, k.2 tog.b., k.1, k.2 tog., k.14.

2nd row: P.13, p.2 tog., p.1, p.2 tog.b., p.31.

3rd row: K.30, k.2 tog.b., k.1, k.2 tog., k.12.

4th row: P.11, p.2 tog., p.1, p.2 tog.b., p.29.

5th row: K.28, k.2 tog.b., k.1, k.2 tog., k.10.

6th row: P.9, p.2 tog., p.1, p.2 tog.b., p.27.

7th row: K.26, k.2 tog.b., k.1, k.2 tog., k.8.

On these 37 sts., p.1 row.

** Beginning right-side rows with k.1 and wrong-side rows with p.1, work 6 rows in single rib.

Beginning with a k. row, st.st. 4 rows.

Continuing in st.st. inc. 1 st. at each end of next and every following 4th row until the 6th inc. row has been worked – 49 sts.

P.1 row, then inc. 1 st. at each end of next and following 25 right-side rows – 101 sts.

Work 7 rows straight. Mark each end of work with a coloured thread to denote end of leg seam.

To shape front and back seams: Dec. 1 st. at each end of next and every following 6th row until the 3rd dec. row has been worked – 95 sts.

Work 7 rows straight, then dec. 1 st. at each end of next and every following 8th row until a further 3 dec. rows have been completed – 89 sts. **.

Next row: All p.

To shape for extra length on back:

Navy dungarees; striped jersey (pattern p. 171).

1st and 2nd (turning) rows: K.40 for 1st row, turn and p. to end for 2nd row.

3rd and 4th rows: K.30, turn and p. to end.

5th and 6th rows: K.20, turn and p. to end.

7th and 8th rows: K.10, turn and p. to end.

Next row: All k. across 89 sts. picking up a thread at each point where work was turned and taking this together with next st. to avoid a gap in the knitting.

Break off wool and leave sts. on spare needle.

The Right Leg

With No. 10 needles cast on 39 sts. and k.1 row.

To shape the foot:

1st row: K.13, up 1, k.1, up 1, k.19, up 1, k.1, up 1, k.5.

2nd and 4th rows: All p.

3rd row: K.14, up 1, k.1, up 1, k.21, up 1, k.1, up 1, k.6.

5th row: K.15, up 1, k.1, up 1, k.23, up 1, k.1, up 1, k.7.

6th row: All p.

On these 51 sts., k.1 row and p.1 row.

Next row (right side): All p.

Next row: All k.

Next row: All p.

The last 3 rows form a ridge.

Beginning with a p. row, st.st. 5 rows.

To shape the instep:

1st row: K.14, k.2 tog.b., k.1, k.2 tog., k.32.

2nd row: P.31, p.2 tog., p.1, p.2 tog.b., p.13.

3rd row: K.12, k.2 tog.b., k.1, k.2 tog., k.30.

4th row: P. 29, p.2 tog., p.1, p.2 tog.b., p.11.

5th row: K.10, k.2 tog.b., k.1, k.2 tog., k.28.

6th row: P.27, p.2 tog., p.1, p.2 tog.b., p.9.

7th row: K.8, k.2 tog.b., k.1, k.2 tog., k.26.

On these 37 sts., p.1 row.

Now work as given for left leg from ** to **.

To shape for extra length on back:

1st and 2nd (turning) rows: P.40 for 1st row, turn and k. to end for 2nd row.

3rd and 4th rows: P.30, turn and k. to end.

5th and 6th rows: P.20, turn and k. to end.

7th and 8th rows: P.10, turn and k. to end.

Next row: P. across all sts. closing gaps, then with wrong side of left leg facing, onto same needle, p. the 89 sts. of left leg. You now have 178 sts. on needle joined at centre front.

Change to No. 12 needles and work 16 rows in single rib.

Next 2 rows: Cast off 61 sts., rib to end.

Now work on 56 sts. for top.

Change to No. 10 needles.

1st row: All k.

2nd row: K.12, p.32, k.12.

Repeat these 2 rows 16 times more, then work 1st row again.

Beginning on wrong side of work, k.5 rows.

Now divide sts. for neck.

Next row: K.15, cast off next 26 sts., k. to end and work on these 15 sts. for 1st strap. K.15 rows ending at inner edge.

Break off wool and leave sts. on spare needle.

With wrong side of work facing, rejoin wool to other set of 15 sts. and, using No. 10 needles, k.16 rows ending at inner edge, turn, cast on 26 sts., turn and k. across 15 sts. of 1st strap – 56 sts.

K.6 rows, ending with a right-side row.

Next row: K.12, p.32, k.12.

Next row: All k.

Repeat these 2 rows 23 times more.

Change to No. 12 needles.

Work 7 rows in single rib.

Next (buttonhole) row: Rib 6, * cast off 2 – 1 st. left on right-hand needle not included in next item, rib 18; repeat from * once, cast off 2, rib to end.

Next row: Rib 6, turn, cast on 2, turn, rib 19, turn, cast on 2, turn, rib 19, turn, cast on 2, turn, rib 6.

Work a further 7 rows in single rib.

Cast off.

To Make Up The Dungarees

Press on wrong side, avoiding the ribbing, using a warm iron over a damp cloth. Join inner leg and underfoot seams, then join front and back seams. Sew buttons to waist band at back. Sew motif to front.

Striped Jersey

(see illustration p. 169)

Materials

Two 50-gramme balls of Patons Purple Heather 4-ply in main colour and one ball in contrast colour for 1st size; three balls in main and one ball in contrast for 2nd and 3rd sizes. For any one size: a pair each of No. 10 and No. 12 knitting needles; 3 buttons.

Tension

Work at a tension of 7 stitches and 9 rows to 1 inch, over the stocking stitch, using No. 10 needles, to obtain the following measurements:

Measurements

INCHES

	1st size	2nd size	3rd size
All round at under-arms	$21\frac{1}{4}$	$23\frac{1}{2}$	26
Side seam	$6\frac{1}{2}$	$7\frac{1}{4}$	8
Length	11	12	$13\frac{1}{4}$
Sleeve seam	7	$8\frac{1}{2}$	$9\frac{3}{4}$

Abbreviations

K., knit; p., purl; st., stitch; tog., together; inc., increase (by working twice into same st.); w.fwd., wool forward to make a st.; s.k.p.o., slip 1, k.1, pass slipped st. over; st.st., stocking st. (k. on right side and p. on wrong side); single rib is k.1 and p.1 alternately; m., main colour; c., contrast colour.

● *The instructions are given for 1st size. Where they vary, work figures in first brackets for 2nd size; figures in second brackets for 3rd size.*

The Back

With No. 12 needles and c., cast on 75 (83) (91) sts. and, beginning right-side rows with k.1 and wrong-side rows with p.1, work 14 rows in single rib.

Break off c., join on m.

Change to No. 10 needles and, beginning with a k. row, st.st. 46 (52) (58) rows.

To shape the raglan armholes:

1st row: Cast off 5 (6) (7) sts., k. to end.

2nd row: Cast off 5 (6) (7) sts., p. to end.

3rd row: K.1, k.2 tog., k. to last 3 sts., s.k.p.o., k.1.

4th row: K.1, p. to last st., k.1 **

Repeat 3rd and 4th rows 6 (8) (10) times more, then work 3rd row again – 49 (51) (53) sts.

Now divide sts. for back opening.

Next row: K.1, p.21 (22) (23) and leave these sts. on spare needle for left side, p. to last st., k.1 and work on these 27 (28) (29) sts. for right side.

The right side:

1st row: K.1, k.2 tog., k. to end.

2nd row: K.2, p. to last st., k.1.

Repeat these 2 rows 3 times more.

Next (buttonhole) row: K.1, k.2 tog., k. to last 4 sts., k.2 tog., w.fwd., k.2.

Work 2nd row, then repeat 1st and 2nd rows 3 times more.

Work buttonhole row; work 2nd row, then work 1st and 2nd rows twice more.

Cast off remaining 16 (17) (18) sts.

The left side: With right side of work facing, rejoin wool to 22 (23) (24) sts. on spare needle, cast on 5 sts. for underlap.

1st row: K. to last 3 sts., s.k.p.o., k.1.

2nd row: K.1, p. to last 2 sts., k.2.

Repeat these 2 rows 10 times more.

Cast off remaining 16 (17) (18) sts.

The Front

Work as given for back to **.

Repeat 3rd and 4th rows 10 (12) (14) times more, then work 3rd row again — 41 (43) (45) sts.

Now divide sts. for front neck.

Next row: K.1, p.13 and leave these 14 sts. on spare needle for right side, cast off next 13 (15) (17) sts., p. to last st., k.1 and work on these 14 sts. for left side.

The left side: To shape neck and continue shaping raglan:

1st row: K.1, k.2 tog., k. to end.

2nd row: P. 2 tog., p. to last st., k.1.

Repeat these 2 rows 4 times more — 4 sts.

Next row: K.1, k.2 tog., k.1.

Next row: P.2, k.1.

Next row: K.1, k.2 tog.

Take remaining 2 sts. tog. and fasten off.

The right side: With right side of work facing, rejoin wool to the 14 sts. on spare needle.

1st row: K. to last 3 sts., s.k.p.o., k.1.

2nd row: K.1, p. to last 2 sts., p.2 tog.

Repeat these 2 rows 4 times more — 4 sts.

Next row: K.1, s.k.p.o., k.1.

Next row: K.1, p.2.

Next row: S.k.p.o., k.1.

Take remaining 2 sts. tog. and fasten off.

The Sleeves (both alike)

With No. 12 needles and c., cast on 43 (45) (47) sts. and work 14 rows in single rib as given for back.

Break off c.; join on m.

Change to No. 10 needles.

Beginning with a k. row, st.st. 6 rows, then inc. 1 st. at each end of next row.

St.st. 3 rows.

Rejoin c., and work 2 rows.

With m., inc. 1 st. at each end of next row, then work 3 rows straight.

With c., work 2 rows straight.

With m., inc. 1 st. at each end of next row, then work 3 rows straight.

With c., work 2 rows straight. This completes the 3 stripes. Break off c.

Inc. 1 st. at each end of next and every following 6th row until a further 3 (5) (7) inc. rows have been worked — 55 (61) (67) sts.

Work 13 rows straight.

To shape the raglan sleeve top:

1st row: Cast off 5 (6) (7) sts., k. to end.

2nd row: Cast off 5 (6) (7) sts., p. to end.

3rd row: K.1, k.2 tog., k. to last 3 sts., s.k.p.o., k.1.

4th row: K.1, p. to last st., k.1.

Repeat 3rd and 4th rows 18 (20) (22) times more.

Cast off remaining 7 sts.

The Neck Band

First join raglan seams. With right side of work facing, rejoin c., to centre back and, using No. 12 needles, pick up and k.16 (17) (18) sts. across back, 5 sts. from top of sleeve, 15 sts. down left side of neck, 13 (15) (17) sts. across centre front, 15 sts. from right side of neck, 5 sts. from sleeve and finally 16 (17) (18) sts. across back — 85 (89) (93) sts.

Beginning 1st row with p.1, work 2 rows in single rib.

Next row: Rib 2, w.fwd., k.2 tog., rib to end.

Rib a further 3 rows.

Cast off in rib.

To Make Up The Jersey

Press on wrong side, avoiding the ribbing, using a warm iron over a damp cloth. Join sleeve and side seams. Neaten lower edge of back opening. Sew on buttons.

His First Suit

Jersey and Pants

Materials

Five 50-gramme balls of Patons Trident Double Knitting; a pair each of No. 8 and No. 10 knitting needles; a cable needle; a 4-inch zip fastener; a waist length of elastic.

Tension

Work at a tension of 11 stitches and 15 rows to 2 inches, over the stocking stitch, using No. 8 needles, to obtain the following measurements:

Measurements

	INCHES
The Jersey	
All round at underarms	22
Side seam	$6\frac{1}{2}$
Length	$11\frac{3}{4}$
Sleeve seam	$7\frac{1}{2}$
The Pants	
All round at widest part	25
Side seam	$7\frac{1}{2}$

Abbreviations

K., knit; p., purl; st., stitch; tog., together; dec., decrease (by working 2 sts. tog.); inc., increase (by working twice into same st.); k.2 tog.b., k.2 sts. tog. through back of loops; sl., slip; s.k.p.o., sl.1, k.1, pass slipped st. over; p.s.s.o., pass slipped st. over; y.fwd., yarn forward to make a st.; tw.2 rt., twist 2 right (sl. next st. onto cable needle and leave at back of work, k.1 then p. st. from cable needle); tw.2 lt., twist 2 left (sl. next st. onto cable needle and leave at front of work, p.1 then k. st. from cable needle); st.st., stocking st. (k. on right side and p. on wrong side); single rib is k.1 and p.1 alternately.

The Jersey

The Back

With No. 10 needles cast on 63 sts. and, beginning right-side rows with k.1 and wrong-side rows with p.1, work 12 rows in single rib **.

Change to No. 8 needles and, beginning with a k. row, st.st. 38 rows.

To shape the raglan armholes:

1st row: Cast off 3 sts., k. to end.

2nd row: Cast off 3 sts., p. to end.

3rd row: K.2, k.2 tog., k. to last 4 sts., k.2 tog.b., k.2.

4th row: All p.

5th row: All k.

6th row: All p.

Repeat 3rd to 6th rows once more – 53 sts.

Now work 3rd and 4th rows only 15 times.

Break off yarn and leave remaining 23 sts. on spare needle.

The Front

Work as back to **.

Change to No. 8 needles and work in pattern as follows:

1st row: K.23, p.6, tw.2 rt., p.1, tw.2 lt., p.6, k.23.

2nd row: P.23, k.6, p.1, k.3, p.1, k.6, p.23.

3rd row: K.23, p.5, tw.2 rt., p.3, tw.2 lt., p.5, k.23.

4th row: P.23, k.5, p.1, k.5, p.1, k.5, p.23.

5th row: K.23, p.4, tw.2 rt., p.5, tw.2 lt., p.4, k.23.

6th row: P.23, k.4, p.1, k.7, p.1, k.4, p.23.

7th row: K.23, p.3, tw.2 rt., p.7, tw.2 lt., p.3, k.23.

8th row: P.23, k.3, p.1, k.9, p.1, k.3, p.23.

9th row: K.23, p.3, tw.2 lt., p.7, tw.2 rt., p.3, k.23.

10th row: P.23, k.4, p.1, k.7, p.1, k.4, p.23.

11th row: K.23, p.4, tw.2 lt., p.5, tw.2 rt., p.4, k.23.

12th row: P.23, k.5, p.1, k.5, p.1, k.5, p.23.

13th row: K.23, p.5, tw.2 lt., p.3, tw.2 rt., p.5, k.23.

14th row: P.23, k.6, p.1, k.3, p.1, k.6, p.23.

15th row: K.23, p.6, tw.2 lt., p.1, tw.2 rt., p.6, k.23.

16th row: P.23, k.7, p.1, k.1, p.1, k.7, p.23.

These 16 rows form the pattern; repeat them once more, then work first 6 rows again.

Keeping continuity of pattern continue as follows:

To shape the raglan armholes:

1st row: Cast off 3 sts., pattern to end.

2nd row: Cast off 3 sts., pattern to end.

3rd row: K.2, k.2 tog., pattern to last 4 sts., k.2 tog.b., k.2.

4th row: Work in pattern.

5th row: Work in pattern.

6th row: Work in pattern.

Repeat 3rd to 6th rows once more – 53 sts.

Now work 3rd and 4th rows only 6 times, then work 3rd row again – 39 sts.

Now divide sts. for front neck.

Next row: Pattern 13 and leave these sts. on spare needle for right side, pattern next 13 sts. and leave these on a stitch-holder for neck band, pattern to end and work on these 13 sts. for left side.

The left side: To shape the neck: Work 6 rows decreasing 1 st. at armhole edge, as before, and 1 st. at neck edge on each right-side row – 7 sts.

Now dec. 1 st. at armhole edge only on next and following 3 alternate rows – 3 sts. ***.

Next row: P.3.

Next row: K.1, k.2 tog.

Next row: P.2.

Take remaining 2 sts. tog. and fasten off.

The right side: With right side of work facing, rejoin yarn to the 13 sts. on spare needle and work as given for left side to ***

Next row: P.3.

Next row: K.2 tog.b., k.1.

Next row: P.2.

Take remaining 2 sts. tog. and fasten off.

The Sleeves (both alike)

With No. 10 needles cast on 38 sts. and work 12 rows in single rib.

Change to No. 8 needles and, beginning with a k. row, st.st. 8 rows.

Inc. 1 st. at each end of next and every following 8th row until the 5th inc. row has been worked – 48 sts.

St.st. 5 rows.

To shape the raglan sleeve top: Work exactly as given for raglan armhole shaping on back when 8 sts. will remain.

Break off yarn and leave sts. on safety-pin.

The Neck Band

First join right raglan seams, then join left sleeve to front only. With right side of work facing, rejoin yarn to sts. at top of left sleeve and, using No. 10 needles, k. these 8 sts., pick up and k.12 sts. down left side of neck, k. the 13 sts. at centre front, pick up and k.12 sts. from right side of neck, k. the 8 sts. of right sleeve and finally k. across the 23 sts. at back – 76 sts.

Work 7 rows in single rib.
Cast off in rib.

To Make Up The Jersey

Press on wrong side, avoiding the ribbing, using a warm iron over a damp cloth. Join remaining raglan seam leaving 4 inches free at top for zip. Join sleeve and side seams. Insert zip.

The Pants

The Back

With No. 8 needles cast on 19 sts.
1st row: K. to end, turn and cast on 6 sts.
2nd row: P. to end, turn and cast on 6 sts.
3rd row: K.6, s.k.p.o., k.15, k.2 tog., k.6, turn and cast on 6 sts.
4th row: P. to end, turn and cast on 6 sts.
5th row: K.12, s.k.p.o., k.13, k.2 tog., k.12, turn and cast on 8 sts.
6th row: P. to end, turn and cast on 8 sts.
7th row: K.20, s.k.p.o., k.11, k.2 tog., k.20, turn and cast on 8 sts.
8th row: P. to end, turn and cast on 8 sts.
9th row: K.28, s.k.p.o., k.9, k.2 tog., k.28, turn and cast on 6 sts.
10th row: P. to end, turn and cast on 6 sts.
11th row: K.34, s.k.p.o., k.7, k.2 tog., k.34.
12th row: All p.
13th row: K.34, s.k.p.o., k.5, k.2 tog., k.34.
14th row: All p.
15th row: K.34, s.k.p.o., k.3, k.2 tog., k.34.
16th row: All p.
17th row: K.34, s.k.p.o., k.1, k.2 tog., k.34.
18th row: All p.
19th row: K.34, sl.1, k.2 tog., p.s.s.o., k.34.
20th row: All p. – 69 sts.
St.st. 34 rows **.

To shape for extra length on back:
1st and 2nd (turning) rows: K.60 for 1st row, turn sl.1, p.50 for 2nd row, turn.
3rd and 4th rows: Sl.1, k.40, turn, sl.1, p.30, turn.
5th and 6th rows: Sl.1, k.20, turn, sl.1, p.10, turn.
7th row: K. across all sts.
8th row: P. across all sts.
Change to No. 10 needles.
*** **1st row:** K.1, * p.1, k.1 ; repeat from * to end.
2nd row: P.1, * k.1, p.1 ; repeat from * to end.
Repeat these 2 rows once more.
Next (slot) row: Rib 3, * y.fwd., k.2 tog., rib 4 ; repeat from * to end.
Rib a further 3 rows.
Cast off in rib.

The Front

Work as back to **
Work a further 2 rows straight.
Change to No. 10 needles and work as back from *** to end.

The Leg Bands (both alike)

First join crotch seam. With right side of work facing, rejoin yarn to lower edge of side, and using No. 10 needles, pick up and k.68 sts. along entire leg edge.

Work 5 rows in single rib.
Cast off in rib.

To Make Up The Pants

Press as given for jersey. Join side seams. Insert elastic at waist.

Ribbed Sweater, Tights and Tabard

Contributed by Eugenie Hammond

Materials

The Tabard: Two 50-gramme balls of Patons Double Knitting for the 1st size; three balls for the 2nd size. For either size: one 50-gramme ball of Patons Purple Heather 4-ply in a contrast colour; a pair each of No. 8 No. 10 and No. 12 knitting needles; 2 button moulds; 1 large press fastener.

The Tights: Four 50-gramme balls of Patons Purple Heather 4-ply; a pair of No. 12 knitting needles; a waist length of elastic.

The Sweater: For either size: Three 50-gramme balls of Patons Purple Heather 4-ply; a pair each of No. 10 and No. 12 knitting needles.

Abbreviations

K., knit; p., purl; st., stitch; tog., together; dec., decrease (by working 2 sts. tog.); inc., increase (by working twice into same st.); w.fwd., wool forward to make a st.; s.k.p.o., slip 1, k.1, pass slipped st. over; st.st., stocking st. (k. on right side and p. on wrong side); single rib is k.1 and p.1 alternately.

● *The instructions are given for 1st size. Where they vary, work figures in brackets for 2nd size.*

Tension and Size

Worked at a tension of 7 stitches and 9 rows to 1 inch over ribbing, stretched, using No. 10 needles and 11 stitches and 15 rows to 2 inches over stocking stitch using No. 8 needles the set will be suitable for the 2 and 3-year-olds.

The Tabard

The Back

With No. 8 needles and Double Knitting cast on 40 sts. and k.1 row and p.1 row.

Continuing in st.st., inc. 1 st. at each end of next and following 9 alternate rows – 60 sts.

Work 41 (47) rows straight, ending with a p. row.

Dec. 1 st. at each end of the next 7 rows – 46 sts. **.

Work 38 (44) rows straight, ending with a k. row.

Now divide sts. for back neck.

Next row: P.18, cast off 10, p. to end and work on these 18 sts. for the right back shoulder.

The right back shoulder: Dec. 1 st. at neck edge on each of the next 8 rows – 10 sts.

Work 5 rows, then dec. 1 st. at each end of the next 3 rows.

Cast off remaining 4 sts.

The left back shoulder: With right side of work facing, rejoin wool to the 18 sts. and work as given for right back shoulder to end.

The Front

Work as given for back to **.

Work 34 (40) rows straight.

Now divide sts. for front neck.

Next row: P.18, cast off 10, p. to end and work on these 18 sts. for the left front shoulder.

The left front shoulder: Dec. 1 st. at neck edge on each of the next 8 rows – 10 sts.

Work 9 rows, then dec. 1 st. at each end of the next 3 rows.

Cast off remaining 4 sts.

The right front shoulder: With right side of working facing, rejoin wool to the 18 sts. and work as given for left front shoulder to end.

The Bias Edging

With No. 10 needles and 4-ply, cast on 7 sts.

1st row: All p.

2nd row: Inc. in 1st st., k.4, k.2 tog.

Repeat these 2 rows until bias strip is long enough to fit all round outer edge of back.

Cast off.

Work another piece in the same way to fit all round front.

The Front Tabs (make 2)

With No. 10 needles and Double Knitting, cast on 7 sts. and beginning right-side rows with k.1 and wrong-side rows with p.1, work 18 rows in single rib. Dec. 1 st. at beginning of next 4 rows.

Take remaining 3 sts. tog. and fasten off.

The Back Tabs (make 2)

With No. 10 needles and Double Knitting, cast on 7 sts. and work 16 rows in single rib.

Cast off.

The Button Covers (make 2)

With No. 12 needles and 4-ply cast on 8 sts. and, beginning with a k. row, st.st. 10 rows.

Cast off.

To Make Up The Tabard

Press on wrong side, using a warm iron over a damp cloth. Sew one edge of binding all round outer edge of back and front, fold to wrong side and slip st. in place. Sew tabs in place and add buckle to back tab.

Run gathering thread round edge of button cover, insert button mould and draw up. Overlap right shoulder and secure with button. Sew button to front shoulder at left side and fasten to back with press fastener.

The Tights

The First Leg

With No. 12 needles and 4-ply cast on 89 sts.

1st row: K.1, * p.1, k.1; repeat from * to end.

2nd row: P.1, * k.1, p.1; repeat from * to end.

Continuing in single rib work a further 4 rows.

Next (slot) row: K.1, * w.fwd., k.2 tog., p.1, k.1 ; repeat from * to end.
Work a further 5 rows.

To shape for extra length on back:
1st and 2nd (turning) rows: Rib 10 for 1st row, turn and rib to end for 2nd row.
3rd and 4th rows: Rib 20, turn and rib to end.
5th and 6th rows: Rib 30, turn and rib to end.
7th and 8th rows: Rib 40, turn and rib to end.
9th and 10th rows: Rib 50, turn and rib to end.
11th and 12th rows: Rib 60, turn and rib to end.
Work 2 rows across all sts.

Inc. 1 st. at beginning of next row and every following 6th row until the 12th inc. row has been worked – 101 sts.

Work 1 row, then inc. 1 st. at each end of the next and following 2 alternate rows – 107 sts.

Work 1 row, then dec. 1 st. at each end of the next 5 rows – 97 sts.

Work 1 row, then dec. 1 st. at each end of the next row and following 9 alternate rows – 77 sts.

Work 3 rows, then dec. 1 st. at each end of the next row and every following 4th row until a further 5 dec. rows have been worked – 67 sts.

Work 7 rows, then dec. 1 st. at each end of next row and every following 8th row until a further 9 dec. rows have been worked – 49 sts.

Work 31 rows straight – adjust length of leg here if required.

To shape the heel:
1st and 2nd (turning) rows: Rib 17, turn, rib 11, turn.

3rd and 4th rows: Rib 12, turn, rib 13, turn.
5th and 6th rows: Rib 14, turn, rib 15, turn.
7th and 8th rows: Rib 16, turn, rib 17, turn.
9th and 10th rows: Rib 18, turn, rib 19, turn.
11th and 12th rows: Rib 20, turn, rib 21, turn.
13th and 14th rows: Rib 22, turn, rib to end.
Work 36 rows across all sts., adjust length of foot here if required.

To shape the toe:
1st row: Dec., rib 20, dec., dec., rib 20, dec., rib 1.
2nd and every alternate row: Work without shaping.
3rd row: Dec., rib 18, dec., dec., rib 18, dec., rib 1.
5th row: Dec., rib 16, dec., dec., rib 16, dec., rib 1.
7th row: Dec., rib 14, dec., dec., rib 14, dec., rib 1.
9th row: Dec., rib 12, dec., dec., rib 12, dec., rib 1.
10th row: Work without shaping.
Cast off remaining 29 sts.

The Second Leg

Work exactly the same as first leg as the fabric is reversible.

To Make Up The Tights

Do not press. Join inner leg and underfoot seams, then join front and back seams. Insert elastic.

The Sweater

The Back

With No. 12 needles and 4-ply cast on 81 (89) sts.
1st row: K.1, * p.1, k.1 ; repeat from * to end.

2nd row: P.1, * k.1, p.1 ; repeat from * to end.

Mark right side of work with a coloured thread for easier identification.

Repeat these 2 rows 5 times more.

Change to No. 10 needles and continuing in rib work a further 58 (62) rows.

To shape the raglan armholes:

1st and 2nd rows: Cast off 3 (4), rib to end.

3rd row: K.2, k.2 tog., rib to last 4 sts., s.k.p.o., k.2.

4th row: K.1, p.2, rib to last 3 sts., p.2, k.1 **.

Repeat 3rd and 4th rows 24 (26) times.

Break off wool and leave remaining 25 (27) sts. on a spare needle.

The Front

Work as given for back to **.

Repeat 3rd and 4th rows 17 (19) times more, then work 3rd row again – 37 (39) sts.

Now divide sts. for front neck.

Next row: K.1, p.2, rib 10 and leave these 13 sts. on a spare needle for right side, rib next 11 (13) sts. and leave these on a safety-pin for neck band, rib 10, p.2, k.1 and work on these 13 sts. for left side.

The left side: Still decreasing for raglan on each right-side row, dec. 1 st. at neck edge on each of next 5 rows – 5 sts.

Work 1 row, then dec. 1 st. at armhole edge only on the next row and following 2 right-side rows.

Work 1 row, then take these 2 sts. tog. and fasten off.

The right side: With right side of work facing, rejoin wool to the 13 sts. on spare needle and work as given for the left side.

The Sleeves (both alike)

With No. 12 needles and 4-ply cast on 45 (47) sts. and work 12 rows in rib as given for back.

Change to No. 10 needles and rib 2 rows.

Inc. 1 st. at each end of the next row and every following 6th row until the 9th (11th) inc. row has been worked – 63 (69) sts.

Work 13 (9) rows straight.

To shape the raglan sleeve top: Work exactly as given for raglan armhole shaping on back when 7 sts. will remain.

Break off wool and leave sts. on a safety-pin.

The Neck Band

First join right raglan seams, then join left sleeve to front only. With right side of work facing, rejoin wool to sts. of left sleeve and, using No. 12 needles, rib the 7 sts. of left sleeve, pick up and k.15 sts. down left side of neck, rib the 11 (13) sts. at centre front, pick up and k.15 sts. from right side of neck, rib the 7 sts. of right sleeve and rib the 25 (27) sts. at back – 80 (84) sts.

Work 7 rows in single rib.

Cast off very loosely in rib.

To Make Up The Sweater

Do not press. Join remaining raglan seam and neck band. Join side and sleeve seams.

Opposite – Hooded sweater and skirt (pattern p. 182).

Hooded Sweater and Skirt

(see illustration p. 181)

The stitch gives the effect of all-round pleats

Contributed by Eugenie Hammond

Materials

For the sweater: Ten 25-gramme balls of Wendy Double Knit Nylonised for 1st size; eleven balls for 2nd size. For either size: a pair each of No. 8 and No. 10 knitting needles; a 4-inch zip.

For the skirt: Five balls of the same wool for 1st size; six balls for 2nd size. For either size: a pair each of No. 8 and No. 10 knitting needles; waist length of 1-inch wide elastic.

Tension

Work at a tension of 11 stitches and 15 rows to 2 inches, over the stocking stitch, using No. 8 needles, to obtain the following measurements:

Abbreviations

K., knit; p., purl; st., stitch; tog., together; dec., decrease (by working 2 sts. tog.); inc., increase (by working twice into same st.); k.2 tog.b., k.2 tog. through back of loops; y.fwd., yarn forward to make a st.; s.k.p.o., slip 1, k.1, pass slipped st. over; st.st., stocking st. (k. on right side and p. on wrong side); single rib is k.1 and p.1 alternately.

● *The instructions are given for 1st size. Where they vary, work figures in brackets for 2nd size.*

Measurements

INCHES

	1st size	2nd size
The Sweater		
All round at underarms	24	26
Side seam	$7\frac{3}{4}$	$8\frac{1}{4}$
Length	$12\frac{1}{4}$	13
Sleeve seam	$8\frac{1}{2}$	$8\frac{3}{4}$
The Skirt		
All round at lower edge	28	30
Length	$9\frac{1}{4}$	$9\frac{1}{2}$

The Sweater

The Back

With No. 10 needles cast on 66 (72) sts. and work 4 rows in single rib.

Change to No. 8 needles and, beginning with a k. row, st.st. 54 (58) rows.

To shape the square armholes: Cast off 7 (8) sts. at beginning of next 2 rows – 52 (56) sts.

St.st. 32 (34) rows.

To slope the shoulders: Cast off 7 (8) sts. at beginning of next 4 rows.

Break off yarn and leave remaining 24 sts. on a spare needle.

The Pocket Backs (make 2)

With No. 8 needles cast on 16 (18) sts. and, beginning with a k. row, st.st. 16 (18) rows.

Break off yarn and leave sts. on a spare needle.

The Front

With No. 10 needles cast on 66 (72) sts. and work 4 rows in single rib.

Change to No. 8 needles and st.st. 16 (18) rows.

Next (pocket) row: K.3, slip next 16 (18) sts. onto a stitch-holder and, in their place, k. across the 16 (18) sts. of one pocket back, k. next 28 (30) sts. slip next 16 (18) sts. onto a stitch-holder and k. across the 16 (18) sts. of other pocket back then k. remaining 3 sts. of row – 66 (72) sts.

Beginning with a p. row, st.st. 37 (39) rows.

To shape the square armholes: Cast off 7 (8) sts. at beginning of next 2 rows – 52 (56) sts.

St.st. 3 (5) rows.

Now divide sts. for front opening.

Next row: P.26 (28) and leave these sts. on a spare needle for right side, p. to end and work on these 26 (28) sts. for left side.

The left side:
1st row: All k.
2nd row: K.1, p. to end.

Repeat these 2 rows 8 times more, then work 1st row again to end at neck edge.

To shape the neck: Cast off 6 sts. at beginning of next row, then dec. 1 st. at neck edge on next 6 rows – 14 (16) sts.

Work 2 rows straight.

To slope the shoulder: Cast off 7 (8) sts. at beginning of next row; work 1 row, then cast off remaining 7 (8) sts.

The right side: With right side of work facing, rejoin yarn to sts. on spare needle.
1st row: All k.
2nd row: P. to last st., k.1.

Repeat these 2 rows 9 times more.

To shape the neck and slope shoulder: Work as given for left side.

The Sleeves (both alike)

With No. 10 needles cast on 38 (40) sts. and work 8 rows in single rib.

Change to No. 8 needles.

Next (inc.) row: K.5 (3), * inc. in next st., k.2; repeat from * 8 (10) times, inc. in next st., k. 5 (3) – 48 (52) sts.

Beginning with a p. row, st.st. 55 (57) rows. Mark each end of work with a coloured thread to denote end of sleeve seam, then work a further 8 (10) rows.

Cast off loosely.

The Neck Band

First join shoulder seams. With right side of work facing, rejoin yarn to neck edge at centre front and, using No. 10 needles, pick up and k.16 sts. along shaped edge then, increasing 1 st. in centre, k. the 24 sts. at back and pick up and k.16 sts. from shaped edge – 57 sts.

Beginning wrong-side rows with p.1 and right-side rows with k.1, work 5 rows in single rib.

Cast off loosely in rib.

The Pocket Tops (both alike)

Slip the 16 (18) sts. of pocket tops onto No. 10 needles, rejoin yarn and k. across these sts. increasing 1 st. in centre – 17 (19) sts.

Work 3 rows in single rib as given for neck band.

Cast off.

The Hood

With No. 8 needles cast on 92 (98) sts. and, beginning with a k. row, st.st. 10 rows.

Next (hem) row: Fold work in half so that cast-on edge lies behind sts. on needle then k.1 st. on needle together with corresponding loop along cast-on edge to form hem.

Beginning with a p. row, st.st. 35 (39) rows.

To shape for back: Cast off 31 (33) sts. at beginning of next 2 rows.

On remaining 30 (32) sts., st.st. 14 (16) rows.

Now shape back section as follows:

1st row: K.5, k.2 tog.b., k.5, k.2 tog.b., k.2 (4), k.2 tog., k.5, k.2 tog., k.5.

2nd and every alternate row: All p.

3rd row: K.4, k.2 tog.b., k.4, k.2 tog.b., k.2 (4), k.2 tog., k.4, k.2 tog., k.4.

5th row: K.3, k.2 tog.b., k.3, k.2 tog.b., k.2 (4), k.2 tog., k.3, k.2 tog., k.3.

7th row: K.2, k.2 tog.b., k.2, k.2 tog.b., k.2 (4), k.2 tog., k.2, k.2 tog., k.2.

9th row: K.1, k.2 tog.b., k.1, k.2 tog.b., k.2 (4), k.2 tog., k.1, k.2 tog., k.1.

11th row: K.2 tog.b., k.2 tog.b., k.2 (4), k.2 tog., k.2 tog.

13th row: K.2 tog.b., k.2 (4), k.2 tog.

15th row: K.2 tog. twice (k.2 tog. 3 times).

16th row: P.2 (3).

Cast off.

To Make Up The Sweater

Press on wrong side, avoiding the ribbing, using a warm iron over a damp cloth.

Set in sleeves sewing the row ends above the markers to the sts. cast off for armholes on back and front. Join sleeve and side seams. Sew down pocket backs and neaten row ends of pocket tops on right side. Join row ends of back section of hood to the cast-off groups at each side. Beginning and ending 1 inch in from centre front edges sew the cast on edge of hood to neck ribbing stretching the ribbing to fit the hood. Insert zip. Make a length of twisted cord; thread through hem at face edge and finish with tassels.

The Skirt

The Back and Front (both alike)

With No. 8 needles cast on 97 (105) sts.

1st row: K.1, * y.fwd., s.k.p.o., k.6; repeat from * to end.

2nd row: * P.7, k.1; repeat from * to last st., p.1.

3rd row: K.1, * p.1, with yarn at front to make a st., s.k.p.o., k.5; repeat from * to end.

4th row: * P.6, k.2; repeat from * to last st., p.1.

5th row: K.1, * p.2, with yarn at front to make a st., s.k.p.o., k.4; repeat from * to end.

6th row: * P.5, k.3; repeat from * to last st., p.1.

7th row: K.1, * p.3, with yarn at front to make a st., s.k.p.o., k.3; repeat from * to end.

8th row: * P.4, k.4; repeat from * to last st., p.1.

9th row: K.1, * p.4, with yarn at front to make a st., s.k.p.o., k.2; repeat from * to end.

10th row: * P.3, k.5; repeat from * to last st., p.1.

11th row: K.1, * p.5, with yarn at front to make a st., s.k.p.o., k.1; repeat from * to end.

12th row: * P.2, k.6; repeat from * to last st., p.1.

13th row: K.1, * p.6, with yarn at front to make a st., s.k.p.o.; repeat from * to end.

14th row: * P.1, k.7; repeat from * to last st., p.1.

These 14 rows form the pattern of imitation pleats.

Repeat them 3 times more, then work first 6 (8) rows again.

184

Opposite – Jersey, skirt and trouser (pattern p. 186).

Change to No. 10 needles and beginning right-side rows with k.1 and wrong-side rows with p.1, work 8 rows in single rib.
Cast off loosely in rib.

To Make Up The Skirt

Press very lightly on wrong side taking care not to stretch the knitting, using a warm iron over a damp cloth. Join side seams. Join elastic into a circle and secure inside waist ribbing with a herringbone st. casing.

Jersey, Skirt and Trousers

(see illustration p. 185)

Matching Sweaters with Skirt or Trousers

Materials

For the Jersey: Seven 25 gramme balls of Lister Lavenda Double Knitting Wool in main colour and four balls in a contrast colour; a pair each of No. 8 and No. 10 knitting needles; 2 buttons.

For the Skirt: Five balls of the same wool in main colour; a pair each of No. 8 and No. 10 knitting needles; a waist length of elastic.

For the Trousers: Four balls of the same wool in main colour; a pair each of No. 8 and No. 10 knitting needles; a waist length of elastic.

Tension

Work at a tension of 11 stitches and 15 rows to 2 inches, over the stocking stitch and 19 stitches and 34 rows to 3 inches over the pattern, using No. 8 needles, to obtain the following measurements:

Measurements

	INCHES
The Jersey	
All round at underarms	25
Side seam	8
Length	13
Sleeve seam	$8\frac{1}{2}$
The Skirt	
Length	$9\frac{3}{4}$
The Trousers	
All round at widest part	$25\frac{1}{2}$
Length	$8\frac{1}{2}$

Abbreviations

K., knit; p., purl; st., stitch; tog., together; dec., decrease (by working 2 sts. tog.); inc., increase (by working twice into same st.); sl., slip; w.o.n., wool over needle to make a st.; k.2 tog.b., k.2 sts. tog. through back of loops; p.s.s.o., pass slipped st. over; w.t.f., wool to front; w.t.b., wool to back; st.st., stocking st. (k. on right side and p. on wrong side); single rib is k.1 and p.1 alternately; m., main colour; c., contrast colour.

The Jersey

The Back

With No. 10 needles and m., cast on 79 sts. and, beginning right-side rows with k.1 and wrong-side rows with p.1, work 14 rows in single rib.

Change to No. 8 needles and work in pattern as follows:

1st row: With m., all k.
2nd row: With m., all p.
3rd row: With c., k.1, * sl.1 p.wise, k.1; repeat from * to end.
4th row: With c., k.1, * w.t.f., sl.1 p.wise, w.t.b., k.1; repeat from * to end.

These 4 rows form the pattern; repeat them 17 times more.

To shape the armholes: Keeping continuity of pattern cast off 3 sts. at beginning of next 2 rows, then dec. 1 st. at each end of next and following 6 right-side rows – 59 sts. **

Work 35 rows straight.

To slope the shoulders: Cast off 6 sts. at beginning of next 4 rows and 7 sts. on following 2 rows.

Cast off remaining 21 sts.

The Front

Work as given for back to **

On these 59 sts., work 2 rows, ending with a right-side row.

Now divide sts. for front opening.

Next row: P. 27 and leave these sts. on spare needle for right side, p. next 5 sts. and leave on safety-pin for buttonhole band, p. to end and work on these 27 sts. for left side.

The left side: Work 25 rows straight, ending at neck edge.

To shape the neck: Cast off 3 sts. at beginning of next row, then dec. 1 st. at neck edge on each of next 5 rows – 19 sts.

Work 1 row to finish at armhole edge.

To slope the shoulder: Cast off 6 sts. at beginning of next and following alternate row; work 1 row, then cast off remaining 7 sts.

The right side: With right side of work facing, rejoin wool to 27 sts. on spare needle and work to end of row.

Now work as given for left side to end.

The Sleeves (both alike)

With No. 10 needles and m., cast on 43 sts. and work 14 rows in single rib as given for back.

Change to No. 8 needles and work the 4 pattern rows given for back 3 times.

Keeping continuity of the pattern, inc. 1 st. at each end of next 2 rows and every following 11th and 12th rows until the 12th inc. row has been worked – 67 sts.

Work 2 rows straight.

To shape the sleeve top: Cast off 3 sts. at beginning of next 2 rows, then dec. 1 st. at each end of next and following 6 right-side rows – 47 sts.

Work 1 row, then dec. 1 st. at each end of next 8 rows.

Cast off remaining 31 sts.

The Collar

With No. 10 needles and m., cast on 99 sts. and work 2 rows in single rib as given for back.

Next (dec.) row: Rib 3, sl.1, k.2 tog., p.s.s.o., rib to last 6 sts., k.3 tog., rib 3.

Next row: Work in rib.

Repeat last 2 rows 10 times more.

Cast off remaining 55 sts. loosely.

The Buttonhole Band

Rejoin m. to the 5 sts. at centre and, using No. 10 needles, work as follows:

1st row: K.1, then inc. in each of next 4 sts. – 9 sts.

Work 7 rows in single rib.

Next (buttonhole) row: Rib 4, w.o.n., k.2 tog., rib 3.

Rib 11 rows.

Work buttonhole row, then rib 3 rows.

Cast off.

The Button Band

With No. 10 needles and m. cast on 9 sts. and work 24 rows in single rib.

Cast off.

To Make Up The Jersey

Press on wrong side, avoiding the ribbing, using a warm iron over a damp cloth. Join shoulder seams, set in sleeves, then join sleeve and side seams. Sew bands to respective fronts and neaten lower edge of opening. Sew cast-off edge of collar evenly to neck edge. Sew on buttons.

The Skirt

The Back and Front (both alike)

With No. 10 needles and m. cast on 94 sts. and work 6 rows in single rib.

Change to No. 8 needles, beginning with a k. row, st.st. 16 rows.

Next (shaping) row: K.22, k.2 tog.b., k. to last 24 sts., k.2 tog., k.22.

St.st. 5 rows.

Repeat last 6 rows 6 times more, then work shaping row again – 78 sts.

P.1 row.

Change to No. 10 needles and work 4 rows in single rib.

Next (slot) row: Rib 2, * w.o.n., k.2 tog., rib 2; repeat from * to end.

Work a further 3 rows in single rib.

Cast off in rib.

To Make Up The Skirt

Press as given for jersey. Join side seams. Thread elastic through holes at waist.

The Trousers

The Right Leg

With No. 10 needles and m. cast on 94 sts. and work 4 rows in single rib.

Change to No. 8 needles and k.1 row – omit this row when working left leg.

To shape the back and front: Continuing in st.st. cast off 2 sts. at beginning of next 3 rows, then dec. 1 st. at each end of next 3 rows.

On these 82 sts., work 1 row.

Dec. 1 st. at each end of next and following 2 alternate rows – 76 sts.

Work 3 rows.

Dec. 1 st. at each end of next and 2 following 4th rows – 70 sts.

Work 26 rows ending with a right-side row – end with a wrong-side row here on left leg.

To shape for extra length on back:

1st and 2nd (turning) rows: P.54 for 1st row, turn and k. to end for 2nd row.

3rd and 4th rows: P.35, turn and k. to end.

5th and 6th rows: P.16, turn and k. to end.

P.1 row across all sts. picking up a thread at each point where work was turned and taking this together with next st. to avoid a gap in the knitting.

Change to No. 10 needles and work 4 rows in single rib.

Next (slot) row: Rib 2, * w.o.n., k.2 tog., rib 2; repeat from * to end.

Work 3 rows in single rib.

Cast off loosely in rib.

The Left Leg

Work as given for right leg noting the row to be omitted before working the shaping.

This will reverse the shapings and the turning rows will read:

1st and 2nd rows: K.54, turn and p. to end.

3rd and 4th rows: K.35, turn and p. to end.

5th and 6th rows: K.16, turn and p. to end.

K.1 row across all sts. closing gaps.

To Make Up The Trousers

Press as given for jersey. Join inner leg seams, then join front and back seams. Thread elastic through holes at waist.

Cabled Jacket and Trousers

Materials

For the Jacket: Ten 25 gramme balls of Wendy Double Knit Nylonised for 1st size; eleven balls for 2nd size; for either size: a pair each of No. 8 and No. 10 knitting needles; a cable needle; 6 buttons.

For the Trousers: Ten balls of the same wool for 1st size; eleven balls for 2nd size; for either size a pair each of No. 8 and No. 10 knitting needles; a cable needle; waist length of 1 inch wide elastic.

Tension

Work at a tension of 11 stitches and 15 rows to 2 inches, over the stocking stitch, using No. 8 needles, to obtain the following measurements:

Abbreviations

K., knit; p., purl; st., stitch; tog., together; dec., decrease (by working 2 sts. tog.); inc., increase (by working twice into same st.); sl., slip; c.6f., cable 6 front (sl. next 3 sts. onto cable needle and leave at front of work, k.3, then k.3 from cable needle); c.6b., cable 6 back (sl. next 3 sts. onto cable needle and leave at back of work, k.3, then k.3 from cable needle); st.st., stocking st. (k. on right side and p. on wrong side); single rib is k.1 and p.1 alternately.

● *The instructions are given for 1st size. Where they vary, work figures in brackets for 2nd size.*

Measurements

	INCHES	
	1st size	2nd size
The Jacket		
All round at underarms	24	26
Side seam	$8\frac{1}{4}$	$9\frac{1}{4}$
Length	13	$14\frac{1}{2}$
Sleeve seam	$9\frac{1}{4}$	$10\frac{1}{4}$
The Trousers		
Inside leg seam	14	$15\frac{1}{2}$
Outside leg seam	20	$21\frac{1}{2}$

The Jacket

The Back

With No. 10 needles cast on 75 (81) sts. and, beginning right-side rows with k.1 and wrong-side rows with p.1, work 10 rows in single rib.

Change to No. 8 needles.

1st foundation row: K.8 (10), p.2, k.6, p.2, k.7 (8), p.2, k.6, p.2, k.5, p.2, k.6, p.2, k.7 (8), p.2, k.6, p.2, k.8 (10).

2nd foundation row: P.8 (10), k.2, p.6, k.2, p.7 (8), k.2, p.6, k.2, p.5, k.2, p.6, k.2, p.7 (8), k.2, p.6, k.2, p.8 (10).

Repeat these 2 foundation rows once more.

Now work in pattern as follows:

1st row: K.8 (10), p.2, c.6b., p.2, k.7 (8), p.2, c.6b., p.2, k.5, p.2, c.6f., p.2, k.7 (8), p.2, c.6f., p.2, k.8 (10).

2nd row: P.8 (10), k.2, p.6, k.2, p.7 (8), k.2, p.6, k.2, p.5, k.2, p.6, k.2, p.7 (8), k.2, p.6, k.2, p.8 (10).

3rd row: K.8 (10), p.2, k.6, p.2, k.7 (8), p.2, k.6, p.2, k.5, p.2, k.6, p.2, k.7 (8), p.2, k.6, p.2, k.8 (10).

4th row: As 2nd row.

5th to 8th rows: Repeat 3rd and 4th rows twice.

These 8 rows form the pattern; repeat them 5 (6) times more.

To shape the armholes: Keeping continuity of pattern, cast of 4 sts. at beginning of next 2 rows, then dec. 1 st. at each end of the next row and following 3 (4) right-side rows — 59 (63) sts.

Work 25 rows straight.

To slope the shoulders: Cast off 9 (10) sts. at beginning of next 2 rows and 10 sts. on following 2 rows.

Break off wool and leave remaining 21 (23) sts. on a spare needle.

The Left Front

With No. 10 needles cast on 37 (39) sts. and, beginning right-side rows with k.1 and wrong-side rows with p.1, work 10 rows in single rib, decreasing 1 st. in centre of last row on the 1st size only — 36 (39) sts. **

Change to No. 8 needles.

1st foundation row: K.8 (10), p.2, k.6, p.2, k.7 (8), p.2, k.6, p.2, k.1.

2nd foundation row: P.1, k.2, p.6, k.2, p.7 (8), k.2, p.6, k.2, p.8 (10).

Repeat these 2 rows once more.

Now work in pattern as follows:

1st row: K.8 (10), p.2, c.6b., p.2, k.7 (8), p.2, c.6b., p.2, k.1.

2nd row: P.1, k.2, p.6, k.2, p.7 (8), k.2, p.6, k.2, p.8 (10).

3rd row: K.8 (10), p.2, k.6, p.2, k.7 (8), p.2, k.6, p.2, k.1.

4th row: As 2nd row.

5th to 8th rows: Repeat 3rd and 4th rows twice.

Repeat these 8 rows 5 (6) times more.

To shape the armhole: Cast off 4 sts. at beginning of next row; work 1 row, then dec. 1 st. at armhole edge on next and following 3 (4) right-side rows — 28 (30) sts.

Work 14 rows straight, ending at front edge.

To shape the neck: Cast off 2 (3) sts. at beginning of next row, then dec. 1 st. at neck edge on next 7 rows — 19 (20) sts.

Work 3 rows straight, ending at armhole edge.

To slope the shoulder: Cast off 9 (10) sts. at beginning of next row; work 1 row, then cast off remaining 10 sts.

The Right Front

Work as left front to **.

Change to No. 8 needles.

1st foundation row: K.1, p.2, k.6, p.2, k.7 (8), p.2, k.6, p.2, k.8 (10).

2nd foundation row: P.8 (10), k.2, p.6, k.2, p.7 (8), k.2, p.6, k.2, p.1.

Repeat these 2 rows once more.

Now work in pattern as follows:

1st row: K.1, p.2, c.6f., p.2, k.7 (8), p.2, c.6f., p.2, k.8 (10).

2nd row: P.8 (10), k.2, p.6, k.2, p. 7(8), k.2, p.6, k.2, p.1.

3rd row: K.1, p.2, k.6, p.2, k.7 (8), p.2, k.6, p.2, k.8 (10).

4th row: As 2nd row.

5th to 8th rows: Repeat 3rd and 4th rows twice.

Repeat these 8 rows 5 (6) times more, then work 1st row again.

To shape the armhole: Cast off 4 sts. at beginning of next row, then dec. 1 st. at armhole edge on next and following 3 (4) right-side rows – 28 (30) sts.

Work 15 rows straight, ending at front edge.

To shape the neck and shoulder: Work as left front to end.

The Left Sleeve

With No. 10 needles cast on 40 sts. and work 12 rows in single rib.

Change to No. 8 needles.

1st foundation row: K.15, p.2, k.6, p.2, k.15.

2nd foundation row: P.15, k.2, p.6, k.2, p.15.

Repeat these 2 rows once more.

Now work in pattern as follows:

1st row: K.15, p.2, c.6b., p.2, k.15.

2nd row: P.15, k.2, p.6, k.2, p.15.

These 2 rows set position of sts. for the cable panel. Keeping continuity of the panel by working the c.6b. on every 8th row from previous cable row, inc. 1 st. at each end of next and every following 8th row until the 7th (8th) inc. row has been worked – 54 (56) sts.

Work 3 rows straight.

To shape the sleeve top: Cast off 4 sts. at beginning of next 2 rows, then dec. 1 st. at each end of next and following 5 (6) alternate rows – 34 sts.

Work 1 row, then dec. 1 st. at each end of next 8 rows.

Cast off remaining 18 sts.

The Right Sleeve

Work as given for left sleeve but work c.6f. instead of c.6b.

The Button Band

With No. 10 needles cast on 9 sts.

1st row: K.1, * p.1, k.1 ; repeat from * to end.

2nd row: K.2, p.1, k.1, p.1, k.1, p.1, k.2.

Repeat these 2 rows 41 (46) times more.

Break off wool and leave sts. on safety-pin.

The Buttonhole Band

With No. 10 needles cast on 9 sts. and rib 6 rows as given for button band.

1st (buttonhole) row: Rib 3, cast off 3, rib to end.

2nd (buttonhole) row: Rib 3, turn, cast on 3, turn, rib to end.

Rib 14 (16) rows.

Repeat last 16 (18) rows 3 times more, then work buttonhole rows again.

Rib 12 (14) rows.

Break off wool and leave sts. on safety-pin.

The Neck Band

First join shoulder seams. Slip sts. of right front band onto No. 10 needle, rejoin wool to neck edge of right front and onto this needle pick up and k.18 (19) sts. from right front neck edge, k. across the 21 (23) sts. of back and pick up and k.18 (19) sts. from left front neck edge, then rib across the 9 sts. of left front band – 75 (79) sts.

Rib 1 row.

Work buttonhole over next 2 rows, then rib 3 rows.

Cast off in rib.

To Make Up The Jacket

Press on wrong side, avoiding the ribbing, using a warm iron over a damp cloth. Set in sleeves, join sleeve and side seams. Sew front bands in place. Sew on buttons.

The Trousers

The Right Leg

With No. 10 needles cast on 56 (60) sts. and, beginning with a k. row, st.st. 9 rows.

Next row: All k. on wrong side to mark hemline.

Change to No. 8 needles.

1st foundation row: K.23 (25), p.2, k.6, p.2, k.23 (25).

2nd foundation row: P.23 (25), k.2, p.6, k.2, p.23 (25).

Repeat these 2 rows once more.

Now work in pattern as follows:

1st row: K.23 (25), p.2, c.6f., p.2, k.23 (25).

2nd row: P.23 (25), k.2, p.6, k.2, p.23 (25).

3rd row: K.23 (25), p.2, k.6, p.2, k.23 (25).

4th row: P.23 (25), k.2, p.6, k.2, p.23 (25).

5th to 8th rows: Repeat 3rd and 4th rows twice.

Keeping continuity of the cable panel inc. 1 st. at each end of the next row and every following 6th (8th) row until the 6th inc. row has been worked – 68 (72) sts.

Work 5 rows straight, then inc. 1 st. at each end of the next row and every following 6th row until a further 6 inc. rows have been completed – 80 (84) sts.

Work 1 row, then inc. 1 st. at each end of the next row and following 9 alternate rows – 100 (104) sts.

Work 1 row **.

*** **To shape the centre front and back seams:**

1st row: Cast off 3, pattern to end.

2nd row: Cast off 2, pattern to end.

3rd row: Cast off 3, pattern to end.

4th row: Dec., pattern to end.

5th row: Cast off 3, pattern to end.

6th row: Dec., pattern to end.

7th row: Cast off 3, pattern to end.

Dec. 1 st. at beginning only of the next row and following alternate row – 82 (86) sts.

Dec. 1 st. at each end of the next row and every following 4th row until the 9th dec. row has been worked – 64 (68) sts.

Work 2 rows straight, ending with a right-side row (end with a wrong-side row when working left leg).

To shape for extra length on back:

1st and 2nd (turning) rows: Pattern 57 (60) for 1st row, turn and pattern to end for 2nd row.

3rd and 4th rows: Pattern 50 (52), turn and pattern to end.

5th and 6th rows: Pattern 43 (44), turn and pattern to end.

7th and 8th rows: Pattern 36, turn and pattern to end.

9th and 10th rows: Pattern 29, turn and pattern to end.

11th and 12th rows: Pattern 22, turn and pattern to end.

13th and 14th rows: Pattern 15, turn and pattern to end.

15th and 16th rows: Pattern 8, turn and pattern to end.

Work 1 row across all 64 (68) sts. picking up a thread at each point where work was turned and taking this together with next st. to avoid a gap in the knitting.

Change to No. 10 needles and work 8 rows in single rib.

Cast off loosely in rib.

The Left Leg

Work as given for right leg to ** but work c.6b. instead of c.6f.

Work 1 row more, to end with a right-side row.

Now work as given for right leg from *** to end noting that you end with a wrong-side row before shaping for extra length on back.

To Make Up The Trousers

Press on wrong side, avoiding the ribbing, using a warm iron over a damp cloth. Join inner leg seams, then join front and back seams. Turn up hems and sew in place. Join elastic into a circle and secure inside waist ribbing with a herringbone st. casing. Press centre creases.

Opposite – Party dress and co (pattern p. 194).

Party Dress and Coat

(see illustration p. 193)

Matching Dress and Coat for the Special Occasion. The sleeveless coat makes an excellent pinafore dress to wear with sweater or blouse

Contributed by Eugenie Hammond

Materials

For the Dress: Seven 23.25-gramme balls of Wendy Courtelle 4-ply Crêpe; a pair of No. 10 knitting needles; 3 buttons; $1\frac{1}{2}$ yards of ribbon.
For the Coat: Five 23.25-gramme balls of Wendy Courtelle 4-ply Crêpe; a pair of No. 10 knitting needles; 6 buttons.

Tension

Work at a tension of 13 stitches and 18 rows to 2 inches, over the stocking stitch, using No. 10 needles, to obtain the following measurements:

Abbreviations

K., knit; p., purl; st., stitch; tog., together; dec., decrease (by working 2 sts. tog.); y.fwd., yarn forward to make a st.; k.2 tog.b., k.2 sts. tog. through back of loops; st.st., stocking st. (k. on right side and p. on wrong side); m.st., moss st. (k.1 and p.1 alternately and on subsequent rows the sts. are reversed).

● *Instructions given in brackets must be worked the number of times stated after second bracket.*

Measurements

	INCHES
The Dress	
All round at underarms	*24*
Side seam	$11\frac{3}{4}$
Length	$16\frac{1}{2}$
Sleeve seam	$6\frac{1}{2}$
The Coat	
All round at underarms	$25\frac{1}{2}$
Side seam	$11\frac{3}{4}$
Length	$16\frac{1}{2}$

The Dress

The Back

With No. 10 needles cast on 113 sts.

M.st. row: K.1, * p.1, k.1 ; repeat from * to end.

Repeat this row 5 times more.

Next row: All k.

Next row: All p.

Now shape skirt as follows :

Next (shaping) row: K.24, k.2 tog., k. to last 26 sts., k.2 tog.b., k.24.

Beginning with a p. row, st.st. 5 rows.

Repeat last 6 rows 15 times more, then work shaping row again – 79 sts. **

P.1 row.

To shape the raglan armholes:

1st row: Cast off 5, k. to end.

2nd row: Cast off 5, p. to end.

3rd row: K.2, k.2 tog., k. to last 4 sts., k.2 tog.b., k.2.

4th row: K.1, p. to last st., k.1 ***

Repeat 3rd and 4th rows 4 times more, then work 3rd row again – 57 sts.

Now divide sts. for back opening.

Next row: K.1, p.26 and leave these 27 sts. on spare needle for left side, p. to last st., k.1 and work on these 30 sts. for right side.

The right side:

1st row: K.2, k.2 tog., k. to end.

2nd row: K.2, p. to last st., k.1.

Repeat these 2 rows 4 times more.

Next (buttonhole) row: K.2, k.2 tog., k. to last 4 sts., k.2 tog., y.fwd., k.2.

Next row: As 2nd row.

Repeat 1st and 2nd rows 4 times more, then work buttonhole row again.

Next row: As 2nd row.

Repeat 1st and 2nd rows twice more.

Cast off remaining 17 sts.

The left side: With right side of work facing, rejoin yarn to 27 sts. left on spare needle, cast on 3 sts. for underlap.

1st row: K. to last 4 sts., k.2 tog.b., k.2.

2nd row: K.1, p. to last 2 sts., k.2.

Repeat these 2 rows 12 times more.

Cast off remaining 17 sts.

The Front

Work as given for back to ***

Repeat 3rd and 4th rows 13 times more, then work 3rd row again – 39 sts.

Now divide sts. for front neck.

Next row: K.1, p.11 and leave these 12 sts. on spare needle for right side, cast off next 15 sts., p. to last st., k.1 and work on these 12 sts. for left side.

The left side: To shape the neck and continue shaping raglan: Work 6 rows decreasing 1 st. for raglan, as before, on each right-side row and dec. 1 st. at neck edge on each of these rows – 3 sts. ****

Next row: K.1, k.2 tog.

Next row: P.1, k.1.

Take remaining 2 sts. tog. and fasten off.

The right side: With right side of work facing, rejoin yarn to the 12 sts. on spare needle and work as given for left side to ****

Next row: K.2 tog.b., k.1.

Next row: K.1, p.1.

Take remaining 2 sts. tog. and fasten off.

The Sleeves (both alike)

With No. 10 needles cast on 89 sts. and work 4 rows in m.st. increasing 1 st. at end of last row – 90 sts.

Now work in pattern as follows :

1st row: K.1, k.2 tog., k.2 tog., * (y.fwd., k.1) 3 times, y.fwd., (k.2 tog.) 4 times; repeat from * to last 8 sts., (y.fwd., k.1) 3 times, y.fwd., k.2 tog., k.2 tog., k.1.

2nd row: All p.

3rd row: All k.

4th row: All p.

Repeat these 4 rows 12 times more, then work 1st and 2nd rows again.

Next (dec.) row: * (k.1, k.2 tog.) 4 times, k.1, k.3 tog.; repeat from * 4 times more, (k.1, k.2 tog.) 3 times, k.1 – 57 sts.

Next row (wrong side): All k.

Next (slot) row: K.1, * y.fwd., k.2 tog.; repeat from * to end.

Next row (wrong side): All k.

To shape the raglan sleeve top:
1st row: Cast off 5, k. to end.
2nd row: Cast off 5, p. to end.
3rd row: K.2, k.2 tog., k. to last 4 sts., k.2 tog.b., k.2.
4th row: K.1, p. to last st., k.1.
Repeat 3rd and 4th rows 18 times more.
Cast off remaining 9 sts.

The Collar

With No. 10 needles cast on 123 sts. and work the 4 pattern rows given for sleeves twice, then work 1st and 2nd rows again.
Next (dec.) row: * K.3 tog., k.2 tog., k.2 tog.; repeat from * to last 4 sts., k.2 tog., k.2 tog. – 53 sts.

Next row: Work in m.st.
Next (buttonhole) row: Work in m.st. to last 4 sts., k.2 tog., y.fwd., m.st.2.
Work 3 rows in m.st.
Cast off.

To Make Up The Dress

Press lightly on wrong side using a cool iron over a dry cloth.
Join raglan seams, then join sleeve and side seams. Neaten lower edge of back opening. Sew collar evenly to neck edge taking the sts. along the first m.st. row so that the m.st. band forms the neck edge. Sew on buttons. Thread ribbon through sleeves.

The Coat

The Back

With No. 10 needles cast on 117 sts. and work as given for back of dress to **.
On these 83 sts., p.1 row.
To shape the armholes: Cast off 5 sts. at beginning of next 2 rows, then dec. 1 st. at each end of next and following 4 right-side rows – 63 sts.
St.st. 29 rows straight.
To slope the shoulders: Cast off 8 sts. at beginning of next 4 rows.
Cast off remaining 31 sts.

The Left Front

With No. 10 needles cast on 61 sts. and work 6 rows in m.st.
Now continue as follows:
1st row: K. to last 4 sts., m.st.4.
2nd row: M.st.4, p. to end.
Next (shaping) row: K.24, k.2 tog., k. to last 4 sts., m.st.4.
Keeping m.st. border as set, st.st. 5 rows.
Repeat last 6 rows 15 times more, then work shaping row again – 44 sts.
Work 1 row to end at side edge.
To shape the armhole and slope front edge:
1st row: Cast off 5, k. to last 6 sts., k.2 tog.b., m.st.4.
2nd row: M.st.4, p. to end.
3rd row: K.2 tog., k. to last 6 sts., k.2 tog.b., m.st.4.

4th row: M.st.4, p. to end.
Repeat 3rd and 4th rows 3 times more, then work 3rd row again – 28 sts.
This completes armhole shaping.
Work 1 row, then dec. 1 st. at front edge, inside border as before, on next and following alternate row – 26 sts.
Work 3 rows, then dec. 1 st. at front edge on next and every following 4th row until a further 6 dec. rows have been worked – 20 sts.
Work 1 row to end at armhole edge.
To slope the shoulder:
1st row: Cast off 8, k. to last 4 sts., m.st.4.
2nd row: M.st.4, p. to end.
3rd row: Cast off 8, m.st. to end.
On remaining 4 sts. work 14 rows in m.st. for front band extension.
Cast off.

The Right Front

With No. 10 needles cast on 61 sts. and work 6 rows in m.st.
Next row: M.st.4, k. to end.
Next row: P. to last 4 sts., m.st.4.
Next (shaping) row: M.st.4, k. to last 26 sts., k.2 tog.b., k.24.
Keeping m.st. border as set, st.st. 5 rows.
Now, making a buttonhole on next and every following 18th row by working m.st.4, y.fwd., k.2 tog. at beginning of row, repeat last 6 rows 15 times more, then work

196

**Opposite – Poncho and hat (patte
p. 198).**

shaping row again. For your guidance the buttonholes are worked on every 3rd shaping row and the final buttonhole is worked on the last shaping row – 44 sts.

Work 1 row to end at front edge.

To shape the armhole and slope front edge:

1st row: M.st.4, k.2 tog., k. to end.
2nd row: Cast off 5, p. to last 4 sts., m.st.4.
3rd row: M.st.4, k.2 tog., k. to last 2 sts., k.2 tog.
4th row: P. to last 4 sts., m.st.4.

Repeat 3rd and 4th rows 3 times more, then work 3rd row again – 28 sts.

This completes armhole shaping.

Work 1 row, then dec. 1 st. at front edge, as before, on next and following alternate row – 26 sts.

Work 3 rows, then dec. 1 st. at front edge, as before, on next and every following 4th row until a further 6 dec. rows have been worked – 20 sts.

Work 2 rows, ending at armhole edge.

To slope the shoulder:
1st row: Cast off 8, p. to last 4 sts., m.st.4.
2nd row: M.st.4, k. to end.
3rd row: Cast off 8, m.st. to end.

On remaining 4 sts., work 14 rows in m.st. for front band extension.
Cast off.

The Armhole Bands (both alike)

First join shoulder seams. With right side of work facing, rejoin yarn at underarm and, using No. 10 needles, pick up and k.79 sts. along entire armhole edge.

Work 4 rows in m.st. decreasing 1 st. at each end of every row.
Cast off.

To Make Up The Coat

Press as given for dress. Join side seams. Join cast-off edges of front band extensions together and sew in place across back neck. Sew on buttons.

Poncho and Hat

(see illustration p. 197)

**Shaped shoulders and snug fitting neckline
make this poncho something really different.
Matching hat adds the final touch**

Materials

Five 1-ounce balls of Double Knitting
Wool in grey; four balls in orange and
three balls in white; a pair of No. 9
knitting needles; a button mould.

Tension and Size

Worked at a tension of 6 stitches and 8
rows to 1 inch, over the stocking stitch, using
No. 9 needles the Poncho will measure 57
inches all round lower edge and 16 inches
in depth at centre front. The Hat will fit an
average size head.

Abbreviations

K., knit; p., purl; st., stitch; tog., together;
dec., decrease (by working 2 sts. tog.); inc.,
increase (by working twice into same st.);
k. or p.2 tog.b., k. or p.2 sts. tog. through
back of loops; st.st., stocking st. (k. on
right side and p. on wrong side); single rib
is k.1 and p.1 alternately; garter st. is k.
on every row.

The Poncho

The Back and Front (both alike)

With No. 9 needles and grey cast on 171
sts.
1st row: K.83, k.2 tog.b., k.1 and mark this
st. with a coloured thread for centre,
k.2 tog., k.83.
2nd, 3rd and 4th rows: All k.
5th row: K. to within 2 sts. of centre st.,
k.2 tog.b., k.1, k.2 tog., k. to end.
6th, 7th and 8th rows: All k.
9th row: As 5th row.
10th row: All k.
This completes garter st. border.
Beginning with a k. row, st.st. 2 rows, then
dec. 1 st. at each side of centre st. as before,
on next and 2 following 4th rows – 159 sts.
P.1 row. Break off grey; join in orange.
Work 2 rows, then dec. 1 st. at each side
of centre st. on next and 4 following 4th
rows – 149 sts.

P.1 row. Break off orange; join in white.
Dec. 1 st. at each side of centre st. on
next and following 9 alternate rows – 129
sts.
P.1 row. Break off white; join in grey.
Dec. 1 st. at each side of centre on next
and following 9 alternate rows – 109 sts.
P.1 row. Break off grey; join in orange.
Dec. 1 st. at each side of centre on next
and following 6 alternate rows – 95 sts.
P.1 row.
Now shape for shoulder line as follows:
Next row: K.3, k.2 tog.b., k. to within 2 sts.
of centre, k.2 tog.b., k.1, k.2 tog., k. to last
5 sts., k.2 tog., k.3.
Next row: All p.
Repeat last 2 rows twice more – 83 sts.
Break off orange; join in white.
Repeat last 2 rows 4 times more, then
work the first of these rows again – 63 sts.

Continue as follows:

1st row: P.3, p.2 tog., p. to last 5 sts., p.2 tog.b., p.3.

2nd row: K.3, k.2 tog.b., k. to within 2 sts. of centre, k.2 tog.b., k.1, k.2 tog., k. to last 5 sts., k.2 tog., k.3.

3rd row: As 1st row.

On remaining 55 sts., beginning right-side rows with k.1 and wrong-side rows with p.1, work 10 rows in single rib.

Cast off loosely in rib.

To Make Up The Poncho

Press on wrong side using a warm iron over a damp cloth.

Join side seams carefully matching colours.

The Hat

To Make

With No. 9 needles and grey cast on 96 sts. and work 8 rows in single rib.

Now, joining colours as required, using separate balls of wool for each section, work as follows:

1st row: K.16 with grey, join orange, twist wools to avoid gap and with orange k.16, join white and k.16, join grey and k.16, join orange and k.16, join white and k.16.

Beginning with a p. row, st.st. 3 rows working the colour panels as set and twisting wools at each change to avoid gaps in knitting.

Next (inc.) row: * Inc. in 1st st., k. to last 2 sts. of grey section, inc. in next st., k.1; repeat from * across each section.

St.st. 5 rows straight.

Repeat the last 6 rows once more, then work the increase row again – 132 sts.

Break off orange and white.

With grey k.15 rows for garter st. band.

Next row: K.22 grey, join orange and k.22, join white and k.22, join grey and k.22, join orange and k.22, join white and k.22.

P.1 row changing colours as set.

Now shape crown:

Next (dec.) row: * K.1, k.2 tog.b., k. to last 3 sts. of grey section, k.2 tog., k.1; repeat from * across each section.

St.st. 3 rows.

Repeat last 4 rows twice more, then work decrease row again – 84 sts.

P.1 row, then dec. as before. across each section on next and following 3 right-side rows – 36 sts.

Break off wool; run end through remaining sts., draw up and fasten securely.

To Make Up The Hat

Press on wrong side using a warm iron over a damp cloth. Join row ends to form back seam.

The button cover: With grey cast on 8 sts. and work 10 rows in st.st. Cast off. Run a gathering thread all round outer edge, insert button mould; draw up and fasten securely, then sew to top of hat.

Bolero and Skirt

**Even without the fringe this set will look
lovely worked in one colour and worn with
a frilly blouse**

Materials

For the Bolero: Four 25-gramme
balls of Lee Target Motoravia Double
Knitting Wool for either size; a pair
each of No. 8 and No. 9 knitting
needles; oddment of contrast colour
for tassels.
For the Skirt: Five 25-gramme balls
of Lee Target Motoravia Double
Knitting Wool for either size; oddment
of contrast colour for tassels; a pair
each of No. 8 and No. 9 knitting
needles; waist length of 1-inch wide
elastic.

Tension

Work at a tension of 11 stitches and 15
rows to 2 inches, over the stocking stitch,
using No. 8 needles, to obtain the following
measurements:

Measurements

	INCHES	
	1st size	2nd size
The Bolero		
All round at underarms	23½	25
Side seam	6¾	7¼
The Skirt		
All round lower edge	31½	33
Length	8¾	9

Abbreviations

K., knit; p., purl; st., stitch; tog., together;
dec., decrease (by working 2 sts. tog.); inc.,
increase (by working twice into same st.);
k.2 tog.b., k.2 tog. through back of loops;
st.st., stocking st. (k. on right side and p. on
wrong side); garter st. is every row k.

● *The instructions are given for 1st size.
Where they vary, work figures in brackets
for 2nd size.*

The Bolero

The Back

With No. 8 needles cast on 66 (70) sts.
and, beginning with a k. row, st.st. 36 (40)
rows.
To shape the armholes: Cast off 6 (7)
sts. at beginning of next 2 rows, then dec.
1 st. at each end of next and following 6
right-side rows – 40 (42) sts.
St.st. 10 rows ending with a k. row.
Now divide sts. for back neck.

Next row: P.13 (14) cast off next 14 sts.,
p. to end and work on these 13 (14) sts.
for 1st shoulder.
1st shoulder: Dec. 1 st. at neck edge on
next and following 2 (3) right-side rows.
P.1 row, then cast off remaining 10 sts.
2nd shoulder: With right side of work
facing, rejoin wool to the 13 (14) sts. and
work as given for 1st shoulder.

**Opposite – Bolero and skirt; sailor su
(pattern p. 234).**

The Left Front

With No. 8 needles cast on 20 (22) sts. and k.1 row and p.1 row.

Continuing in st.st. inc. 1 st. at end — front edge — on next and following 7 right-side rows — 28 (30) sts.

St.st. 19 (23) rows.

To shape the armhole and slope front edge:

1st row: Cast off 6 (7) sts., k. to last 2 sts., dec.

2nd row: All p.

Work 13 rows decreasing 1 st. at armhole edge on each right-side row and 1 st. at front edge on the 5th and 11th of these rows — 12 (13) sts. This completes armhole shaping.

St.st. 3 rows.

Dec. 1 st. at front edge on next row and following 6th row — 10 (11) sts.

St.st. 7 (9) rows, decreasing 1 st. at front edge on the 6th of these rows on the 2nd size only — 10 sts.

Cast off.

The Right Front

With No. 8 needles cast on 20 (22) sts. and k.1 row and p.1 row.

Inc. 1 st. at beginning – front edge – on next and following 7 right-side rows – 28 (30) sts.

St.st. 20 (24) rows.

To shape the armhole and slope front edge:

1st row: Cast off 6 (7) sts., p. to last 2 sts., p.2 tog.

Work 13 rows decreasing 1 st. at armhole edge on each right-side row and 1 st. at front edge on the 6th and 12th of these rows – 12 (13) sts. This completes armhole shaping.

St.st. 4 rows.

Dec. 1 st. at front edge on next row and following 6th row – 10 (11) sts.

St.st. 7 (9) rows, decreasing 1 st. at front edge on the 6th of these rows on 2nd size only – 10 sts.

Cast off.

The Armhole Bands (both alike)

First join shoulder seams. With right side of work facing, rejoin wool at underarm and, using No. 9 needles, pick up and k.70 (72) sts. along entire armhole edge.

K.3 rows decreasing 1 st. at each end of each row.

Cast off.

The Front Band

First join side seams. With No. 9 needles cast on 8 sts. and slipping first st. on every row work in garter st. until band is long enough, when slightly stretched, to fit all round outer edge of bolero. Cast off when correct length is assured.

To Make Up The Bolero

Press on wrong side, using a warm iron over a damp cloth. Beginning at centre back sew border in place stretching slightly along straight edges and easing to a round shape at lower edge of each front. With contrast colour work a row of chain st. along the border seam on each front. Cut 6-inch lengths of contrast colour and using 2 strands together, work tassels through the chain st. as shewn in photograph.

The Skirt

The Back and Front (both alike)

With No. 8 needles cast on 88 (92) sts. and k.13 rows.

Beginning with a p. row, st.st. 3 (5) rows.

Next (shaping) row: K.23, k.2 tog.b., k. to last 25 sts., k.2 tog., k.23.

St.st. 5 rows.

Repeat shaping row.

Next row: All k. on wrong side to make ridge for fringe.

St.st. 4 rows.

Work the shaping row, then st.st. 5 rows.

Repeat last 6 rows 4 times more, then work shaping row again – 72 (76) sts.

St.st. 8 rows.

Next row: All k. on wrong side to mark fold line.

Change to No. 9 needles and st.st. a further 8 rows.

Cast off loosely.

To Make Up The Skirt

Press as given for bolero. Join side seams. Trim with contrast tassel fringe along the ridge at lower edge. Fold along line at waist and slip st. in place leaving a small opening. Insert elastic. Close opening.

Cowboy Suit

(see illustration p. 204)

Two-colour jersey and plain trousers to keep him warm. Add the fringe and accessories and he's a happy cowboy.

Materials

The Sweater: Seven 25-gramme balls of Wendy Double Knit Nylonised in main colour and three balls in a contrast colour for either size.

The Trousers: Ten balls in main colour for either size.

For either size or garment: a pair each of No. 8 and No. 10 knitting needles; a medium-size crochet hook; a waist length of 1-inch wide elastic for trousers.

Tension

Work at a tension of 11 stitches and 15 rows to 2 inches, over the stocking stitch, using No. 8 needles, to obtain the following measurements:

Abbreviations

K., knit; p., purl; st., stitch; tog., together; dec., decrease (by working 2 sts. tog.); inc., increase (by working twice into same st.); k.2 tog.b., k.2 sts. tog. through back of loops; y.fwd., yarn forward to make a st.; sl., slip; p.s.s.o., pass slipped st. over; st.st., stocking st. (k. on right side and p. on wrong side); single rib is k.1 and p.1 alternately; m., main colour; c., contrast colour.

● *The instructions are given for 1st size. Where they vary, work figures in brackets for 2nd size.*

Measurements

INCHES

	1st size	2nd size
The Sweater		
All round at underarms	24	$25\frac{1}{4}$
Side seam	$7\frac{3}{4}$	$8\frac{3}{4}$
Length	$12\frac{3}{4}$	14
Sleeve seam	8	9
The Trousers		
Inside leg seam	14	$15\frac{1}{2}$
Outside leg	20	$21\frac{1}{2}$

The Sweater

The Back

With No. 10 needles and m., cast on 66 (70) sts. and work 10 rows in single rib.

Change to No. 8 needles and, beginning with a k. row, st.st. 50 (56) rows.

To shape the armholes: Cast off 4 sts. at beginning of next 2 rows, then dec. 1 st. at each end of next and following 2 (3) right-side rows — 52 (54) sts.

P.1 row. Break of m. and join on c.
Next row: All k.
Next row (wrong side): All k. **.

Beginning with a k. row, st.st. 24 rows.

To slope the shoulders: Cast off 7 (8) sts. at beginning of next 2 rows and 8 sts. on the following 2 rows.

Cast off the remaining 22 sts.

The Front

Work as given for back to **
Now divide sts. for front opening.
Next row: K.26 (27) turn and work on these sts. for the 1st half.
1st half:
1st row: K.4, p. to end.
2nd (slot) row: K. to last 2 sts., y.fwd., k.2 tog.
*** Keeping garter st. border, work 5 rows, then work slot row.
Repeat last 6 rows once more.
Work 2 rows, ending at front edge (work 3 rows here when working 2nd half).
To shape the neck: Cast off 8 sts. at beginning of next row, then dec. 1 st. at neck edge on next and following 2 alternate rows – 15 (16) sts.
Work 1 row to finish at armhole edge.
To slope the shoulder: Cast off 7 (8) sts. at beginning of next row; work 1 row, then cast off remaining 8 sts.
2nd half: With right side of work facing, rejoin yarn to remaining sts.
1st row: All k.
2nd row: P. to last 4 sts., k.4.
3rd (slot) row: K.2 tog., y.fwd., k. to end.
Now work as given for 1st half from ***
to end.

The Sleeves (both alike)

With No. 10 needles and m., cast on 40 sts. and work 10 rows in single rib.
Change to No. 8 needles and, beginning with a k. row, st.st. 10 rows.
Inc. 1 st. at each end of the next row and every following 8th row until the 5th (6th) inc. row has been worked – 50 (52) sts.

Work 7 rows.
To shape the sleeve top: Cast off 4 sts. at beginning of next 2 rows, then dec. 1 st. at each end of next and following 7 (8) alternate rows – 26 sts.
Work 1 row, then dec. 1 st. at each end of the next 5 rows – 16 sts.
Work 1 row, then cast off.

The Collar

With No. 10 needles and c., cast on 99 sts. and beginning right-side rows with k.1 and wrong-side rows with p.1, work 2 rows in single rib.
Next (shaping) row: Rib 3, sl.1, k.2 tog., p.s.s.o., rib to last 6 sts., k.3 tog., rib 3.
Next row: Work in rib.
Repeat last 2 rows 10 times more.
Cast off the remaining 55 sts. loosely in rib.

To Make Up The Sweater

Press on wrong side, avoiding the ribbing, using a warm iron over a damp cloth. Join shoulder seams, set in sleeves, then join sleeve and side seams. Beginning and ending in centre of front bands, sew cast-off edge of collar to neck edge.
Trim front and back with fringe as follows: Cut c. into 4-inch lengths and using 2 strands together, fold in half and draw looped end through a st. along garter st. ridge on yoke, put cut ends through loop and pull tight to form tassel.
Make a twisted cord with main colour and use to fasten front.

The Trousers

The Right Leg

With No. 10 needles and m. cast on 67 (71) sts. and, beginning with a k. row, st.st. 9 rows.
Next row: All k. on wrong side to mark hemline.
Change to No. 8 needles.
1st row: K.26 (28), p.1, k.13, p.1, k.26 (28).

2nd row: P.26 (28), k.1, p.13, k.1, p.26 (28).
To shape the inset:
1st row: K.26 (28), p.1, k.2 tog.b., k.9, k.2 tog., p.1, k.26 (28).
2nd row: P.26 (28), k.1, p.11, k.1, p.26 (28).
3rd row: K.26 (28), p.1, k.11, p.1, k.26 (28).

Repeat 2nd and 3rd rows once (twice) more, then work 2nd row again — 65 (69) sts.

To shape inside leg and continue shaping inset:

Next row: Inc. in 1st st., k.25 (27), p.1, k.2 tog.b., k.7, k.2 tog., p.1, k.25 (27), inc. in last st.

Keeping the 'p' st. at each side on inset, work 5 (7) rows straight.

Next row: Inc. 1 st. at each end and dec. 1 st. at each side of inset as before.

Repeat last 6 (8) rows twice more — 65 (69) sts.

Work 5 (7) rows straight.

Next row: Inc. in 1st st., k.29 (31), p.1, sl.1, k.2 tog., p.s.s.o., p.1, k.29 (31), inc. in last st.

Next row: P.31 (33), k.1, p.1, k.1, p.31 (33).

Work 4 (6) rows straight.

Next row: Inc. in 1st st., k.30 (32), sl.1, k.2 tog., p.s.s.o., k.30 (32), inc. in last st. — 65 (69) sts.

Beginning with a p. row, st.st. 5 rows.

Inc. 1 st. at each end of the next row and every following 6th row until the 6th inc. row has been worked — 77 (81) sts.

Work 1 row, then inc. 1 st. at each end of next row and the following 9 alternate rows — 97 (101) sts.

Work 1 row **

*** **To shape the centre front and back seams:**

1st row: Cast off 3, work to end.
2nd row: Cast off 2, work to end.
3rd row: Cast off 3, work to end.
4th row: Dec., work to end.
5th row: Cast off 3, work to end.
6th row: Dec., work to end.
7th row: Cast off 3, work to end.

Dec. 1 st. at beginning of the next row and following alternate row — 79 (83) sts.

Dec. 1 st. at each end of the next row and every following 4th row until the 9th dec. row has been worked — 61 (65) sts.

Work 2 rows straight, ending with a right-side row (end with a wrong-side row here when working left leg).

To shape for extra length on back:

1st and 2nd (turning) rows: Work 54 (60) for 1st row, turn and work to end for 2nd row.

3rd and 4th rows: Work 46 (52), turn and work to end.

5th and 6th rows: Work 38 (44), turn and work to end.

7th and 8th rows: Work 32 (36), turn and work to end.

9th and 10th rows: Work 26 (29), turn and work to end.

11th and 12th rows: Work 20 (22), turn and work to end.

13th and 14th rows: Work 14 (15), turn and work to end.

15th and 16th rows: Work 8, turn and work to end.

Work 1 row across all sts. picking up a thread at each point where work was turned and taking this together with the next st. to avoid a gap in the knitting.

Change to No. 10 needles and work 8 rows in single rib.

Cast off loosely in rib.

The Left Leg

Work as given for right leg to ** then work 1 row more to end with a right-side row.

Now work as given for right leg from *** to end noting that you end with a wrong-side row before shaping for extra length on back.

To Make Up The Trousers

Press as given for sweater. Join inside leg seams, then join front and back seams. Join elastic into a circle and secure inside waist ribbing with a herringbone st. casing. Trim with fringe along 'p' st. ridge at each side of inset at lower edge. Turn up hems and sew in place. Press crease.

Hat and Coat

(see illustration p. 209)

Materials

Fourteen 25-gramme balls of Emu Scotch Superwash Double Knitting Wool for the 1st size; fifteen balls for the 2nd size. For either size: a pair each of No. 8 and No. 10 knitting needles; a cable needle; 4 buttons; alice band for hat.

Tension

Work at a tension of 11 stitches and 15 rows to 2 inches, over the stocking stitch, using No. 8 needles, to obtain the following measurements:

Measurements

	INCHES	
	1st size	2nd size
All round at underarms- fastened	24	26
Side seam	$10\frac{3}{4}$	$11\frac{3}{4}$
Length	18	$19\frac{1}{2}$
Sleeve seam	8	9

Abbreviations

K., knit; p., purl; st., stitch; tog., together; dec., decrease (by working 2 sts. tog.); inc., increase (by working twice into same st.); k.2 tog.b., k.2 sts. tog. through back of loops; sl., slip; p.s.s.o., pass slipped st. over; c.6f., cable 6 front (sl. next 3 sts. onto cable needle and leave at front of work, k.3, then k.3 from cable needle); c.6b., cable 6 back (sl. next 3 sts. onto cable needle and leave at back of work, k.3, then k.3 from cable needle); st.st., stocking st. (k. on right side and p. on the wrong side); single rib is a k.1 and p.1 alternately; up 1 (pick up the thread which lies between the needles and k. into back of it, thus making a st.).

● *The instructions are given for the 1st size. Where they vary, work the figures within the brackets for the 2nd size.*

The Coat

The Back

With No. 10 needles cast on 89 (97) sts. and, beginning with a k. row, st.st. 9 rows.
Next row: All k. on wrong side to mark hemline.
Change to No. 8 needles.
1st foundation row: K.12 (14), p.2, k.6, p.2, k.45 (49), p.2, k.6, p.2, k.12 (14).
2nd foundation row: P.12 (14), k.2, p.6, k.2, p.45 (49), k.2, p.6, k.2, p.12 (14).

Repeat these 2 rows once more.
Now work in pattern and shape as follows:
1st (shaping) row: K.12 (14), p.2, c.6f., p.2, k.4, k.2 tog.b., k. to last 28 (30) sts., k.2 tog., k.4, p.2, c.6b., p.2, k.12 (14).
2nd row: P.12 (14), k.2, p.6, k.2, p. to last 22 (24) sts., k.2, p.6, k.2, p.12 (14).
3rd row: K.12 (14), p.2, k.6, p.2, k. to last 22 (24) sts., p.2, k.6, p.2, k.12 (14).
4th row: As 2nd row.

5th to 8th rows: Repeat 3rd and 4th rows twice.

These 8 rows form the pattern and the shaping; repeat them 8 (9) times more, then work the 1st row again – 69 (75) sts. This completes shaping.

Keeping continuity of the cable panels work a further 3 rows.

To shape the raglan armholes: Dec. 1 st. at each end of the next row and following 26 (28) right-side rows.

On 15 (17) sts., work 1 row.

Cast off.

The Left Front

With No. 10 needles cast on 54 (57) sts. and st.st. 9 rows.

Next row: Cast on 17 for front facing then k. to end of row to mark hemline.

Change to No. 8 needles.

1st foundation row: K.12 (14), p.2, k.6, p.2, k.32 (33), sl.1 p.wise, k.16.

2nd foundation row: K.2, p. to last 22 (24) sts., k.2, p.6, k.2, p.12 (14).

Repeat these 2 rows once more.

Now work in pattern and shape as follows:

1st (shaping) row: K.12 (14), p.2, c.6f., p.2, k.4, k.2 tog.b., k. to last 17 sts., sl.1, k.16.

2nd row: K.2, p. to last 22 (24) sts., k.2, p.6, k.2, p.12 (14).

3rd row: K.12 (14), p.2, k.6, p.2, k. to last 17 sts., sl.1, k.16.

4th row: As 2nd row.

5th to 8th rows: Repeat 3rd and 4th rows twice.

Repeat these 8 rows 8 (9) times more, then work the 1st row again – 61 (63) sts. This completes shaping.

Keeping continuity of the cable panel work a further 3 rows, ending at side edge.

To shape the raglan armhole: Dec. 1 st. at armhole edge on the next row and following 19 (21) right-side rows – 41 sts.

To shape the neck:

Next row: K.2, p.15 and leave these 17 sts. on a stitch-holder for facing, cast off next 8 sts. for neck, pattern to end.

Now work 7 rows decreasing 1 st. at neck edge on each of these rows and 1 st. at armhole edge on each right-side row – 5 sts.

Work 1 row, then dec. 1 st. at armhole edge only on the next row and following 2 alternate rows.

Take remaining 2 sts. tog. and fasten off.

The facing: With right side of work facing, rejoin wool to the 17 sts. left on stitch-holder, cast off 9 sts., k. to end.

Work 1 row, then dec. 1 st. at beginning of the next row and following 5 right-side rows.

Take remaining 2 sts. tog. and fasten off.

The Right Front

With No. 10 needles cast on 54 (57) sts., and st.st. 9 rows.

Next row: All k. on wrong side to mark hemline, turn and cast on 17 sts. for front facing.

Change to No. 8 needles.

1st foundation row: K.16, sl.1, k.32 (33), p.2, k.6, p.2, k.12 (14).

2nd foundation row: P.12 (14), k.2, p.6, k.2, p. to last 2 sts., k.2.

Repeat these 2 rows once more.

Now work in pattern and shape as follows:

1st (shaping) row: K.16, sl.1, k.26 (27), k.2 tog., k.4, p.2, c.6b., p.2, k.12 (14).

2nd row: P.12 (14), k.2, p.6, k.2, p. to last 2 sts., k.2.

3rd row: K.16, sl.1, k. to last 22 (24) sts., p.2, k.6, p.2, k.12 (14).

4th row: As 2nd row.

5th to 8th rows: Repeat 3rd and 4th rows twice.

Repeat these 8 rows 5 times more, then work the first 4 rows again.

Next (double buttonhole) row: K.8, cast off 4 – 1 st. left on right-hand needle – k. next 3 sts., sl.1, k.4, cast off 4, pattern to end.

Next row: Work in pattern casting on 4 sts. over those cast off on previous row.

Still shaping as before, work 20 (28) rows making buttonholes on the 19th/20th (23rd/24th) of these rows. This completes shaping.

On 61 (63) sts., work a further 2 rows, ending at front edge.

To shape the raglan armhole: Work 40 (44) rows decreasing 1 st. at armhole edge on each right-side row and making buttonholes on the 17th/18th and 37th/38th (17th/18th and 41st/42nd) of these rows – 41 sts.

Opposite – Girl's hat and coat; boy cap, coat and trousers (pattern p. 21

To shape the neck:

Next row: K.17 and leave these sts. on a stitch-holder for facing, cast off next 8 sts., pattern to last 2 sts., k.2 tog.

Work 7 rows decreasing 1 st. at neck edge on each row and 1 st. at armhole edge on each right-side row – 5 sts.

Now dec. 1 st. at armhole edge on next row and following 2 right-side rows.

Take remaining 2 sts. tog. and fasten off.

The facing: With wrong side of work facing, rejoin wool to the 17 sts. left on stitch-holder, cast off 9, p. to last 2 sts., k.2.

Work 1 row, then dec. 1 st. at beginning of the next row and following 5 alternate rows.

Take remaining 2 sts. tog. and fasten off.

The Sleeves (both alike)

With No. 10 needles cast on 45 (49) sts. and st.st. 9 rows.

Next row: All k. on wrong side to mark hemline.

Change to No. 8 needles and, beginning with a k. row, st.st. 4 rows.

Inc. 1 st. at each end of the next row and every following 12th (14th) row until the 5th inc. row has been worked.

On 55 (59) sts., st.st. 7 rows.

To shape the raglan sleeve top: Dec. 1 st. at each end of the next row and every following 3rd row until the 13th dec. row has been worked – 29 (33) sts.

Work 1 row, then dec. 1 st. at each end of the next row and following 7 (9) right-side rows.

On 13 sts., p.1 row, then cast off.

The Collar

With No. 8 needles cast on 55 (59) sts. and, beginning with a k. row, st.st. 4 rows.

Next (inc.) row: K.2, up 1, k.1, up 1, k. to last 3 sts., up 1, k.1, up 1, k.2.

St.st. 5 rows.

Repeat last 6 rows once more, then work the increase row again.

On 67 (71) sts., st.st. 4 rows, then k.1 row on wrong side to mark fold line.

Beginning with a k. row, st.st. 4 rows.

Next (dec.) row: K.2, sl.1, k.2 tog., p.s.s.o., k. to last 5 sts., k.3 tog., k.2.

St.st. 5 rows.

Repeat last 6 rows once more, then work the decrease row again – 55 (59) sts.

St.st. 3 rows.

Cast off.

To Make Up The Coat

Press on wrong side, using a warm iron over a damp cloth.

Join raglan seams, then join sleeve and side seams.

Fold collar at fold line and join row ends; turn to right side and press.

Turn facings back to right side and pin collar in place at neck edge, then sew in place taking each end between the facings.

Fold facings to wrong side; press and slip st. in position.

Turn up hem at lower edge and on sleeves and sew in place.

Neaten double buttonholes.

Sew on buttons.

The Hat

To Make

With No. 10 needles cast on 76 (82) sts. and, beginning with a k. row, st.st. 7 rows.

Next row: All k. on wrong side to mark hemline.

Beginning with a k. row, st.st. 6 rows.

Next (hem) row: Fold work in half so that the cast-on edge lies behind the sts. on the needle and form hem by knitting 1 st. on needle together with the corresponding st. along cast-on edge.

Change to No. 8 needles; p.1 row, then work in pattern as follows:

1st row: K.24 (26), p.2, k.6, p.2, k.8 (10), p.2, k.6, p.2, k.24 (26).

2nd row: P.24 (26), k.2, p.6, k.2 p.8 (10), k.2, p.6, k.2, p.24 (26).

3rd and 4th rows: As 1st and 2nd rows.

5th row: K.24 (26), p.2, c.6f., p.2, k.8 (10), p.2, c.6b., p.2, k.24 (26).

6th row: As 2nd row.

7th and 8th rows: As 1st and 2nd rows.

Repeat these 8 rows 4 times more (4 times and first 4 rows again).

To shape the back:

1st and 2nd rows: Cast off 27 (29) sts., k. to end.

You now have a ridge across centre 22 (24) sts.

On remaining 22 (24) sts., beginning with a k. row, st.st. 14 rows.

Dec. 1 st. at each end of the next row and following 6th row.

On 18 (20) sts., st.st. 13 (15) rows.

Cast off.

The back edging: With right side of work facing, rejoin wool to outer edge of the first cast-off group and, using No. 10 needles, pick up and k.27 (29) sts. from those cast off, pick up and k.22 (24) sts.

along ridge at centre and 27 (29) sts. from other side.

On these 76 (82) sts., beginning with a p. row, st.st. 10 rows.

Cast off.

To Make Up The Hat

Press. Join row ends of back section to sides along the original cast-off edges allowing the st.st. rows of edging to roll to wrong side and form a band round back of hat.

Catch this edging in place.

With No. 10 needles, working through one thickness only at hem to leave opening for alice band, pick up and k.81 (87) sts. along neck edge.

Beginning wrong-side rows with p.1 and right-side rows with k.1, work 5 rows in single rib.

Cast off.

Slide alice band through hem at face edge.

Boy's Cap, Coat and Trousers

(see illustration p. 209)

**Peaked Cap, Double Breasted Coat and
Long Trousers**

Materials

For the Coat: Fourteen 25-gramme balls of Emu Scotch Superwash Double Knitting Wool for 1st size; fifteen balls for 2nd size.
For the Trousers: Eight balls of the same wool for 1st size; nine balls for 2nd size.
For the Cap: Two balls for 1st size; three balls for 2nd size.
For either size set: One ball of the same wool in a contrast colour; a pair each of No. 8 and No. 10 knitting needles; 10 medium size buttons; 2 small buttons; waist length of 1-inch wide elastic; large press fastener; canvas and lining for cap.

Tension

Work at a tension of 11 stitches and 15 rows to 2 inches, over the stocking stitch, using No. 8 needles, to obtain the following measurements:

Measurements

INCHES

	1st size	2nd size
The Coat		
All round at underarms	25	27
Side seam	$10\frac{3}{4}$	$11\frac{3}{4}$
Length	18	$19\frac{1}{2}$
Sleeve seam	8	9
The Trousers		
Inside leg seam	14	$15\frac{1}{2}$
Outside leg seam	20	$21\frac{1}{2}$
The Hat		
All round head edge	20	21

Abbreviations

K., knit; p., purl; st., stitch; tog., together; dec., decrease (by working 2 sts. tog.); inc., increase (by working twice into same st.); k.2 tog.b., k.2 sts. tog. through back of loops; up 1 (pick up the thread which lies between the needles and k. into back of it, thus making a st.); tw.2, twist 2 (k. into front of 2nd st. on left-hand needle, then k. 1st st. and slip both sts. off needle tog.); sl., slip; w.fwd., wool forward to make a st.; st.st., stocking st. (k. on right side and p. on wrong side); garter st. is k. on every row; single rib is k.1 and p.1 alternately.

● *Instructions are given for 1st size. Where they vary, work figures in brackets for 2nd size.*

The Coat

The Back

With No. 10 needles cast on 106 (112) sts. and, beginning with a k. row, st.st. 9 rows.

Next row: All k. on wrong side to mark hemline.

Change to No. 8 needles and work in pattern as follows:

1st row: K.31 (34), p.1, * tw.2; repeat from * 20 times more, p.1, k.31 (34).

2nd row: P.31 (34), k.2, * p.1, k.1; repeat from * 20 times more, p.31 (34).

These 2 rows form the pattern; repeat them 3 times more.

Keeping continuity of the centre panel, shape as follows:

Next (shaping) row: K.5, k.2 tog.b., pattern to last 7 sts., k.2 tog., k.5.

Work 13 (15) rows straight.

Repeat last 14 (16) rows twice then work shaping row again – 98 (104) sts.

Work 13 (15) rows straight.

Next (dec.) row: K. nil (2), * k.2 tog., k.1; repeat from * 7 times, k.2 tog., k.1 (2) then, across centre panel work k.1, ** k.2 tog., k.2; repeat from ** 9 times, k.2 tog., k.1, across other side work k.1 (2), *** k.2 tog., k.1; repeat from *** 7 times, k.2 tog., k. nil (2) – 69 (75) sts.

Beginning wrong-side rows with p.1 and right-side rows with k.1, work 7 rows in single rib.

Beginning with a k. row, st.st. 8 rows.

To shape the raglan armholes: Dec. 1 st. at each end of next row and following 26 (28) right-side rows – 15 (17) sts.

Work 1 row.

Cast off.

The Right Front

With No. 10 needles cast on 74 (76) sts. and, beginning with a k. row, st.st. 9 rows.

Next row: All k. on wrong side to mark hemline.

Change to No. 8 needles.

1st row: K.1, * tw.2; repeat from * 19 times, p.1, k.32 (34).

2nd row: P.32 (34), k.2, * p.1, k.1; repeat from * to end.

Repeat these 2 rows 3 times more.

Next (shaping) row: Pattern to last 7 sts., k.2 tog., k.5.

Work 13 (15) rows straight.

Repeat last 14 (16) rows twice more, then work shaping row again – 70 (72) sts.

Work 13 (15) rows straight.

Next (dec.) row: Pattern 42, k.3 (4), * k.2 tog., k.3; repeat from * 3 times, k.2 tog., k.3 (4) – 65 (67) sts.

Continue as follows:

1st row (wrong side): P.1, * k.1, p.1; repeat from * 10 (11) times more, k.2, ** p.1, k.1; repeat from ** to end.

2nd row: Pattern 42, * k.1, p.1; repeat from * to last st., k.1.

Repeat these 2 rows twice more, then work 1st row again.

Next row: Pattern 42, k. to end.

Next row: P.23 (25), pattern to end.

Repeat last 2 rows 3 times more.

To shape the raglan armhole: Keeping continuity of pattern, dec. 1 st. at end of next and following 20 (22) right-side rows – 44 sts.

Work 1 row to finish at front edge.

To shape the neck:

Next row: Cast off 25, pattern to last 2 sts., dec.

Work 10 rows decreasing 1 st. at armhole edge on each right-side row and 1 st. at neck edge on each of these 10 rows – 3 sts.

Cast off.

The Front Edging

With right side of work facing, join contrast to hemline at lower edge and, using No. 10 needles, pick up and k.92 (100) sts. evenly along front edge – for your guidance, pick up 1 st. from each of 3 row ends then miss 1 row end – pick up and k.25 sts. along cast-off group at neck – 117 (125) sts.

K.1 row, then cast off.

The Left Front

With No. 10 needles cast on 74 (76) sts. and, beginning with a k. row, st.st. 9 rows.

Next row: All k. on wrong side to mark hemline.

Change to No. 8 needles.

1st row: K.32 (34), p.1, * tw.2; repeat from * 19 times more, k.1.

2nd row: K.2, * p.1, k.1; repeat from * 19 times more, p.32 (34).

Repeat these 2 rows 3 times more.

Next (shaping) row: K.5, k.2 tog.b., pattern to end.

Work 13 (15) rows straight.

Repeat last 14 (16) rows twice more, then work shaping row again – 70 (72) sts.

Work 5 (7) rows straight.

1st (buttonhole) row: K.28 (30), p.1, pattern 8, cast off 4 – 1 st. left on right-hand needle not included in next item, pattern 15, cast off 4, pattern to end.

2nd (buttonhole) row: Work in pattern casting on 4 sts. over each group cast off on previous row.

Work 6 rows straight.

Next (dec.) row: K.3 (4), * k.2 tog., k.3; repeat from * 3 times more, k.2 tog., k.3 (4), pattern 42 – 65 (67) sts.

Continue as follows:

1st row (wrong side): K.2, * p.1, k.1; repeat from * to last st., p.1.

2nd row: Rib 23 (25), pattern to end.

Repeat these 2 rows twice more, then work 1st row again.

Next row: K.23 (25), pattern to end.

Next row: Pattern 42, p. to end.

Repeat last 2 rows twice more.

Work buttonholes, as before, over next 2 rows.

To shape the raglan armhole: Working buttonholes on the 19th/20th (21st/22nd) rows from previous buttonholes, dec. 1 st. at beginning of next and following 20 (22) right-side rows – 44 sts.

To shape the neck: Cast off 25 sts. at beginning of next row, then work 11 rows decreasing 1 st. at armhole edge on each right-side row and 1 st. at neck edge on first 10 of these rows – 3 sts.

Cast off.

The Front Edging

Work as right front but begin at neck edge.

The Sleeves (both alike)

With No. 10 needles cast on 41 (45) sts. and, beginning with a k. row, st.st. 9 rows.

Next row: All k. on wrong side to mark hemline.

Change to No. 8 needles and, beginning with a k. row, st.st. 4 rows.

Inc. 1 st. at each end of next and every following 8th row until the 7th inc. row has been worked – 55 (59) sts.

Work 7 (15) rows straight.

To shape the raglan sleeve top: Dec. 1 st. at each end of next and every following 3rd row until the 13th dec. row has been worked – 29 (33) sts. – work 1 row, then dec. 1 st. at each end of next and following 7 (9) right-side rows.

Work 1 row.

Cast off remaining 13 sts.

The Collar

With No. 8 needles cast on 55 (59) sts. and, beginning with a k. row, st.st. 4 rows.

Next (inc.) row: K.6, up 1, k. to last 6 sts., up 1, k.6.

Next row: All p.

Repeat these 2 rows 7 times more – 71 (75) sts.

Next row: All k.

Next row (wrong side): All k. to mark fold line.

Continue as follows:

1st row: K.1, * tw.2; repeat from * twice, k.2 tog.b., k. to last 9 sts., k.2 tog., ** tw.2; repeat from ** twice, k.1.

2nd row: K.2, p.1, k.1, p.1, k.1, p. to last 7 sts., k.1, p.1, k.1, p.1, k.1, p.1, k.1.

Repeat these 2 rows 7 times more – 55 (59) sts.

Work 2 rows straight.

Cast off.

The edging: With right side facing join contrast to patterned side edge of collar and, using No. 10 needles, pick up and k.20 sts. from cast-off edge to fold line.

K.1 row.

Cast off.

Work along other side in the same way.

The Belt

With No. 8 needles and contrast cast on 4 sts. and k.2 rows.

Inc. 1 st. at each end of next and following alternate row – 8 sts.

K.156 rows.

Dec. 1 st. at each end of next and following alternate row – 4 sts.

K.1 row.

Cast off.

To Make Up The Coat

Press on wrong side, using a warm iron over a damp cloth. Join raglan seams, then join sleeve and side seams. Fold collar at fold line and join side edges. Beginning and ending at inner edge of contrast border, sew collar evenly to neck edge. Turn up hems and slip st. in place. Sew on buttons. Secure neck with press fastener. Attach belt at each side of front panel with buttons.

The Trousers

The Right Leg

With No. 10 needles cast on 57 (61) sts. and, beginning with a k. row, st.st. 9 rows.

Next row: All k. on wrong side to mark hemline ******.

Change to No. 8 needles.

1st row: K.13 (15), sl.1, k. to end.

2nd row: All p.

Repeat these 2 rows 4 times more.

*** Keeping continuity of the sl. st., inc. 1 st. at each end of next and every following 6th (8th) row until the 6th inc. row has been worked – 69 (73) sts.

Work 5 rows, then inc. 1 st. at each end of next and every following 6th row until a further 6 inc. rows have been completed – 81 (85) sts.

Work 1 row, then inc. 1 st. at each end of next and following 9 alternate rows – 101 (105) sts.

Work 1 row to end with a p. row – work 2 rows here on left leg to end with a k. row.

To shape the crotch:

1st row: Cast off 3, work to end.

2nd row: Cast off 2, work to end.

3rd row: Cast off, 3 work to end.

4th row: Dec., work to end.

5th to 8th rows: Repeat 3rd and 4th rows twice.

9th row: Work without shaping.

10th row: Dec., work to end – 83 (87) sts.

Dec. 1 st. at each end of next and every following 4th row until the 9th dec. row has been worked – 65 (69) sts.

Work 2 rows ending with a right-side row – ending with a wrong-side row on left leg *******

To shape for extra length on back:

1st and 2nd (turning) rows: P.60, for 1st row, turn and k. to end for 2nd row.

3rd and 4th rows: P.52, turn and k. to end.

5th and 6th rows: P.44, turn and k. to end.

7th and 8th rows: P.36, turn and k. to end.

9th and 10th rows: P.29, turn and k. to end.

11th and 12th rows: P.22, turn and k. to end.

13th and 14th rows: P.15, turn and k. to end.

15th and 16th rows: P.8, turn and k. to end.

P.1 row across all sts. picking up a thread at each point where work was turned and taking this together with next st. to avoid a gap in the knitting.

Change to No. 10 needles and, beginning right-side rows with k.1 and wrong-side rows with p.1, work 8 rows in single rib.

Cast off loosely in rib.

The Left Leg

Work as right leg to ******.

Change to No. 8 needles.

1st row: K.43 (45), sl.1, k. to end.

2nd row: All p.

Repeat these 2 rows 4 times more.

Now work as given for right leg from ******* to ******* noting the extra row to be worked before shaping the crotch.

To shape for extra length on back: Work as right leg but read k. for p. and p. for k. throughout.

Change to No. 10 needles and work 8 rows in single rib.

Cast off.

To Make Up The Trousers

Press. Join inner leg and front and back seams. Turn up hems and slip st. in place.

Secure elastic inside waist ribbing with a herringbone st. casing. Press creases on sl.st.

The Cap

To Make

First half of back ribbing:
With No. 10 needles cast on 40 sts.

1st and 2nd (turning) rows: * K.1, p.1 ; repeat from * to last 2 sts., turn and rib to end.

3rd and 4th rows: Rib 36, turn and rib to end.

5th and 6th rows: Rib 34, turn and rib to end.

7th and 8th rows: Rib 32, turn and rib to end.

9th and 10th rows: Rib 30, turn and rib to end.

11th and 12th rows: Rib 28, turn and rib to end.

Break off wool and leave sts. on spare needle.

Second half of back ribbing:
Work as first half. Do not break off wool.

Next (joining) row: Rib 40, turn, cast on 40 (48) sts. for centre front, turn and, onto same needle, beginning at short edge, rib the 40 sts. of first half – 120 (128) sts.

Rib 1 row.

Change to No. 8 needles.

1st row: K.1, * tw.2 ; repeat from * to last st., k.1.

2nd row: K.2, * p.1, k.1 ; repeat from * to end.

Repeat these 2 rows 8 (10) times more.

Join on contrast colour and k.2 rows for garter st. band. Break off contrast.

To shape the crown:
1st (shaping) row: * K.2 tog., k.11 (12), k.2 tog.b. ; repeat from * 7 times.
St.st. 3 rows.

2nd (shaping) row: * K.2 tog., k.9 (10), k.2 tog.b. ; repeat from * 7 times.
St.st. 3 rows.

Repeat last 4 rows 3 times more working 2 sts. less between the decreases on each repeat of the shaping row, then work shaping row again – 24 (32) sts.

Next row: * P.2 tog. ; repeat from * to end – 12 (16) sts.

Break off wool ; run end through remaining sts. draw up and fasten off securely.

The Peak

With right side of work facing, rejoin main colour to cast-on edge at front and, using No. 10 needles, pick up and k.40 (48) sts. along the edge between the ribbing.
P.1 row.

1st and 2nd (turning) rows: K.38 (46), turn, p.36 (44) turn.

3rd and 4th rows: K.34 (42), turn, p.32 (40), turn.

5th and 6th rows: K.30 (38), turn, p.28 (36), turn.

7th and 8th rows: K.26 (34), turn, p.24 (32), turn.

9th and 10th rows: K.22 (30), turn and p.20 (28), turn.

11th and 12th rows: K.18 (26), turn, p.16 (24), turn.

13th row: K. to end.

14th row: P. to end.

Continue as follows:

1st and 2nd (turning) rows: K.28 (36), turn, p.16 (24), turn.

3rd and 4th rows: K.18 (26), turn, p.20 (28), turn.

5th and 6th rows: K.22 (30), turn, p.24 (32), turn.

7th and 8th rows: K.26 (34), turn, p.28 (36), turn.

9th and 10th rows: K.30 (38), turn, p.32 (40), turn.
11th and 12th rows: K.34 (42), turn, p.36 (44), turn.
13th row: K. to end.
14th row: P. to end.
K.1 row and p.1 row.
   Cast off.

The Strap

   With No. 10 needles and contrast colour, cast on 5 sts. and k.6 rows.
Next (buttonhole) row: K.2, w.fwd., k.2 tog., k.1.

K.92 rows.
Work the buttonhole row, then k.5 rows.
Cast off

To Make Up The Cap

   Press. Join row ends to form back seam. Cut canvas shape to fit peak, insert and sl.st. facing to inside of cap. Cut circle of canvas and lining to fit crown and sew in place. Sew button to each side of cap and add front strap.

Bobble Cap and Scarf

(see illustration p. 156)

Materials

Four 25-gramme balls of Lister Lavenda Double Knitting Wool in main colour and two balls in a contrast colour for the set; a pair of No. 8 knitting needles.

Abbreviations

K., knit; p., purl; st., stitch; tog., together; dec., decrease (by working 2 sts. tog.); m., main colour; c., contrast colour.

Tension and Size

Worked at a tension of 16 stitches and 15 rows to 2 inches, the scarf will measure 6½ inches wide and 37 inches long including fringe and hat will fit the 2–3-year-olds.

The Scarf

To Make

With No. 8 needles and m., cast on 51 sts.
1st row: K.3, * p.1, k.3; repeat from * to end.
2nd row: K.1, * p.1, k.3; repeat from * to last 2 sts., p.1, k.1.
These 2 rows form the ribbed pattern; repeat them 12 times more.

Break off m., join on c. and work 6 rows.
Break off c., join on m. and work 26 rows.
Joining colours as required, work 6 rows c., 104 rows m., 6 rows c., 26 rows m., 6 rows c. and 26 rows m.
Cast off.

The Cap

To Make

With No. 8 needles and c., cast on 107 sts. and work 26 rows in rib pattern as given for scarf.

Now work 6 rows m. and 4 rows c.
Break off m. and continue with c. only.
To shape the crown:
Next (dec.) row: K.35, k.2 tog., k.34, k.2 tog., k.34 – 105 sts.
Next row: All p.
Continue as follows:
1st row: K.1, * k.2 tog., k.6; repeat from * to end.
2nd and every alternate row: All p.
3rd row: K.1, * k.2 tog., k.5; repeat from * to end.
5th row: K.1, * k.2 tog., k.4; repeat from * to end.
7th row: K.1, * k.2 tog., k.3; repeat from * to end.
9th row: K.1, * k.2 tog., k.2; repeat from * to end.
11th row: K.1, * k.2 tog., k.1; repeat from * to end.
12th row: All p. – 27 sts.

Next row: K.1, * k.2 tog.; repeat from * to end – 14 sts.

Next row: * P.2 tog.; repeat from * to end.

Break off wool; run end through remaining 7 sts. draw up and fasten securely, then join row ends to form back seam.

To Make Up The Scarf and Cap

Press lightly on wrong side, using a warm iron over a damp cloth.

Make and add pom-pon to cap and trim each end of scarf with tassels.

Classic Twin Set

Long sleeved 'V' neck cardigan and short sleeved sweater for both boys and girls

Materials

Four ounces of Sirdar Fontein Crêpe 4-ply equivalent for 1st size; five ounces for 2nd size. For either size; a pair each of No. 10 and No. 12 knitting needles; 5 buttons.

Tension

Work at a tension of 7 stitches and 9 rows to 1 inch, over the stocking stitch, using No. 10 needles, to obtain the following measurements:

Measurements

	INCHES	
	1st size	2nd size
All round at underarms	$22\frac{1}{2}$	$24\frac{3}{4}$
Side seam	$7\frac{1}{4}$	8
Length	13	14
Sleeve seam	9	10

Abbreviations

K., knit; p., purl; st., stitch; tog., together; dec., decrease (by working 2 sts. tog.); inc., increase (by working twice into same st.); k.2 tog.b., k.2 sts. tog. through back of loops; st.st., stocking st. (k. on right side and p. on wrong side); single rib is k.1 and p.1 alternately.

● *The instructions are given for 1st size. Where they vary, work figures in brackets for 2nd size.*

The Cardigan

The Back

With No. 12 needles cast on 72 (80) sts. and work 27 rows in single rib.

Next (inc.) row: Rib 9 (10), * inc. in next st., rib 8 (9); repeat from * to end – 79 (87) sts.

Change to No. 10 needles and, beginning with a k. row, st.st. 44 (50) rows.

To shape the raglan armholes:

1st row: Cast off 3 (4) sts., k. to end.

2nd row: Cast off 3 (4) sts., p. to end.

3rd row: K.1, k.2 tog.b., k. to last 3 sts., k.2 tog., k.1.

4th row: All p.

Repeat 3rd and 4th rows 24 (25) times more.

Cast off remaining 23 (27) sts.

The Left Front

With No. 12 needles cast on 34 (38) sts. and work 27 rows in single rib.

Next (inc.) row: Rib 7 (8), * inc. in next st., rib 8 (9); repeat from * to end – 37 (41) sts.

Change to No. 10 needles and, beginning with a k. row, st.st. 44 (50) rows **

To shape the raglan armhole and slope front edge:

1st row: Cast off 3 (4) sts., k. to last 2 sts., dec.

2nd row: All p.

3rd row: K.1, k.2 tog.b., k. to end.

4th row: All p.

5th row: K.1, k.2 tog.b., k. to end.

6th row: All p. – 31 (34) sts.

*** Continuing to dec. 1 st. at armhole edge on each right-side row, dec. 1 st. at front edge on next and every following 8th (6th) row until a further 6 (8) front edge dec. rows have been worked – 4 sts.

Work 1 row, then dec. 1 st. at armhole edge only on next and following right-side row.

Next row: P.2 and take these 2 sts. tog. and fasten off.

The Right Front

Work as given for left front to **.

To shape the raglan armhole and slope front edge:

1st row: Dec., k. to end.

2nd row: Cast off 3 (4) sts., p. to end.

3rd row: K. to last 3 sts., k.2 tog., k.1.

4th row: All p.

5th row: K. to last 3 sts., k.2 tog., k.1.

6th row: All p. – 31 (34) sts.

Now work as given for left front from *** to end.

The Sleeves (both alike)

With No. 12 needles cast on 40 (42) sts. and work 21 rows in single rib.

Next (inc.) row: Rib 1 (2), * inc. in next st., rib 8; repeat from * 3 times more, inc. in next st., rib 2 (3) – 45 (47) sts.

Change to No. 10 needles and, beginning with a k. row, st.st. 4 rows.

Inc. 1 st. at each end of next and every following 6th row until the 9th (10th) inc. row has been worked – 63 (67) sts.

St.st. 11 (13) rows.

To shape the raglan sleeve top: Work exactly as given for raglan armhole shaping on back when 7 sts. will remain.

Cast off.

The Front Band

First join raglan seams. With No. 12 needles cast on 9 sts.

1st row: K.1, * p.1, k.1; repeat from * to end.

2nd row: K.2, * p.1, k.1; repeat from * ending last repeat with k.2.

Repeat these 2 rows once more.

1st (buttonhole) row: Rib 3, cast off 3, rib to end.

2nd (buttonhole) row: Rib 3, turn, cast on 3, turn, rib to end.

Rib 16 (18) rows.

Repeat last 18 (20) rows 3 times more, then work 2 buttonhole rows again.

Continue in rib until band, when slightly stretched, is long enough to fit all round front edge.

Cast off when correct length is assured.

To Make Up The Cardigan

Press on wrong side, avoiding the ribbing, using a warm iron over a damp cloth. Join side and sleeve seams. Sew front band in place with last buttonhole level with first front shaping. Sew on buttons.

The Sweater

Materials

Three ounces of Sirdar Fontein Crêpe 4-ply equivalent for 1st size; four ounces for 2nd size. For either size: a pair each of No. 10 and No. 12 knitting needles; a 4-inch zip fastener.

Tension

Work at a tension of 7 stitches and 9 rows to 1 inch, over the stocking stitch, using No. 10 needles, to obtain the following measurements:

Measurements

INCHES

	1st size	2nd size
All round at underarms	$22\frac{1}{2}$	$24\frac{3}{4}$
Side seam	$7\frac{1}{4}$	8
Length	13	14
Sleeve seam	$2\frac{3}{4}$	$2\frac{3}{4}$

Abbreviations

K., knit; p., purl; st., stitch; tog., together; inc., increase (by working twice into same st.); k.2 tog.b., k.2 sts. tog. through back of loops; st.st., stocking st. (k. on right side and p. on wrong side); single rib is k.1 and p.1 alternately.

● *The instructions are given for 1st size. Where they vary, work figures in brackets for 2nd size.*

The Back

With No. 12 needles cast on 72 (80) sts. and work 27 rows in single rib.

Next (inc.) row: Rib 9 (10), * inc. in next st., rib 8 (9); repeat from * to end — 79 (87) sts.

Change to No. 10 needles and, beginning with a k. row, st.st. 44 (50) rows.

To shape the raglan armholes:

1st row: Cast off 3 (4) k. to end.

2nd row: Cast off 3 (4), p. to end.

3rd row: K.1, k.2 tog.b., k. to last 3 sts., k.2 tog., k.1.

4th row: All p. **.

Repeat 3rd and 4th rows 10 (11) times more, then work 3rd row again — 49 (53) sts.

Now divide sts. for back opening.

Next row: P.24 (26) and leave these sts. on a spare needle for left side, cast off next st., p. to end and work on these 24 (26) sts. for right side.

The right side:

1st row: K.1, k.2 tog.b., k. to end.

2nd row: K.1, p. to end.

Repeat these 2 rows 12 times more.

Cast off remaining 11 (13) sts.

The left side: With right side of work facing, rejoin wool to sts. on spare needle.

1st row: K. to last 3 sts., k.2 tog., k.1.

2nd row: P. to last st., k.1.

Repeat these 2 rows 12 times more.

Cast off remaining 11 (13) sts.

The Front

Work as given for back to **.

Repeat 3rd and 4th rows 16 (17) times more, then work 3rd row again – 37 (41) sts.

Now divide sts. for front neck.

Next row: P.13 and leave these sts. on spare needle for right side, p. next 11 (15) sts. and leave on stitch-holder for neck band, p. to end and work on these 13 sts. for left side.

The left side:

1st row: K.1, k.2 tog.b., k. to last 2 sts., k.2 tog.

2nd row: All p.

Repeat these 2 rows 3 times more – 5 sts.

Next row: K.1, k.2 tog.b., k.2.

Next row: P.4.

Next row: K.1, k.2 tog.b., k.1.

Next row: P.3.

Next row: K.1, k.2 tog.b.

Next row: P.2.

Take these 2 sts. tog. and fasten off.

The right side: With right side of work facing, rejoin wool to 13 sts. on spare needle.

1st row: K.2 tog.b., k. to last 3 sts., k.2 tog., k.1.

2nd row: All p.

Repeat these 2 rows 3 times more – 5 sts.

Next row: K.2, k.2 tog., k.1.

Next row: P.4.

Next row: K.1, k.2 tog., k.1.

Next row: P.3.

Next row: K.2 tog., k.1.

Next row: P.2.

Take remaining 2 sts. tog. and fasten off.

The Sleeves (both alike)

With No. 12 needles cast on 50 (52) sts. and work 8 rows in single rib, increasing 1 st. at end of last row – 51 (53) sts.

Change to No. 10 needles and, beginning with a k. row, st.st. 2 rows.

Inc. 1 st. at each end of next and following 5 (6) right-side rows – 63 (67) sts.

St.st. 5 (3) rows.

To shape the raglan sleeve top:

1st row: Cast off 3 (4) sts., k. to end.

2nd row: Cast off 3 (4) sts., p. to end.

3rd row: K.1, k.2 tog.b., k. to last 3 sts., k.2 tog., k.1.

4th row: All p.

Repeat 3rd and 4th rows 24 (25) times more.

Cast off remaining 7 sts.

The Neck Band

First join raglan seams. With right side of work facing, rejoin wool to neck edge at centre back and, using No. 12 needles, pick up and k. 10(12) sts. from left side, 6 sts. from sleeve, 13 sts. down left side of front neck, k. the 11 (15) sts. at centre front, pick up and k.13 sts. from right side of neck, 6 sts. from sleeve and 10 (12) sts. from right side of back – 69 (77) sts.

1st row: K.1, * p.1, k.1; repeat from * to end.

2nd row: K.2, * p.1, k.1; repeat from * ending last repeat with k.2.

Repeat these 2 rows 3 times more.

Cast off in rib.

To Make Up The Sweater

Press on wrong side, avoiding the ribbing, using a warm iron over a damp cloth. Join sleeve and side seams. Insert zip fastener.

Cape and Hat

**An up-to-the minute Maxi-Cape with
Matching Hat**

Contributed by Eugenie Hammond

Materials

For the Cape: Eleven 50-gramme
balls of Patons Trident Double
Knitting for 1st size; twelve balls for
2nd size. For either size: a pair of
No. 8 knitting needles; 9 buttons.
For the Hat: Two balls of the same
yarn; a pair of No. 8 and No. 10
knitting needles; 1 button.

Tension

Work at a tension of 21 stitches and 22
rows to 3 inches, over the pattern, using
No. 8 needles, to obtain the following
measurements:

Measurements

	INCHES	
	1st size	2nd size
All round at chest level	32	33
Length without hem	28½	30

Abbreviations

K., knit; p., purl; st., stitch; tog., together;
dec., decrease (by working 2 sts. tog.); tw.2,
twist 2 (p. into front of 2nd st. on left-hand
needle then p. into front of 1st st. and slip
both sts. off needle together); y.fwd., yarn
forward to make a st.; up 1 (pick up the
thread which lies between the needles and
k. into back of it, thus making a st.).

● *The instructions are given for 1st size.
Where they vary, work figures in brackets
for 2nd size.*

The Cape

The Main Panels (make 4)

With No. 8 needles cast on 76 (78) sts. and p.1 row.

Now work in pattern as follows:

1st row (right side): All k.

2nd row: K.1, * tw.2; repeat from * to last st., k.1.

3rd row: All k.

4th row: K.1, p.1, * tw.2; repeat from * to last 2 sts., p.1, k.1.

Repeat these 4 rows 6 times more **.

Keeping continuity of the pattern dec. 1 st. at each end of next and every following 10th row until the 16th (17th) dec. row has been worked – 44 sts.

Work 7 rows straight.

Dec. 1 st. at each end of next and following 13 right-side rows – 16 sts.

Work 1 row.

Cast off.

The Right Front Panel

With No. 8 needles cast on 36 (38) sts. and work as given for main panels to **.

To shape the side: Dec. 1 st. at *end* of next row and every following 10th row until the 10th (11th) dec. row has been worked – 26 (27) sts.

Work 6 rows straight.

Mark end of last row to denote beginning of arm opening – mark beginning of row on left-front panel.

Work 3 rows straight.

Dec. 1 st. at *end* of next row and every following 10th row until a further 3 dec. rows have been worked – 23 (24) sts.

Work 4 rows straight. Mark end of last row to denote end of arm opening – mark beginning of row on left-front panel.

Work 5 rows straight.

Dec. 1 st. at *end* of next row and every following 10th row until a further 3 dec. rows have been worked – 20 (21) sts.

Work 7 rows straight.

Dec. 1 st. at *end* of next and every following 8th row until a further 3 dec. rows have been worked – 17 (18) sts. ***.

Work 1 row to end at straight front edge.

To shape the neck:

Next row: Cast off 6 (7), work to last 2 sts., dec.

Work 1 row, then dec. 1 st. at each end of next and following 3 alternate rows.

Take remaining 2 sts. tog. and fasten off.

The Left Front Panel

Work as given for right front panel to *** but dec. at *beginning* of the rows instead of end.

To shape the neck:

Next row: Cast off 6 (7) sts., work to end.

Next row: Dec., work to end.

Work 1 row, then dec. 1 st. at each end of next and following 3 alternate rows.

Take remaining 2 sts. tog. and fasten off.

The Button Band

With No. 8 needles cast on 6 sts. and k.212 (224) rows.

Cast off.

The Buttonhole Band

With No. 8 needles cast on 6 sts. and k.32 (44) rows.

Next (buttonhole) row: K.3, y.fwd., k.2 tog., k.1.

K.21 rows.

Repeat last 22 rows 7 times more, then work buttonhole row again.

K.3 rows. Cast off.

The Front-Opening Bands (make 2)

With No. 8 needles cast on 8 sts. and k.35 rows.

Cast off.

To Make Up The Cape

Pin out and press on wrong side using a warm iron over a damp cloth. Join the four main panels together then join right and left front panels leaving seam open between the markers for front openings. Sew bands to openings and attach the cast-on and cast-off edges neatly to right side of front panels. Sew front bands in place.

The neck band: With right side of work facing, rejoin wool to inner edge of button-hole band and, using No. 8 needles, pick up and k.50 sts. all round neck edge to inner edge of button band.

K.19 rows.
Cast off.
Fold neck band in half and slip st. to wrong side, then join row-ends.

Sew on buttons. Press seams. Turn up to required length.

The Hat

The Main Part

With No. 8 needles cast on 120 sts. and k.6 rows.

Work the 4 pattern rows given for cape 4 times, then work first 2 rows again.

Cast off.

The Crown

With No. 8 needles cast on 100 sts. and k.2 rows then p.1 row.

Now shape as follows.

1st row: K.1, * k.2 tog., k.9 ; repeat from * to end – 91 sts.

2nd row: All p.

3rd row: K.1, * k.2 tog., k.8 ; repeat from * to end – 82 sts.

4th row: All p.

Repeat 3rd and 4th rows 6 times more working 1 st. less between the decreases on each successive repeat, then work the 3rd row again – 19 sts.

Next row: P.1, * p.2 tog. ; repeat from * to end – 10 sts.

Break off yarn ; run end through remaining sts. draw up and fasten off securely, then join row-ends.

The Ear Flaps (make 2)

With No. 10 needles cast on 4 sts. and k.46 rows.

1st (shaping) row: K.2, up 1, k.2.
K.3 rows.

2nd (shaping) row: K.2, up 1, k.1, up 1, k.2.
K.3 rows.

3rd (shaping) row: K.2, up 1, k. to last 2 sts., up 1, k.2.
K.3 rows.

Repeat last 4 rows 7 times more, then work shaping row again – 25 sts.
K.1 row.
Cast off.

To Make Up The Hat

Join row ends of main part to form a circle. Press crown flat, then sew in place.

Sew ear flaps in position. Sew button to centre of crown.

Striped Jersey and Matching Pants

(see illustration p. 229)

in 4-ply

Materials

For the Jersey: For either size: Three 25-gramme balls of Bairnswear Pleasure 4-ply Wool in main colour and two balls in a contrast colour; a pair each of No. 10 and No. 12 knitting needles; a 4-inch zip fastener.
For the Pants: Three balls of the same wool in main colour for 1st size; four balls for 2nd size. For either size: a pair each of No. 10 and No. 12 knitting needles; a waist length of elastic.

Tension

Work at a tension of 7 stitches and 9 rows to 1 inch, over the stocking stitch, using No. 10 needles, to obtain the following measurements:

Measurements

	INCHES	
	1st size	2nd size
The Jersey		
All round at underarms	$22\frac{1}{2}$	$24\frac{3}{4}$
Side seam	$7\frac{1}{4}$	8
Length	13	14
Sleeve seam	$2\frac{3}{4}$	$2\frac{3}{4}$
The Pants		
All round at widest part	23	$25\frac{1}{2}$
Side seam length	$8\frac{1}{2}$	9

Abbreviations

K., knit; p., purl; st., stitch; tog., together; inc., increase (by working twice into same st.); w.fwd., wool forward to make a st.; k.2 tog.b., k.2 tog. through back of loops; sl., slip; p.s.s.o., pass slipped st. over; st.st., stocking st. (k. on right side and p. on wrong side); single rib is k.1 and p.1 alternately; m., main colour; c., contrast colour.

● *The instructions are given for 1st size. Where they vary, work figures in brackets for 2nd size.*

The Jersey

The Back

With No. 12 needles and m., cast on 72 (80) sts. and work 27 rows in single rib.
Next (inc.) row: Rib 9 (10), * inc. in next st., rib 8 (9); repeat from * to end – 79 (87) sts.
Change to No. 10 needles and k.1 row and p.1 row.

Join on c. and, working in a stripe sequence of 2 rows c. and 2 rows m., work 42 (50) rows in st.st. ending with 2 rows c.
To shape the raglan armholes:
1st row: Cast off 3 (4) sts., k. to end.
2nd row: Cast off 3 (4) sts., p. to end.
3rd row: K.1, k.2 tog.b., k. to last 3 sts., k.2 tog., k.1.

227

4th row: All p. **.

Repeat 3rd and 4th rows 10 (11) times more, then work 3rd row again – 49 (53) sts.

Now divide sts. for back opening.

Next row: P.24 (26) and leave these sts. on a spare needle for left side, cast off next st., p. to end and work on these 24 (26) sts. for right side.

The right side:

1st row: K.1, k.2 tog.b., k. to end.

2nd row: K.1, p. to end.

Repeat these 2 rows 12 times more.

Cast off remaining 11 (13) sts.

The left side: With right side of work facing, rejoin wool to the 24 (26) sts. on spare needle.

1st row: K. to last 3 sts., k.2 tog., k.1.

2nd row: P. to last st., k.1.

Repeat these 2 rows 12 times more.

Cast off remaining 11 (13) sts.

The Front

Work as back to **.

Repeat 3rd and 4th rows 16 (17) times more, then work 3rd row again – 37 (41) sts.

Now divide sts. for front neck.

Next row: P.13 and leave these sts. on spare needle for right side, p. next 11 (15) sts. and leave on stitch-holder for neck band, p. to end and work on these 13 sts. for left side.

The left side:

1st row: K.1, k.2 tog.b., k. to last 2 sts., k.2 tog.

2nd row: All p.

Repeat these 2 rows 3 times more – 5 sts.

Next row: K.1, k.2 tog.b., k.2.

Next row: P.4.

Next row: K.1, k.2 tog.b., k.1.

Next row: P.3.

Next row: K.1, k.2 tog.b.

Next row: P.2.

Take these 2 sts. tog. and fasten off.

The right side: With right side of work facing, rejoin wool to the 13 sts. on spare needle.

1st row: K.2 tog.b., k. to last 3 sts., k.2 tog., k.1.

2nd row: All p.

Repeat these 2 rows 3 times more – 5 sts.

Next row: K.2, k.2 tog., k.1.

Next row: P.4.

Next row: K.1, k.2 tog., k.1.

Next row: P.3.

Next row: K.2 tog., k.1.

Next row: P.2.

Take these 2 sts. tog. and fasten off.

The Sleeves (both alike)

With No. 12 needles and m. cast on 50 (52) sts. and work 8 rows in single rib increasing 1 st. at end of last row – 51 (53) sts.

Change to No. 10 needles and k.1 row and p.1 row.

Join on c.

Continuing in stripe sequence of 2 rows c. and 2 rows m., inc. 1 st. at each end of next and following 5 (6) right-side rows – 63 (67) sts.

Work 3 (1) row(s) straight, ending with 2 rows c.

To shape the raglan sleeve top:

1st row: Cast off 3 (4) sts., k. to end.

2nd row: Cast off 3 (4) sts., p. to end.

3rd row: K.1, k.2 tog.b., k. to last 3 sts., k.2 tog., k.1.

4th row: All p.

Repeat 3rd and 4th rows 24 (25) times more.

Cast off remaining 7 sts.

The Neck Band

First join raglan seams. With right side of work facing, join m. to centre back and, using No. 12 needles, pick up and k.10 (12) sts. across back, 6 sts. from left sleeve, 13 sts. down left side of neck, k. the 11 (15) sts. at centre front, pick up and k.13 sts. from right side of neck, 6 sts. from right sleeve and finally 10 (12) across back – 69 (77) sts.

1st row: K.1, * p.1, k.1; repeat from * to end.

2nd row: K.2, * p.1, k.1; repeat from * ending last repeat with k.2.

Repeat these 2 rows 3 times more.

Cast off in rib.

To Make Up The Jersey

Press on wrong side, avoiding the ribbing, using a warm iron over a damp cloth. Join sleeve and side seams. Insert zip.

The Pants

The Front

With No. 10 needles and m., cast on 17 sts. and, beginning with a k. row, st.st. 6 rows.

Now shape for legs and gusset as follows:

1st row: Cast on 4 sts., k. to end.
2nd row: Cast on 4 sts., p. to end.
3rd row: Cast on 4, k.8, k.2 tog.b., k.13, k.2 tog., k. to end.
4th row: Cast on 4, p. to end.
5th row: Cast on 4, k.12, k.2 tog.b., k.11, k.2 tog., k. to end.
6th and every following alternate row: Cast on 4, p. to end.
7th row: Cast on 4, k.16, k.2 tog.b., k.9, k.2 tog., k. to end.
9th row: Cast on 4, k.20, k.2 tog.b., k.7, k.2 tog., k. to end.
11th row: Cast on 4, k.24, k.2 tog.b., k.5, k.2 tog., k. to end.
13th row: Cast on 4, k.28, k.2 tog.b., k.3, k.2 tog., k. to end.
15th row: Cast on 4, k.32, k.2 tog.b., k.1, k.2 tog., k. to end.
17th row: Cast on 4, k.36, sl.1, k.2 tog., p.s.s.o., k. to end.
18th row: Cast on 4, p. to end – 73 sts.

Cast on 4 sts. at beginning of next 2 (4) rows – 81 (89) sts. **

Work 62 (68) rows in st.st.

*** Change to No. 12 needles and, beginning right-side rows with k.1 and wrong-side rows with p.1, work 4 rows in single rib.

Next (slot) row: K.1, * w.fwd., k.2 tog., p.1, k.1; repeat from * to end.

Rib 3 rows.

Cast off.

The Back

Work as front to **.
Work 60 (66) rows in st.st.

To shape for extra length on back:
1st and 2nd (turning) rows: K.76 (80) for 1st row, turn and p.71 for 2nd row, turn.
3rd and 4th rows: K.66, turn and p.61, turn.
5th and 6th rows: K.56, turn and p.51, turn.

7th and 8th rows: K.46, turn and p.41, turn.
9th and 10th rows: K.36, turn and p.31, turn.
11th and 12th rows: K.26, turn and p.21, turn.
13th row: K. to end.
14th row: P. to end.

Now work as front from *** to end.

The Leg Bands

First join crotch seam. With right side of work facing, join m. wool to side edge and, using No. 12 needles, pick up and k.90 (98) sts. along entire leg edge.

Work 7 rows in single rib.

Cast off.

To Make Up The Pants

Press as given for jersey. Join side seams. Thread elastic through waist.

Poncho and Tights

(*see illustration p. 233*)

Materials

For the Poncho: Seven 25-gramme balls of Patons Baby Quick Colourglow Quickerknit and one ball of Patons Quickerknit Baby Wool; a pair each of No. 4 and No. 8 knitting needles; a 4-inch zip.
For the Tights: Six balls of Patons Quickerknit Baby Wool; a pair each of No. 8 and No. 9 knitting needles; a waist length of elastic.

Tension and Size

Worked at a tension of 8 stitches and 12 rows to 2 inches, over the garter stitch using 2 strands of yarn and No. 4 needles and 16 stitches and 16 rows to 2 inches over the unstretched rib, using No. 8 needles, the set will fit baby aged twelve to eighteen months.

Abbreviations

K., knit; p., purl; st., stitch; tog., together; dec., decrease (by working 2 sts. tog.); inc., increase (by working twice into same st.); y.fwd., yarn forward to make a st.; k.3 tog.b., k.3 sts. tog. through back of loops; k. or p.2 tog.b., k. or p.2 sts. tog. through back of loops; up 1 (pick up the thread which lies between the needles and k. into back of it, thus making a st.); st.st., stocking st. (k. on right side and p. on wrong side); single rib is k.1 and p.1 alternately; garter st. is every row k.

● *Instructions in brackets must be worked number of times stated after 2nd bracket.*

(*worked in one piece with 2 strands of yarn throughout*)

The Poncho

The Front

With No. 4 needles and 2 strands of Colourglow yarn cast on 8 sts. and k.1 row.
Now shape as follows:
1st row: K.3, y.fwd., k.2, y.fwd., k.3.
2nd row: All k.
3rd row: K.3, y.fwd., k.4, y.fwd., k.3.
4th row: All k.
5th row: K.3, y.fwd., k. to last 3 sts., y.fwd., k.3.
6th row: All k.
Repeat 5th and 6th rows 22 times more – 58 sts.
Now divide sts. for front opening.

Next row: K.3, y.fwd., k.26, turn and work on these 30 sts. for 1st side.
1st side:
1st row: All k.
2nd row: K.3, y.fwd., k. to end.
Repeat these 2 rows 6 times more – 37 sts.
– ending at inner edge.
To shape the neck:
1st row: Cast off 4; k. to end.
2nd row: K.3, y.fwd., k. to last 2 sts., k.2 tog.
3rd row: All k.
Repeat 2nd and 3rd rows 3 times more – 33 sts.

Next row: K.3, y.fwd., k. to end – 34 sts.

Break off yarn and leave sts. on spare needle.

Rejoin 2 strands of yarn to inner edge of remaining sts.

2nd side:

1st row: K. to last 3 sts., y.fwd., k.3.

2nd row: All k.

Repeat these 2 rows 7 times more – 37 sts.

To shape the neck:

1st row: Cast off 4, k. to last 3 sts., y.fwd., k.3.

2nd row: K. to last 2 sts., k.2 tog.

3rd row: K. to last 3 sts., y.fwd., k.3.

Repeat 2nd and 3rd rows 3 times more – 34 sts.

Next row: K.34, turn, cast on 16 sts., turn and onto same needle k. the 34 sts. of 1st side – 84 sts.

The Back

1st row: K.3, y.fwd., k.3 tog.b., k. to last 6 sts., k.3 tog., y.fwd., k.3.

2nd row: All k.

Repeat these 2 rows 36 times more – 10 sts.

Next row: K.3, y.fwd., k.2 tog.b., k.2 tog., y.fwd., k.3.

Next row: All k.

Cast off remaining 10 sts.

The Hood

With right side of work facing, rejoin 2 strands of yarn to neck edge and, using No. 8 needles, pick up and k.55 sts. evenly all round neck edge.

Beginning wrong-side rows with p.1 and right-side rows with k.1, work 7 rows in single rib.

Cast off 6 sts. at beginning of next 2 rows – 43 sts.

Change to No. 4 needles.

Next (inc.) row: K.2 (up 1, k.2) 3 times, (up 1, k.3) 9 times, (up 1, k.2) 4 times – 59 sts.

Beginning with a p. row, st.st. 23 rows.

Cast off 20 sts. at beginning of next 2 rows – 19 sts.

St.st. 28 rows.

Cast off.

The Trimming

With No. 8 needles and Quickerknit Baby Wool cast on 80 sts. and k.1 row.

Next (loop st.) row: * Insert needle in st., wind wool clockwise twice round needle and first finger of left hand, then round needle only, draw 3 loops through onto right-hand needle letting original st. drop off left-hand needle in the usual way, sl. the 3 loops back onto left-hand needle and k. them tog. through back of loops; repeat from * in each st. to end.

K.2 rows.

Repeat loop st. row.

Cast off.

To Make Up The Poncho

Do not press. Join row ends of top section of hood to the cast-off groups at each side. Sew cast-off edge of loop st. trimming on the inside round face edge of hood, gathering hood slightly to fit; fold back to right side and catch in place.

Cut remainder of yarn into 5-inch lengths and, using 3 strands together trim all round outer edge with tassels. Sew in zip.

The Tights

The Left Leg

With No. 9 needles and Quickerknit Baby Wool cast on 39 sts. and k.1 row.

To shape the foot:

1st row: K.5, up 1, k.1, up 1, k.19, up 1, k.1, up 1, k.13.

2nd and 4th rows: All p.

3rd row: K.6, up 1, k.1, up 1, k.21, up 1, k.1, up 1, k.14.

5th row: K.7, up 1, k.1, up 1, k.23, up 1, k.1, up 1, k.15.

6th row: All p. – 51 sts.

K.1 row and p.1 row.

Next row: All p. on right side.

Beginning with a p. row, st.st. 7 rows.

To shape the instep:
1st row: K.32, k.2 tog.b., k.1, k.2 tog., k.14.
2nd row: P.13, p.2 tog., p.1, p.2 tog.b., p.31.
3rd row: K.30, k.2 tog.b., k.1, k.2 tog., k.12.
4th row: P.11, p.2 tog., p.1, p.2 tog.b., p.29.
5th row: K.28, k.2 tog.b., k.1, k.2 tog., k.10.
6th row: P.9, p.2 tog., p.1, p.2 tog.b., p.27.
7th row: K.26, k.2 tog.b., k.1, k.2 tog., k.8 –
37 sts.
P.1 row.
*** Change to No. 8 needles and, beginning right-side rows with k.1 and wrong-side rows with p.1, work 10 rows in single rib.

Continuing in single rib, inc. 1 st. at each end of next and every following 4th row until the 6th inc. row has been worked – 49 sts. – work 1 row, then inc. 1 st. at each end of next and following 28 right-side rows – 107 sts.

Work 2 rows ending with a right-side row – work 3 rows here on right leg to end with a wrong-side row.

To shape the crotch:
1st row: Cast off 2, rib to last 2 sts., dec.
2nd row: Work without shaping.
3rd row: Cast off 2, rib to end.
Work 3 rows straight.
Dec. 1 st. at each end of next row and following 6th row – 98 sts.
Work 9 rows straight.
Dec. 1 st. at each end of next and every following 10th row until a further 4 dec. rows have been worked – 90 sts.

To shape for extra length on back:
1st and 2nd (turning) rows: Rib 45 for 1st row, turn and rib to end for 2nd row.
3rd and 4th rows: Rib 35, turn and rib to end.
5th and 6th rows: Rib 25, turn and rib to end.
7th and 8th rows: Rib 15, turn and rib to end.
Rib 1 row across all sts. picking up a thread at each point where work was turned and taking this together with next st. to avoid a gap in the knitting.

Rib 4 rows.
Next (slot) row: Rib 2, * y.fwd., rib 2 tog., rib 4; repeat from * ending last repeat with rib 2.
Rib 3 rows.
Cast off.

The Right Leg

With No. 9 needles and Quickerknit Baby Wool cast on 39 sts. and k.1 row.
To shape the foot:
1st row: K.13, up 1, k.1, up 1, k.19, up 1, k.1, up 1, k.5.
2nd and 4th rows: All p.
3rd row: K.14, up 1, k.1, up 1, k.21, up 1, k.1, up 1, k.6.
5th row: K.15, up 1, k.1, up 1, k.23, up 1, k.1, up 1, k.7.
6th row: All p. – 51 sts.
K.1 row and p.1 row.
Next row: All p. on right side.
Beginning with a p. row, st.st. 7 rows.
To shape the instep:
1st row: K.14, k.2 tog.b., k.1, k.2 tog., k.32.
2nd row: P.31, p.2 tog., p.1, p.2 tog.b., p.13.
3rd row: K.12, k.2 tog.b., k.1, k.2 tog., k.30.
4th row: P.29, p.2 tog., p.1, p.2 tog.b., p.11.
5th row: K.10, k.2 tog.b., k.1, k.2 tog., k.28.
6th row: P.27, p.2 tog., p.1, p.2 tog.b., p.9.
7th row: K.8, k.2 tog.b., k.1, k.2 tog., k.26 –
37 sts.
P.1 row.
Now work as given for left leg from *** to end and noting the extra row to be worked before shaping the crotch.

To Make Up The Tights

Join inner leg and underfoot seams. then join front and back seams. Thread elastic through waist.

Poncho and tights (pattern p. 230).

Sailor Suit

(see illustration p. 201)

Materials

Seventeen 25-gramme balls of Robin Vogue Double Knitting for 1st size; nineteen balls for 2nd size. For either size: a pair each of No. 8 and No. 10 knitting needles; oddments of red and white yarn for trimming; a waist length of 1-inch wide elastic.

Tension

Work at a tension of 11 stitches and 15 rows to 2 inches, over the stocking stitch, using No. 8 needles, to obtain the following measurements:

Abbreviations

K., knit; p., purl; st., stitch; tog., together; dec., decrease (by working 2 sts. tog.); inc., increase (by working twice into same st.); k.2 tog.b., k.2 sts. tog. through back of loops; sl., slip; up 1 (pick up the thread which lies between the needles and k. into back of it, thus making a st.); p.s.s.o., pass slipped st. over; st.st., stocking st. (k. on right side and p. on wrong side); garter st. is k. on every row; single rib is k.1 and p.1 alternately.

● *The instructions are given for 1st size. Where they vary, work figures in brackets for 2nd size.*

Measurements

	INCHES	
	1st size	2nd size
The Top		
All round at underarms	24	26
Side seam	9	$9\frac{1}{2}$
Length	$13\frac{3}{4}$	$14\frac{1}{2}$
Sleeve seam	9	$9\frac{1}{2}$
The Trousers		
Inside leg seam	14	$15\frac{1}{2}$
Outside leg	20	$21\frac{1}{2}$

The Top

The Back

With No. 10 needles cast on 66 (72) sts. and, beginning with a k. row, st.st. 5 rows.

Next row: All k. on wrong side to mark hemline **.

Change to No. 8 needles and, beginning with a k. row, st.st. 68 (72) rows.

To shape the square armholes: Cast off 7 (8) sts. at beginning of next 2 rows — 52 (56) sts.

St.st. 32 (34) rows.

To slope the shoulders: Cast off 7 sts. at beginning of next 2 rows and 7 (8) sts. on following 2 rows.

Cast off remaining 24 (26) sts.

The Front

Work as back to **.

Change to No. 8 needles and, beginning with a k. row, st.st. 59 (63) rows, ending with a k. row.

Now divide sts. for front neck.

Next row: P. 33(36) and leave these sts. on a spare needle for right side. p. to end and work on these 33 (36) sts. for left side.

The left side:

1st row: K. to last 3 sts., k.2 tog., k.1.

2nd row: K.1, p. to end.

Repeat these 2 rows 3 times more – 29 (32) sts.

To shape the square armhole and continue sloping neck:

1st row: Cast off 7 (8) sts., k. to last 3 sts., k.2 tog., k.1.

2nd row: K.1, p. to end.

3rd row: All k.

4th row: K.1, p. to end.

5th row: K. to last 3 sts., k.2 tog., k.1.

Repeat 2nd to 5th rows 6 (7) times more 14 (15) sts.

Work 5 (3) rows, ending at armhole edge.

To slope the shoulder: Cast off 7 sts. at beginning of next row; work 1 row, then cast off remaining 7 (8) sts.

The right side: With right side of work facing, rejoin yarn to sts. on spare needle.

To slope the neck:

1st row: K.1, k.2 tog.b., k. to end.

2nd row: P. to last st., k.1.

Repeat these 2 rows 3 times more, then work 1st row again – 28 (31) sts.

To shape the square armhole:

1st row: Cast off 7 (8) sts., p. to last st., k.1.

2nd row: All k.

3rd row: P. to last st., k.1.

4th row: K.1, k.2 tog.b., k. to end.

5th row: P. to last st., k.1.

Repeat 2nd to 5th rows 6 (7) times more 14 (15) sts.

Work 5 (3) rows, ending at armhole edge.

To slope the shoulder: Cast off 7 sts. at beginning of next row; work 1 row, then cast off remaining 7 (8) sts.

The Sleeves (both alike)

With No. 10 needles cast on 38 (40) sts. and, beginning with a k. row, st.st. 5 rows.

Next row: All k. on wrong side to mark hemline.

Beginning with a k. row, st.st. 12 rows.

Change to No. 8 needles.

Inc. 1 st. at each end of next and every following 8th row until the 5th (6th) inc.

row has been worked – 48 (52) sts.

Work 21 (17) rows straight – mark each end of last row with a coloured thread to denote end of sleeve seam, then work a further 8 (10) rows.

Cast off loosely.

The Collar

With No. 8 needles cast on 50 (52) sts. and k.5 rows.

Now work in st.st. with garter st. borders as follows:

1st row: K.3, p. to last 3 sts., k.3.

2nd row: All k.

Repeat these 2 rows 15 times more, then work 1st row again.

Now divide sts. for back neck.

Next row: K.13, cast off next 24 (26) sts., k. to end and work on these 13 sts. for left side.

The left side:

1st row: K.3, p. to last st., k.1.

2nd row: All k.

Repeat these 2 rows 5 (7) times more, then work 1st row again.

Now shape as follows:

1st row: K.1, up 1, k. to last 5 sts., k.2 tog., k.3.

2nd row: K.3, p. to last st., k.1.

3rd row: K. to last 5 sts., k.2 tog., k.3.

4th row: K.3, p. to last st., k.1.

Repeat these 4 rows 7 times more – 5 sts.

Next row: K.5.

Next row: K.3, p.1, k.1.

Next row: K.2 tog., k.3.

On remaining 4 sts., k.30 rows for front tie.

Cast off.

The right side: With wrong side of work facing, rejoin yarn to the 13 sts.

1st row: K.1, p. to last 3 sts., k.3.

2nd row: All k.

Repeat these 2 rows 5 (7) times more, then work 1st row again.

Now shape as follows:

1st row: K.3, k.2 tog.b., k. to last st., up 1, k.1.

2nd row: K.1, p. to last 3 sts., k.3.

3rd row: K.3, k.2 tog.b., k. to end.

4th row: K.1, p. to last 3 sts., k.3.

Repeat these 4 rows 7 times more – 5 sts.

Next row: K.5.

Next row: K.1, p.1, k.3.

Next row: K.3, k.2 tog.b.

On remaining 4 sts., k.30 rows for front tie.

Cast off.

The Front Tab

With No. 10 needles and red cast on 4 sts. and k.20 rows.

Cast off.

To Make Up The Top

Press on wrong side, using a warm iron over a damp cloth. Join shoulder seams. Set in sleeves sewing the row-ends above the markers to the sts. cast off for armholes on back and front. Sew collar to neck edge. Join tab into ring; pull front ties through and secure.

Turn up hems and slip st. in place. Make a length of twisted cord with white and trim collar.

The Trousers

The Right Leg

With No. 10 needles cast on 67 (71) sts. and, beginning with a k. row, st.st. 9 rows.

Next row: All k. on wrong side to mark hemline.

Change to No. 8 needles and k.1 row and p.1 row.

Now shape flare as follows:

1st (shaping) row: K.27 (29), k.2 tog.b., k.9, k.2 tog., k.27 (29).

St.st. 5 (7) rows.

2nd (shaping) row: Inc. in 1st st., k.26 (28), k.2 tog.b., k.7, k.2 tog., k.26 (28), inc. in last st.

St.st. 5 (7) rows.

3rd (shaping) row: Inc. in 1st st., k.27 (29), k.2 tog.b., k.5, k.2 tog., k.27 (29), inc. in last st.

St.st. 5 (7) rows.

4th (shaping) row: Inc. in 1st st., k.28 (30), k.2 tog.b., k.3, k.2 tog., k.28 (30), inc. in last st.

St.st. 5 (7) rows.

5th (shaping) row: Inc. in 1st st., k.29 (31), k.2 tog.b., k.1, k.2 tog., k.29 (31), inc. in last st.

St.st. 5 (7) rows.

6th (shaping) row: Inc. in 1st st., k.30 (32), sl.1, k.2 tog., p.s.s.o., k.30 (32), inc. in last st. – 65 (69) sts.

St.st. 5 (7) rows.

Inc. 1 st. at each end of next and every following 6th row until the 6th inc. row has been worked – 77 (81) sts.

St.st. 7 rows.

Inc. 1 st. at each end of next and following 9 alternate rows – 97 (101) sts.

Work 1 row, to end with a wrong-side row **.

*** **To shape the front and back seams:**

1st row: Cast off 3, work to end.

2nd row: Cast off 2, work to end.

3rd row: Cast off 3, work to end.

4th row: Dec., work to end.

5th row: Cast off 3, work to end.

6th row: Dec., work to end.

7th row: Cast off 3, work to end.

Dec. 1 st. at beginning of next and following alternate row – 79 (83) sts.

Dec. 1 st. at each end of next and every following 4th row until the 9th dec. row has been worked – 61 (65) sts.

Work 2 rows straight, ending with a right-side row (ending with a wrong-side row here when working left leg).

To shape for extra length on back:

1st and 2nd (turning) rows: Work 54 (60) for 1st row, turn and work to end for 2nd row.

3rd and 4th rows: Work 46 (52), turn and work to end.

5th and 6th rows: Work 38 (44), turn and work to end.

7th and 8th rows: Work 32 (36), turn and work to end.

9th and 10th rows: Work 26 (29), turn and work to end.

11th and 12th rows: Work 20 (22), turn and work to end.

13th and 14th rows: Work 14 (15), turn and work to end.

15th and 16th rows: Work 8, turn and work to end.

Work 1 row across all sts. picking up a

Opposite – Bikini (pattern p. 238 striped beach trunks (pattern p. 240 yellow playsuit (pattern p. 241).

thread at each point where work was turned and taking this together with next st. to avoid a gap in the knitting.

Change to No. 10 needles and work 8 rows in single rib.

Cast off.

The Left Leg

Work as given for right leg to ** then work 1 row more to end with a right-side row.

Now work as given for right leg from *** to end noting that you end with a wrong-side row before shaping for extra length on back

To Make Up The Trousers

Press as given for Top. Join inside leg seams, then join front and back seams. Join elastic into a circle and secure inside waist ribbing with a herringbone st. casing.

Turn up hems and sew in place.

Bikini

(see illustration p. 237)

Contributed by Eugenie Hammond

Materials

One 50-gramme ball of Patons Purple Heather 4-ply; a pair each of No. 10 and No. 12 knitting needles; 3 plastic curtain rings; 2 small buttons; shirring elastic.

Tension and Size

Worked at a tension of 7 stitches and 9 rows to 1 inch, over the stocking stitch, using No. 10 needles, the set will fit the 2–3-year-olds.

Abbreviations

K., knit; p., purl; st., stitch; tog., together; inc., increase (by working twice into same st.); w.fwd., wool forward to make a st.; k. or p.2 tog.b., k. or p.2 sts. tog. through back of loops; st.st., stocking st. (k. on right side and p. on wrong side), single rib is k.1 and p.1 alternately.

The Briefs

The Back and Front (both alike)

With No. 10 needles cast on 20 sts. and k.1 row and p.1 row.

Continuing in st.st., inc. 1 st. at each end of next row and following 23 right-side rows — 68 sts.

P.1 row.

Change to No. 12 needles.

Next 2 rows: Cast on 12 sts., work in single rib to end — 92 sts.

Work 5 rows in single rib.

Cast off loosely in rib.

The Leg Bands (both alike)

First join crotch seam. With right side of work facing, rejoin wool to leg edge and, using No. 12 needles, pick up and k.80 sts. along entire leg edge.

Work 3 rows in single rib.

Cast off in rib.

To Make Up The Briefs

Press on wrong side, avoiding the ribbing, using a warm iron over a damp cloth. Join row-ends of leg bands to waist ribbing. Put tabs at each side through plastic ring and sew tabs in place on wrong side. Run shirring elastic through waist ribbing.

The Top

The Right Side

With No. 12 needles cast on 81 sts. and, beginning right-side rows with k.1 and wrong-side rows with p.1, work 2 rows in single rib.

Next (buttonhole) row: Rib to last 4 sts., w.fwd., k.2 tog., rib 2.

Rib 3 rows.

Change to No. 10 needles.

1st and 2nd (turning) rows: Cast off 10 − 1 st. left on right-hand needle − rib next 5 sts., k.2 tog.b., k. to last 10 sts. for 1st row, leave these 10 sts. on a safety-pin and turn, p. to last 8 sts., p.2 tog.b., rib 6 for 2nd row.

3rd and 4th rows: Rib 6, k.2 tog.b., k.45, turn and p. to last 8 sts., p.2 tog.b., rib 6.

5th and 6th rows: Rib 6, k.2 tog.b., k.37, turn and p. to last 8 sts., p.2 tog.b., rib 6.

7th and 8th rows: Rib 6, k.2 tog.b., k.29, turn and p. to last 8 sts., p.2 tog.b., rib 6.

9th and 10th rows: Rib 6, k.2 tog.b., k.21, turn and p. to last 8 sts., p.2 tog.b., rib 6.

11th and 12th rows: Rib 6, k.2 tog.b., k.13, turn and p. to last 8 sts., p.2 tog.b., rib 6.

13th and 14th rows: Rib 6, k.2 tog.b., k.5, turn and p. to last 8 sts., p.2 tog.b., rib 6.

Change to No. 12 needles.

Next row: Work in single rib across all sts., then onto same needle, rib the 10 sts. left on safety-pin − 57 sts.

Rib 1 row.

Next (buttonhole) row: Rib to last 4 sts., w.fwd., k.2 tog., rib 2.

Rib 2 rows.

Next row: Cast off 49 sts., rib to end.

On the remaining 8 sts. work 52 rows in single rib.

Cast off.

The Left Side

With No. 12 needles cast on 81 sts. and, beginning right-side rows with p.1 and wrong-side rows with k.1, work 6 rows in single rib.

Change to No. 10 needles.

1st and 2nd (turning) rows: Cast off 10 − 1 st. left on right-hand needle − rib next 5 sts., p.2 tog., p. to last 10 sts. for 1st row, leave these 10 sts. on a safety-pin, turn and k. to last 8 sts., k.2 tog., rib 6 for 2nd row.

3rd and 4th rows: Rib 6, p.2 tog., p.45, turn and k. to last 8 sts., k.2 tog., rib 6.

5th and 6th rows: Rib 6, p.2 tog., p.37, turn and k. to last 8 sts., k.2 tog., rib 6.

7th and 8th rows: Rib 6, p.2 tog., p.29, turn and k. to last 8 sts., k.2 tog., rib 6.

9th and 10th rows: Rib 6, p.2 tog., p.21, turn and k. to last 8 sts., k.2 tog., rib 6.

11th and 12th rows: Rib 6, p.2 tog., p.13, turn and k. to last 8 sts., k.2 tog., rib 6.

13th and 14th rows: Rib 6, p.2 tog., p.5, turn and k. to last 8 sts., k.2 tog., rib 6.

Change to No. 12 needles.

Next row: Work in single rib across all sts. then, onto same needle, rib the 10 sts. left on safety-pin − 57 sts.

Rib 4 rows.

Next row: Cast off 49, rib to end.

On the remaining 8 sts., work 52 rows in single rib.

Cast off.

To Make Up The Top

Press. Join centre front tabs to ring. Sew straps to back one inch in from centre. Sew on buttons.

Striped Beach Trunks

(see illustration p. 237)

**Just oddments of yarn in any number of
colours could be used to knit these**

Contributed by Eugenie Hammond

Materials

Approximately one ounce of 4-ply in
main colour; small amount of contrast
colour; a pair each of No. 10 and
No. 12 knitting needles; 2 small
buckles; shirring elastic.

Abbreviations

K., knit; p., purl; st., stitch; inc., increase
(by working twice into same st.); m., main
colour; c., contrast colour; single rib is k.1
and p.1 alternately; st.st., stocking st. (k. on
right side and p. on wrong side).

Tension and Size

Worked at a tension of 7 stitches and 9
rows to 1 inch, over the stocking stitch,
using No. 10 needles, the trunks will fit the
2–3-year-olds.

The Back

With No. 10 needles and m., cast on 20
sts.
1st row: All k.
2nd row: All p.
3rd row: Inc. in 1st st., k. to last st., inc.
4th row: All p.
Join in c.
5th row: With c., inc. in 1st st., k. to last st.,
inc.
6th row: With c., all k.
Continuing in stripe sequence of 4 rows
st.st. with m. and 2 rows k. with c., inc. 1 st.
at each end of next row and following 21
alternate rows – 68 sts.
Break off c. and continue with m. only.
Next row: All p. ******.
Change to No. 12 needles.
1st and 2nd rows: Cast on 12 sts. for
buckle tabs, then work in single rib to
end – 92 sts.
Rib 5 rows.
Cast off in rib.

The Front

Work as back to ******.
Change to No. 12 needles.
1st and 2nd rows: Cast on 16 sts. then
work in single rib to end – 100 sts.
Rib 5 rows.
Cast off.

The Leg Bands (both alike)

First join crotch seam. With right side of
work facing, rejoin m. to leg edge and,
using No. 12 needles, pick up and k.80 sts.
along entire leg edge.
Work 3 rows in single rib.
Cast off.

To Make Up The Trunks

Press on wrong side, avoiding the ribbing,
using a warm iron over a damp cloth. Join
row-ends of leg bands to waist ribbing. Sew
buckles to back tabs. Run shirring elastic
through waist on back and front.

Yellow Playsuit

(see illustration p. 237)

When baby has outgrown the dungaree-style crawlers given on page 168, undo the leg seams, pull a thread tightly across the knitting one inch below crotch shaping. Slip the stitches onto No. 12 needles and work 6 rows in single rib. Cast off and rejoin seams.

Bells

(see illustration p. 25)

Materials

Oddments of Double Knitting Wool ;
a pair of No. 9 knitting needles ;
3 small bells ; curtain or teething ring.

Abbreviations

K., knit ; p., purl ; st., stitch ; tog., together ;
up 1 (pick up the thread which lies between
the needles and k. into back of it thus making
a st.) ; st.st., stocking st. (k. on right side
and p. on wrong side).

To Make

Cast on 42 sts. and k.4 rows.
Next row: All p.
Now shape as follows :
1st row: K.7, * k.2 tog., k.6 ; repeat from *
3 times, k.2 tog., k.1.
2nd and every alternate row: All p.
3rd row: K.6, * k.2 tog., k.5 ; repeat from *
3 times, k.2 tog., k.1.
5th row: K.5, * k.2 tog., k.4 ; repeat from *
3 times, k.2 tog., k.1.
7th row: K.4, * k.2 tog., k.3 ; repeat from *
3 times, k.2 tog., k.1.

8th row: All p.
9th row: * P.2 tog. ; repeat from * 10 times –
11 sts.
10th row: All p.
11th row: K.1, * up 1, k.1 ; repeat from *
to end – 21 sts.
Beginning with a p. row work 9 rows in
st.st.
Break off wool ; run end through remaining
sts. draw up and secure, then join row-ends.
Make another two bells in the same way.
Make 3 lengths of twisted cord, attach bell
to one end and then pull cord through top
of bell and attach to ring.

Carry-All Shoulder Bag

(see illustration p. 25)

**All you need for a day out with baby will
fit in this bag**

Contributed by Eugenie Hammond

Materials

Seven 50-gramme balls of Sirdar
Sportswool in navy; one ball in white;
one ball in red; a pair of No. 9
knitting needles; a 20-inch zip
fastener.

Tension and Size

Worked at a tension of 16 stitches and 20
rows to 3 inches, over the rib pattern, using
No. 9 needles, the bag will measure 35
inches all round and $11\frac{1}{2}$ inches in depth,
excluding the zipped section.

The Circles (make 2)

With No. 9 needles and navy, cast on 20
sts. and k.1 row.

Working in garter st. inc. 1 st. at beginning
only on each of next 28 rows – 48 sts.

Work 24 rows straight.

Dec. 1 st. at beginning only on each of
next 28 rows – 20 sts.

Cast off.

The Gusset and Main Part

With No. 9 needles and navy, cast on 188
sts. and k.10 rows.

With red, k.4 rows.
With white, k.2 rows.
With navy, k.6 rows.
Now divide sts. for zip opening.

Next row: With navy k.44, cast off next
100 sts., k. to end.

Abbreviations

K., knit; p., purl; st., stitch; tog., together;
dec., decrease (by working 2 sts. tog.); inc.,
increase (by working twice into same st.);
w.r.n., wool round needle to make a st.;
garter st. is k. on every row.

Next row: With navy k.44, turn, cast on
100 sts., turn, k. to end.

With navy, k.10 rows.
With red, k.4 rows.
With white, k.2 rows.
With navy, k.10 rows.

Break off red and white and continue with
navy only for main part.

1st row: P.3, * k.6, p.2; repeat from *
ending last repeat with p.3.

2nd row: K.3, * p.6, k.2; repeat from *
ending last repeat with k.3.

Repeat these 2 rows 31 times more.

Next (slot) row: K.3, * w.r.n. twice, k.2
tog., k.5; repeat from * to last 3 sts.,
w.r.n. twice, k.2 tog., k.1.

Next row: All k. working once into the
w.r.n. and letting extra loop drop off
needle to form large holes.

K.10 rows.

Cast off.

To Make Up The Bag

Press on wrong side using a warm iron over a damp cloth. Sew zip fastener into opening, then join row-ends of main part and gusset to form tube shape. Pin one circle in place at base of bag and sew firmly in position, then join other circle inside bag, level with first rib row of main part.

Using 4 strands each of red and white, make a twisted cord and thread through holes at top.

Red Push Chair Bag

(see illustration p. 25)

Contributed by Eugenie Hammond

Materials

Ten 50-gramme balls of Sirdar Sportswool in red; oddment of navy and white; a pair of No. 8 knitting needles.

Abbreviations

K., knit; p., purl; st., stitch; tog., together; dec., decrease (by working 2 sts. tog.); st.st., stocking st. (k. on right side and p. on wrong side); garter st. is k. on every row.

Tension and Size

Worked at a tension of 10 stitches and 13 rows to 2 inches, over the stocking stitch, using No. 8 needles, the bag will fit most normal size push-chairs.

The Back Section

With No. 8 needles and red, cast on 64 sts. and k.3 rows.

Now work in st.st. with garter st. borders as follows:

1st row: All k.

2nd row: K.6, p. to last 6 sts., k.6.

Repeat these 2 rows 15 times more, then work 1st row again.

Next row: All k. on wrong side to mark fold line.

Repeat 1st and 2nd rows 106 times more, when work should measure 39 inches from cast-on edge.

Cast off.

The Front Section

With No. 8 needles and red, cast on 68 sts. and k.7 rows.

With navy, k.4 rows.

With white, k.2 rows.

With red, k.6 rows.

With navy, k.4 rows.

With white, k.2 rows.

Break off navy and white and continue with red only.

K.140 rows. Mark each end of work with a coloured thread to denote end of side seam.

Dec. 1 st. at each end of next and following 8th row – 64 sts.

K.13 rows.

Cast off.

The Gussets (make 2)

With No. 8 needles and red, cast on 18 sts. and k.165 rows.

Cast off.

To Make Up The Bag

Press on wrong side using a warm iron over a damp cloth. Join one side of each gusset to each side of front section from cast-on edge to marking threads, then join remaining row-ends across the cast-off edge of gussets.

With right side of front section facing so that the st.st. side will be the inside of bag, sew the cast-off edge of back section to cast-off edge of front section, then other side of gussets to back section to form bag shape. Turn top of back at fold line and join row ends to form section for slipping over handle of push-chair.

The Rabbit

(see illustration p. 25)

Materials

Oddments of Double Knitting Wool in 2 colours; a pair of No. 9 knitting needles; cotton wool for filling.

Tension and Size

Worked at a tension of 6 stitches and 8 rows to 1 inch the rabbit will measure, when completed, 5½ inches in length and 6 inches from base to top of ears.

Abbreviations

K., knit; p., purl; st., stitch; tog., together; dec., decrease (by working 2 sts. tog.); inc., increase (by working twice into same st.); st.st., stocking st. (k. on right side and p. on wrong side).

To Make

The right side: With No. 9 needles and main colour cast on 30 sts.
1st row: K. to last st., inc.
2nd row: Inc., p. to end.
3rd to 7th rows: Work in st.st.
8th row: Dec., p. to end.
9th row: K. to last 2 sts., dec.
10th row: Cast off 8 sts. for front leg, p. to end.
11th row: All k.
12th row: All p.
To shape for head: St.st. 8 rows increasing 1 st. at front edge – that is the cast-off group edge – on each of these rows – 30 sts.

K.1 row and p.1 row.
Next row: K.15 for back, cast off 2, k. to end and work on these 13 sts. for head.
The head: Cast off 2 sts. at beginning of next row for nose, then work 9 rows decreasing 1 st. at each end of 3rd, 6th and 9th of these rows.

Cast off remaining 5 sts.
The back: Rejoin wool to inner edge of 15 sts. of back and work 4 rows decreasing 1 st. at each end of each of these rows.

Cast off remaining 7 sts.

The left side: Work as given for right side but read p. for k. and k. for p. throughout to reverse the shaping. 1st row will read: P. to last st., inc.
The underbody: With contrast colour cast on 4 sts. and k.1 row and p.1 row.

Inc. 1 st. at each end of next and every following 3rd row until the 7th inc. row has been worked – 18 sts.

St.st. 11 rows ending with a p. row.
Next row: K.8, cast off 2, k. to end and work on these 8 sts. for 1st leg.
1st leg: St.st. 10 rows, then dec. 1 st. at each end of next 2 rows.

Cast off remaining 4 sts.
2nd leg: With wrong side facing, rejoin wool to remaining 8 sts. and work as given for 1st leg.

The Ears (make 2)

With main colour cast on 4 sts. and p.1 row.
** Continuing in st.st. inc. 1 st. at each end of next and following 4 alternate rows – 14 sts.

St.st. 9 rows, then dec. 1 st. at each end of

next and following 4 alternate rows – 4 sts. **.

Break off main colour; join on contrast colour and p.1 row.

Now work from ** to ** once more.

Cast off remaining 4 sts.

The Tail

With contrast colour cast on 4 sts.

** Working in st.st. inc. 1 st. at each end of next 4 rows – 12 sts.

Work 10 rows, then dec. 1 st. at each end of next 4 rows **.

Work from ** to ** once more.

Cast off remaining 4 sts.

To Make Up The Rabbit

Beginning at tail end join the two sides together along top of back, over head and down to division of front legs. Sew underbody in place leaving a small opening. Fill and mould into shape then close seam. Fold ears in half and join side seams. Pleat lower edge and sew in position to back of head. Fold tail in half and join one side, fill and close other side. Sew tail in position. Embroider eyes and nose and add strands of thread for whiskers.

The Ball

(see illustration p. 25)

Materials

Oddments of Double Knitting Wool;
a pair of No. 10 knitting needles;
cotton wool or old nylons for filling.

Abbreviations

K., knit; p., purl; st., stitch; tog., together;
dec., decrease (by working 2 sts. tog.); inc.,
increase (by working twice into same st.);
sl., slip; p.s.s.o., pass slipped st. over; k.2
tog.b., k.2 sts. tog. through back of loops;
st.st., stocking st. (k. on right side and p. on
wrong side); garter st. is k. on every row.

The Section (make 5)

With No. 10 needles cast on 3 sts.
1st row: Inc. in 1st st., inc. in next st., k.1.
2nd row: All p.
3rd row: Inc. in 1st st., k. to last 2 sts., inc.
in next st., k.1.
4th row: All p.
Repeat 3rd and 4th rows once more, then
work 3rd row again – 11 sts.
Continuing in st.st. work 3 rows straight,
then inc. 1 st. at each end as before, on next
and every following 4th row until a further
4 inc. rows have been worked – 19 sts.
K.20 rows for garter st. band.
Next row: All p.
Continuing in st.st. work as follows:
Next (dec.) row: K.1, k.2 tog.b., k. to last
3 sts., k.2 tog., k.1.

St.st. 3 rows, then dec. 1 st. at each end,
as before, on next and every following 4th
row until the 4th dec. row has been worked –
11 sts.
St.st. 3 rows, then dec. 1 st. at each end,
as before, on next and following 2 alternate
rows – 5 sts.
Next row: All p.
Next row: K.1, sl.1, k.2 tog., p.s.s.o., k.1.
Next row: P.3.
Cast off.

To Make Up The Ball

Press each section using a warm iron over
a damp cloth. Join sections together leaving
a small opening. Fill and mould to shape.
Close opening.

Hot Water Bottle Cover

(see illustration p. 25)

Materials

Three 25-gramme balls of Lee Target Motoravia Double Knitting Wool; oddment of pink 3-ply; a pair each of No. 8 and No. 11 knitting needles; 3 large press fasteners; oddment of cotton wool; black cotton; ½ yard of ribbon.

Tension and Size

Worked at a tension of 11 stitches and 15 rows to 2 inches, using No. 8 needles, the cover will measure 15½ inches long and 8 inches wide.

Abbreviations

K., knit; p., purl; st., stitch; tog., together; dec., decrease (by working 2 sts. tog.); inc., increase (by working twice into same st.); st.st., stocking st. (k. on right side and p. on wrong side).

The Body (worked in one piece)

With No. 8 needles and Double Knitting cast on 88 sts. and k.3 rows.
Now work as follows:
1st row: All k.
2nd row: K.3, p. to last 3 sts., k.3.
Repeat these 2 rows 37 times more.
Cast off.

The Head

Back section: With No. 8 needles and Double Knitting cast on 16 sts. and k.1 row and p.1 row.
Continuing in st.st., inc. 1 st. at each end of next and following 7 right-side rows – 32 sts.
Work 5 rows straight.
Dec. 1 st. at each end of next and following 7 right-side rows – 16 sts.
P.1 row.
Cast off.

The Brim

With No. 8 needles and Double Knitting cast on 6 sts. and k.110 rows.
Cast off.

The Face

With No. 11 needles and 3-ply cast on 26 sts. and k.1 row and p.1 row.
Continuing in st.st., inc. 1 st. at each end of next and following 8 right-side rows – 44 sts.
Work 7 rows straight.
Dec. 1 st. at each end of next and following 8 right-side rows – 26 sts.
P.1 row.
Cast off.

The Arms (make 2)

With No. 11 needles and 3-ply cast on 20 sts. and, beginning with a k. row, st.st. 6 rows.

Break off 3-ply and join on Double Knitting.

Change to No. 8 needles and k.5 rows.
Beginning with a p. row, st.st. 5 rows.
Cast off.

The Feet (make 2)

With No. 11 needles and 3-ply cast on 20 sts. and st.st. 6 rows.
Cast off.

To Make Up The Cover

Press on wrong side using a warm iron over a damp cloth. Join row ends of body and fold with seam at centre front, then sew cast-off edges together for 2 inches in from each side to form shoulders leaving centre free for neck edge.

Embroider eyelashes and mouth on face, then join face to back section leaving the cast-on edges free for neck opening. Sew one edge of brim all round this seam. Sew open neck edge of head to open neck edge of body. Run a gathering thread along free edge of brim and draw up to fit round face. Fold arms in half lengthwise and join row ends and cast-on edge; fill lightly with cotton wool and sew to body. Join row-ends and cast-on edge of feet; lightly fill with cotton wool and sew in place on front. Sew press fasteners along lower edge. Trim with ribbon bow.

Pyjama Case

(see illustration p. 25)

Contributed by Eugenie Hammond

Materials

Seven 25-gramme balls of Lee Target Motoravia Double Knitting Wool; oddment of 3-ply in pink; a pair each of No. 8 and No. 10 knitting needles; blue and black cotton for embroidery; cotton wool; ribbon; five press studs.

Abbreviations

K., knit; p., purl; st., stitch; tog., together; dec., decrease (by working 2 sts. tog.); inc., increase (by working twice into same st.); st.st., stocking st. (k. on right side and p. on wrong side).

Tension and Size

Worked at a tension of 11 stitches and 15 rows to 2 inches, over the stocking stitch, using No. 8 needles the case will measure 14 inches across at widest part and 21 inches from top of head to lower edge.

The Body (Back and Front alike)

With No. 8 needles and Double Knitting cast on 80 sts. and k.5 rows.

Beginning with a p. row, st.st. 3 rows.

Continuing in st.st., dec. 1 st. at each end of next and every following 8th row until the 10th dec. row has been worked – 60 sts.

Work 5 rows straight.

To shape for arms: Cast on 15 sts. at beginning of next 2 rows – 90 sts.

Continue as follows:

1st row: All k.

2nd row: K.2, p. to last 2 sts., k.2.

Repeat these 2 rows 8 times more.

Cast off.

The Back of Head

With No. 8 needles and Double Knitting cast on 22 sts. and, beginning with a k. row, st.st. 2 rows.

Inc. 1 st. at each end of next and following 8 right-side rows – 40 sts.

Work 15 rows straight.

Dec. 1 st. at each end of next and following 8 right-side rows – 22 sts.

P.1 row.

Cast off.

The Brim

With No. 8 needles and Double Knitting cast on 8 sts. and k.134 rows.

Cast off.

The Face

With No. 10 needles and 3-ply, cast on 32 sts. and, beginning with a k. row, st.st. 2 rows.

Inc. 1 st. at each end of next and following 9 right-side rows – 52 sts.

Work 17 rows straight.

Dec. 1 st. at each end of next and following 9 right-side rows – 32 sts.

P.1 row.

Cast off.

251

The Hands (make 2)

With No. 10 needles and 3-ply cast on 32 sts. and work 8 rows in st.st.

Cast off.

To Make Up The Case

Press on wrong side using a warm iron over a damp cloth. Embroider eyes and mouth on face. Join head pieces together round outer edge leaving a small opening; fill lightly and close seam. Leaving neck edge free, sew one edge of brim round head seam, run a gathering thread along other side of brim and draw up slightly to fit round face.

Join top and side seams of body. Fold hands in half lengthwise and join row-ends and cast-on edge; fill lightly, close remaining edge and sew in place.

Sew head to body and trim neck with ribbon bow.

Close lower edge with press studs.

Opposite – Headband and muff (pattern p. 254).

Headband and Muff

(see illustration p. 253)

**Picture it in white or red for a winter
bridesmaid**

Contributed by Eugenie Hammond

Materials

For the Muff: Three 25-gramme balls
of Bairnswear Pleasure Double
Knitting Wool; a pair of No. 8
knitting needles.

For the Head Band: One 25-gramme
ball of the same wool; a pair each of
No. 8 and No. 10 knitting needles;
a plain Alice Band; a cable needle.

Tension and Size

Worked at a tension of 11 stitches and 15
rows to 2 inches, over the stocking stitch,
using No. 8 needles, the Muff will measure
7 inches wide and 4½ inches deep.

Abbreviations

K., knit; p., purl; st., stitch; tog., together;
c.4f., cable 4 front (slip next 2 sts. onto
cable needle and leave at front of work, k.2,
then k.2 from cable needle); c.4b., cable 4
back (slip next 2 sts. onto cable needle and
leave at back of work, k.2, then k.2 from
cable needle); st.st., stocking st. (k. on
right side and p. on wrong side).

The Muff

To Make

With No. 8 needles cast on 30 sts. and k.1
row.

Next (loop st.) row: K.1, * insert needle
into next st., wind wool clockwise twice
over needle and first finger of left hand,
then over needle only, draw these 3 loops
through onto left-hand needle letting
original st. drop off needle, slip loops
back onto left-hand needle and k. them
tog. through back of loops; repeat from *
to last st., k.1.

Next row: All k.
Repeat these 2 rows 18 times more, then
work loop st. row again.
Beginning with a k. row, st.st. 48 rows.
Cast off.

To Make Up The Muff

Press st.st. section only, using a warm iron
over a damp cloth. Fold in half with loop st.
to inside and join row-ends. Turn to right
side and join remaining edge. Make a length
of twisted cord and sew in place.

The Headband

The Ear Muffs (make 2)

With No. 8 needles cast on 6 sts. and k.1
row.
Work the 2 rows given for muff 22 times.
Cast off.
Join cast-on and cast-off edges together.
Run a gathering thread round one edge;
draw up to form a circle and secure.

The Plait

With No. 10 needles cast on 12 sts. and
k.1 row and p.1 row.
Now work in pattern as follows:
1st row: K.2, c.4f., k.6.
2nd row: All p.
3rd row: K.5, c.4b., k.3.
4th row: All p.
Repeat these 4 rows 23 times more.
Cast off.

To Make Up The Head Band

Press. Fold lengthwise and join row-ends
to form tube. Insert Alice Band and secure
ear muff to each end.

List of Illustrations

(continued)

List of Illustrations
(continued)